Diana J. Sweeney

DANTE VIVO

THE MACMILLAN COMPANY
NEW YORK · BOSTON · CHICAGO · DALLAS
ATLANTA · SAN FRANCISCO

GIOVANNI PAPINI

Dante Vivo

Translated from the Italian by
ELEANOR HAMMOND BROADUS
and ANNA BENEDETTI

NEW YORK
THE MACMILLAN COMPANY
1935

AWARDED THE PREMIO MUSSOLINI IN 1933

Printed in the United States of America
by the Polygraphic Company of America

GIOVANNI PAPINI was born in Florence, Italy, in 1881. For the picture of his childhood and early manhood one should turn to his great poetic confession, *Un Uomo Finito* (1912), where he tells his own story. In 1902 he founded the review *Leonardo*, which became the organ of Italian pragmatism. In 1906 he published his first collection of stories and his first volume of philosophical essays, *The Twilight of the Philosophers*—a book which, as an intellectual autobiography, brought him wide recognition. There followed in rapid succession stories, poems, literary criticism, and philosophical discussions, in which Papini showed himself the leader of the younger generation in Italy, voicing their doubts, their social discontent, their programme of reform.

During the last twenty-five years, Benedetto Croce and Papini have been the principal figures in philosophical thought in Italy. If Croce, as someone has said, opened to modern Italian culture the doors of philosophy, Papini has given to the movement a deeper understanding and a spiritual intensity. By turn pragmatist, futurist, anti-Catholic, and Catholic, Papini has remained honest with himself through all his spiritual changes, bringing to his investigations and conclusions intense ardour and sincerity and originality of approach. His changes have been a sign of his unrest, his hatred of complacency and mediocrity—a mirror of his own dissatisfaction and that of his iconoclastic generation.

v

Friend of Bergson and of William James, literary correspondent for journals in Italy and in other countries, especially in Moscow and Paris, prolific writer on philosophical subjects, poet of no mean ability, stylist with a genius for paradox and a fury in invective, the end of the year 1914 found him associated with Benito Mussolini on the *Popolo d'Italia* in a campaign for the intervention of Italy in the World War. At the end of the war came his religious conversion, and following this, his *Life of Christ* (1919)—a book which has been translated into twenty-three different languages and has had a world-wide success.

In all his writing Papini has shown the traditional Tuscan strain—impassioned but anti-sentimental, aggressive and pungent in phraseology, independent and sometimes revolutionary in conception, and above all bent on intellectual freedom and justice. These traits he brings to bear on Dante. As a Florentine, an artist, and a Catholic, he examines anew the life, the work, the psychology of his greatest fellow-Florentine. The result is a study, as William James said long ago of Papini's work in another field, 'extraordinarily free and spirited and unpedantic.'

E. H. B.

THE first 'spirito eterno' of poetry which came to dwell with me in the days of my youth was Prince Hamlet. The first philosopher who made a profound impression on my mind was Berkeley, and later I translated his works into Italian. The first poet who took possession of my youthful soul was Walt Whitman. The first foreign review to which I contributed was the *Monist*, published in Chicago. The first thinker of a nation other than my own to whom I was bound by ties of genuine friendship was William James.

There must exist, therefore, a kind of foreordained harmony between the Anglo-Saxon culture and my own mind, and perhaps it is due to this special arrangement of fate that my works have had more readers in Great Britain and North America than in Italy itself.

I am happy that, at the moment when my book on Dante is about to be issued in the language of Shakespeare, an opportunity has been given me to express to this great group of English readers my sincere and fervent gratitude. If these my non-Italian readers may be taken as representing by anticipation the judgement of the future, I take pride in having had an honourable and favourable reception by that immense posterity who live on the shores of all the oceans, and who have always known how to mix in due proportions the venerable traditions of humanism with the bold pursuit of every modernity, to carry side by side a proper conservatism and a necessary radicalism.

No writer can say that he has created and thought for all men until his work has been translated into English, that is, into the language which represents to-day the most universal vehicle of the printed word. What the Greek language was from the time of Alexander the Great to St Paul, what the Latin was during all the Middle Ages and until the final splendours of the Renaissance, that the English language is to-day.

And for me, a Florentine and an Italian, it is a great satisfaction to see—thanks to the labour of Eleanor Hammond Broadus and Anna Benedetti—this book on Dante translated into English. Outside of Italy no other country has so greatly loved and studied the creator of the *Divina Commedia* as have England and America. Not only have they produced accomplished Dante scholars— like the English Lord Vernon, H. C. Barlow, Edward Moore, Paget Toynbee; and the American Longfellow, C. E. Norton, J. R. Lowell—worthy to stand on an equality with the Italian and the German; but the first-hand knowledge of Dante's work, even among those of moderate culture, is more widespread than elsewhere. The English-speaking peoples not only know Dante, but they admire him, appreciate him, understand him, love him.

The literature in English about Dante is extraordinarily rich and abundant. Therefore I count it a great honour that this book of mine should be published in Great Britain and in North America.

Perhaps it merited this fortune because, as the reader will see, it is a little different from other books on Dante in that it tries to bring out new elements through an untrammelled and dispassionate investigation of the secret soul of the divine Poet. Fanatical adulators and pedants with extravagant imaginations have almost buried Dante for a second time under a massive and majestic mausoleum of criticism, erudition, interpretation, and rhetoric.

This book is an attempt to resurrect him. I am confident that its true import will be understood by English and American readers.

GIOVANNI PAPINI.

1 May, 1934
Florence, Italy.

Contents

xi

CONTENTS

Illustrations

BOOK ONE

Prolegomena

INTRODUCTION

IT would be well to say at once, in order to prevent misunderstandings and disappointments, that this is not the book of a professor for his students, of a critic for critics, of a pedant for pedants, of a lazy compiler for lazy readers. It is meant to be the live book of a live man about one who, even after death, has never ceased to live. It is above all the book of an artist about an artist, of a Catholic about a Catholic, of a Florentine about a Florentine.

It is not, nor is it meant to be, one of the numerous lives of Dante—write it LIFE or life!—useful or superfluous, which are published here and there, every year, throughout the world. Of Dante's outward life little is known which is based on documents and is absolutely certain. Yet everyone is given to improvising upon the happenings of his earthly life, upon the places where he was or might have been, upon the men and the events of his time that he may have been acquainted with. On the other hand, from the abundance of first-hand documents, that is, from the written evidence furnished by his own books, we know much about his soul; but there are few men who care to search it deeply and interpret it.

Therefore I would have this book of mine, which is more than a life of Dante, present a living Dante, a Dante *vivo*, the essential Dante, a moral and spiritual portrait. It is an essay of investigation about the things in Dante which really matter to us to-day.

In the best books on Dante there is very little about his real life. A large part of them are filled with historical details concerning the thirteenth and four-teenth centuries; with information, often unnecessary, on the persons who were associated with him; with interpretations, more or less felicitous, of his writings; and above all with too many amplifications, romantic, learned, or eloquent, on matters which are not certain or are insufficiently known. Alighieri's outward life, so far as it is known with certainty, can be told in a few pages;[1] while for the full understanding of his soul and work the whole range of a man's lifetime is insufficient. There is always something new awaiting discovery.

I do not mean to undervalue the patient compilers of critical editions or the tireless investigators and illustrators of historical or biographical details. I honour them as I honour the miller who supplies the flour to be consecrated by the celebrant. The workman who sifts the sand and mixes the mortar performs a necessary labour, but God forbid that he should pass judgement on the architect. These learned labours of preparation are valuable and indispensable whether they are directed toward establishing an authoritative text of the work, or are concerned with fixing, on the data furnished by original documents, the precise meaning of every act or of every line of the poet. To these 'positivist' and patient Dantists—such as Michele Barbi, Francesco Torraca, Giuseppi Vandelli, Nicola Zingarelli, to name only the greatest to-day—we owe just praise and sincere gratitude.

[1] For an admirable brief life of Dante, see the article by M. Barbi in the *Enciclopedia Italiana*, Vol. XII, 327–332.

But these editors themselves are aware that to spend many years making critical editions and heaping up explanatory material would not be worth the trouble unless Dante were something more than a text for language-study or a subject in Romance or Comparative Philology. Beyond and above everything else, Dante is a great soul and a great artist; and to understand these spirits of largest mould, all the sequence of manuscript texts, the early editions, the researches in old chronicles and in mediæval philosophies, are entirely insufficient.

On the other hand, most students of Dante fall into three classes: first, teachers of literature trying to explain what the poet meant and why he said it as he did, and for what reasons that way of saying it is obscure or beautiful; second, minute investigators seeking to know the why and wherefore of every happening, the complete and exact itinerary of his wanderings, and what he did on that day or in that year; third, enigmatographers, erudite or fanciful, who wish above all to display their own learning and skill in revealing the mysteries buried in the poet's work.

These methods, however, are inadequate for the understanding of Dante in his loftiness and in his profundity; for the comprehension of Dante as a man, a poet, a prophet, of Dante alive and entire. We little men must approach as near as is possible for us to the sum of his greatness; we must possess a spirit which will at least reflect something of Dante's spirit and vibrate in sympathy. It is precisely this which is almost always lacking in the professional Dantists,

Dantologists, and Dantomaniacs.[1] They are anæmic creatures confronting a sanguine man; ants around a lion. They can go scouting through its mane, and count the hairs on its tail, but they cannot see the gigantic creature entire in its fearful majesty. And woe to them if the lion should suddenly roar!

These Dantists never warm up, or they get heated unseasonably. Dante is flame and fire; they remain lukewarm or frozen, as if they were in contact with an ageless ruin. He is all life, and they are half-dead. He is light, they are darkness. He is powerful, they are weak and flaccid. He burns with moral and messianic faith; they are usually men who have never known, even from a distance, the torment of the divine. But to borrow Dante's words, 'fastidium etenim est in rebus manifestissimis probationes adducere.'[2]

Thus Dante has remained, for the most part, the choice food of worthy teachers, or the pastime of ambitious amateurs. Only a few ever draw near to him through a certain similarity of temperament and with the purpose, or at least with the desire, of making themselves like to him in order to understand him better. For this they would need to be not only diligent and enthusiastic scholars, but true poets or true philosophers. Outside the circle of professional Dantists, there are two poets and two philosophers— to confine ourselves to Italy and modern times— who have really devoted themselves to a study of

---

[1] Since 1905 I have been denouncing, perhaps with too summary a judgement, the spiritual insufficiency of the professional Dantists: *v.* G. Papini, *Per Dante contro il dantismo*, republished in *Eresie Letterarie.* Florence, Vallecchi, 1932, pp. 13–23.

[2] *De Monarchia,* III, **xiv,** 7. It is a bore to prove the obvious.

6

Dante. These are Carducci and Pascoli, Croce and Gentile.

But Carducci, who wrote some eloquent pages on the place occupied by Dante in Italian literature, and who was worthy, by reason of certain qualities of his mind and spirit, to call Dante his 'great neighbour,' rarely came down to particulars and never, unfortunately for us, had the inclination or the opportunity to devote to Dante a substantial and entire book.

Pascoli, unlike Carducci, was too much given to detail, and not always with happy results, for he was over-subtle and quibbling about the hidden meaning of the *Divina Commedia*, with the declared intention, moreover, of being the first to reveal the most jealously guarded of Dante's secrets. However, as Pascoli was a poet and a humanist, he succeeded in discerning part of the truth or in getting a glimpse of it; nor is all that he wrote on the subject to be discarded without examination.

Croce, who has written a treatise on Æsthetics, although by temperament incapable of understanding a work of art, was the least fitted of these four to deal with Dante's poetry. After having defined the *Commedia* as 'a theological or ethical-political-theological romance' completely dead as to its spiritual content, since Christianity, according to Croce, is now only a mummified body, he set himself the awkward task of selecting by a method resembling that of the Abbot Bettinelli,[1]

[1] Severio Bettinelli, in his *Lettere Virgiliane* (1757), assailed Dante as lacking in good taste, and condemned the *Commedia* as 'a chaos of confusion.' He exampted from this condemnation a few choice fragments which he permitted to appear in his selections from the Italian poets as examples for the young.—Trans.

7

those bits and fragments of genuine poetry which are to be found here and there in the poem.

Giovanni Gentile discussed Dante's conceptions with deeper understanding; and although he never devoted an entire volume to Dante, he had the merit of re-affirming the lasting religious significance of the *Commedia*, and understood clearly that one of the central points of the poem was the desire and the preparation on Dante's part for a thorough reform of the Church of his time.[1]

But, as I pointed out at the beginning, for a full understanding of Dante, one must be a Catholic, an artist, and a Florentine. Dante is not limited to these three qualities, but I do not think it vain boasting to maintain that the possession of all three of them is useful to the man who measures himself with Dante. It is not necessary that the zoologist should be an onager, or the astronomer a satellite, because in these cases men are dealing with external things; but it does no harm for a student of Dante to have a little Christian faith, a little experience in the arts, and to be born in Florence. A Catholic: that is, one who still feels to be true and living that which Dante felt and believed.[2] An artist: since only a poet can penetrate (as a critic can not) the mind and genius of a poet. And finally— let no one take offence!—a Florentine. The Florentines of to-day are very different from those of Dante's time, but not different in every way. And however much Florence may be changed and disfigured, there always

---

[1] G. Gentile, *Dante e Manzoni*. Florence, Vallecchi, 1923.

[2] On the necessity of being a Catholic in order to understand Dante thoroughly, see A. Curtayne, *A Recall to Dante*. London, Sheed and Ward, 1932.

remain in some remote corner the look and the atmosphere of Dante's Trecento. There are still some stones and buildings which Dante may have seen, narrow passages which have changed little since his time. My belief that a Florentine is by nature and experience better fitted than another to understand Dante is not a foolish notion due to parochial pride, but the fruit of reasoning and observation.

Many years ago, in the days of my bibliophagia, I amused myself collecting the most important opinions expressed by men of every nation on Dante and his writings. Ever since then it has seemed to me that very few, especially among foreigners, have really understood Dante.

Although the loftiness of Dante's soul and of his subject-matter make him a universal poet, nevertheless these very qualities which make him universal are bound up with things incident to his humanity, with historical circumstances, with seasonings of native wit which cannot easily be recognized and weighed except by men of his own race. It seemed to me, therefore, that to understand Dante in all the irregularities of his nature, in his cracks and blemishes, it is necessary to be an Italian. And taking the next logical step along this road, I began to think that only a Tuscan, a Tuscan of the pure old stock, could fully understand him. Having reached this point, I could do no less than continue; and finally I was tempted to declare that only a Florentine, one who has preserved some trace at least of the ancient Florentine character, whether for good or ill, could dissect certain aspects of the mind and the art of Dante.

It may be said that I am wrong and that accursed self-love, thinly disguised as love for my own people, is drawing me into a capricious and distorted fantasy. But the truth is that up to the present, neither among the ancients nor the moderns, have we seen an outspoken and worthy Florentine, such as I have in mind, consecrating himself entirely to the study of the great poet.

From this we draw three conclusions: the seed of the Dantesque Florentine is exhausted; or those few worthy ones now living still bear a certain unconscious resentment against the man who called down curses upon Florence; or, finally, my idea is only a foolish delusion.

In any case, although I possess the three qualities named above, being a Catholic, a poet, and a Florentine, I do not pretend that I have written a book which presents with thoroughness the whole range of Dante's universe. I confess that I have tried my best not to be inferior to my subject, but I am not so mad as to think that what I have written renders other books on Dante useless.

However, I am not going to make excuses for having written one book more on Dante. Dante is a subject of such proportions that the passing generations can always discover something new in him or his work. And certainly I should not have written this book if I had not thought that I had something new to say, even if my novelties seem, at first sight, somewhat out of accord with prevailing opinions.

Although for six centuries men have been writing in all the languages of the earth about this my greatest fellow-citizen, I have an impression that there is still much more to be discovered. Dante is, in many ways, a still unexplained mystery. The text has been studied, and the work is still incomplete; the external surroundings have been investigated, and there still remain many obscure points; but upon his fundamental nature (to which biographers devote a few lines or a few pages), upon the innate and essential character of his sentiments and aspirations, upon the secret of his powerful art, all has not yet been said, and perhaps even the most important truths remain unspoken. Usually we move in a circle among the commonplaces of a well-bred convention which tries to hide the shadows and the too human side.

This book of mine is neither a prosecution nor an apotheosis. Dante's fame has survived both efforts. First came the period of his rising glory from the fourteenth to the sixteenth century, then a period of neglect, then one almost of deification, balanced later by stupid disparagement. Now the time of full justice is beginning. I have wished, therefore, to present a 'critical portrait'—just as there are critical editions—making use of all known facts about the man and his work, exaggerating nothing and hiding nothing. If my Dante does not exactly match the standard oleographic pattern which is handed down from centenary to centenary by the collectors and reciters of well-worn phrases, I am at least sure of having on my side every honest and sensible man. I have searched for the truth in the spirit of that love which a genius like Dante deserves, and I hope that I have not betrayed either the truth or him.

For me Dante is not a prescribed subject, or a pretext for writing one book more. Even from boyhood I have honoured him, may I say? as a father and a teacher; and while measuring in all humility the immense distance between him and me, I know that I love him. It is easy to admire and praise Dante, but not so easy to love him. When alive, he could not have been a man who easily confided in others or who made friends with everybody. Dead, he gives to most people the effect of a huge unapproachable statue raised on the heights of glory, awe-inspiring.

For my part, I have always seen and loved in him not only the Titan, but the man with all his human weaknesses, the poet with all his torment before the unutterable; and therefore I have come to love him in very truth. And to those whom we truly love we say everything without fear. God grant that a little of my affection for Dante may be transmitted to those who read this book.

OUR BROTHER

EVERYONE sees you, dear Dante, dressed in your close, long tunic, passing with austere face among your fellow-men without even vouch-safing them a single glance, always absorbed in thoughts loftier than the towers or the clouds. We know almost certainly that you were disdainful and reserved; and we read in the lines and between the lines of your writings in prose and verse that you had no great admiration for your fellow-men.

But no one will ever make me believe—me an Italian, a Tuscan, a Florentine—that you always displayed that forbidding visage of solemn abstraction. That would certainly have been an absurd pretence. It is not possible for a man to be constantly attuned to that which he is in the depths of his being; he can be his real self only in certain hours or at certain periods of his life. He can put on a semblance of being always absorbed and magisterial, but to seem is not to be. So, men are hypocrites, and pedantic hypocrites, which are the worst sort.

But you, Dante, though you were not lacking in faults, were neither hypocrite nor poseur. You did not assume a look in order to inspire reverence or awe in the passing crowd. You were a theologian, a philosopher, a prophet, and above all else you were a poet and had your hours and your days of spiritual struggle, of lonely meditation, perhaps of rapt ecstasy. But you were also a man, and indeed a complete man, with all the desires, the caprices, the temptations, the weaknesses which are inherent in the man not wholly freed from the ferment of the blood and the weight of the flesh. And besides, even the greatest saints, when so inclined, ate with gusto their locusts and dry bread; and they did not hesitate to smile and even to jest.

You were a man, Dante, and you were young. So instead of seeing you always with your head bent over old books or your brow furrowed with thought, it pleases me to recall you in your human moments, even the too human moments, of your familiar, everyday life.

I see you in the prime of youth, in prosperous Florence, the city which you loved, and hated, until you died. I see you with friends, not all of them poets, following through the country-side the solitary by-paths where there were neither walls nor hedges to keep your hands from the lilies and the poppies in the fields. I see you laughing and jesting with your companions, and throwing yourself upon the grass to contemplate at ease the limpid sky above the city of stone encircled by its walls of stone. And there you talked of Monna Berta and Ser Martino[1] and of the reproving face of Master Brunetto, and of the maidens you saw at Holy Mass in the church of Santa Margherita or Santa Reparata. For you, too, made love, and not only in the Platonic, mystic, romantic fashion which you describe in your *Vita Nuova*, all sighs, laments, visions, dreams, salutations, and swoonings. In the *Vita Nuova* you are the artist who selects and changes and recreates at will the actual history of a youthful adoration; but in the

---

[1] The names are taken from Dante's line, *Par.* XIII, 139; while Master Brunetto is the 'schoolmaster,' Brunetto Latini.—Trans.

same book we learn that you liked to play at love with other women and pay court to them, and that by some of them you were courted and well-nigh won over. In short, it was natural that you, like other young men, should not be content solely with angelic smiles, salutations, and rhymed verses; and you yourself have confessed that your path was more than once impeded by sensuous desire. This confession is confirmed by the early biographies and by those little anecdotes which are not wholly true but which contain, at least, the more probable portions of an old tradition. There is no sufficient reason for maintaining that you were not overcome, as a youth and as a man, by sinful temptations.[1]

But turning aside from these not unfounded insinuations, I picture you eyeing the young beauties who quickened your heart-beats as you loitered on the corners or passed on your way through the narrow streets of old Florence—a young poet, a novice in philosophy, a poor gentleman, a partisan biding his time. Now in the bright sunlight of morning, now in the pale light of the moon, I see you peering at a damsel who slips around the corner, or at a window where a fresh face shows itself, delicate and lovely. Even in church (you have written it of yourself) you were not ashamed to stare at the handsome women until even the bystanders noticed it. And if, in truth, your love for the 'youngest of the angels' was never stained by a thought less than angelic, need we assume that you never looked at other girls with the natural disturbance, sinful if you like, which is common to every youth who is neither an icicle nor a saint?

[1] v. G. Papini, *La Leggenda di Dante.* Lanciano, Carabba, 1910.

Even when youth had passed, can we say confidently that during your time of exile you lived in the houses of noblemen and stood in the piazzas of cities always showing that harsh face of a sour spinster? or of a metaphysician in mental travail? On the contrary, it is easy to imagine you chatting with some idle gentlewoman and taking pleasure in public spectacles—in the entrance of a victorious *condottiero*, in a religious procession, in a springtime festival of the people. You cannot make me believe, however grim you look in the old and well-known portraits, that you never answered jest with jest, or that you were not occasionally cheek by jowl with buffoons. And did you never stop by chance to listen to a strolling minstrel who sang himself hoarse at the cross-roads among gaping countryfolk, or enter the circle formed about a juggler or a wayside rope-dancer? And that day when you drank a glass of wine too much at the inn, and stayed joking with the landlady and the donkey-drivers? And that other day in late September when you were parched with thirst, and entered the vineyard in Romagna where you ate your fill of topaz grapes filched by the same hand that wrote the *Divina Commedia*?

I do not mean that you debased yourself like a Folgore or a Cecco.[1] On the contrary, you always preserved your dignity and kept to decency, and your pride and self-respect served as checks. But at times you were just a man; you were hungry and thirsty, you

---

[1] Folgore da San Gimignano and Cecco Angioliere were poets contemporary with Dante. D. G. Rossetti calls Cecco the 'scamp' of the Danteans. A brief account of both men may be found in Rossetti's *Dante and his Circle.*— Trans.

THE YOUNG DANTE

From the fresco by Giotto.   Palace of the Podesta, Florence.
About 1334.   (Before restoration.)   [*Photo Alinari.*]

THE YOUNG DANTE

From the fresco by Giotto.   Palace of the Podestà, Florence
About 1334.   (Before restoration.)   [Photo Alinari.]

*Lucidato col fresco di Giotto
da Seymour Kirkup, il primo
promotore della ricerca, prima
della riscoperta nel 1841 c.*

longed for smiles and kisses, and you could jest or, at least, share in the jests of others.

The misfortunes of your life brought you to the need for powerful friends, and one cannot always show to the powerful a face wrathful or preoccupied. They might mistake an expression of mental absorption for a sign of boredom, and hold it an offence. So you must have had to speak empty and foolish words, and smile or make pretence of smiling.

After days and nights of meditation, of study, of reading, of poetic labour, you would feel the longing to see a little open sky, a stretch of green fields, to lie at ease under a tree, to listen to the song of a country-girl, to gather a rose just bursting into bloom, to sit beside a stream, to follow with the eye the moving and changing clouds, to eat ripe fruit, to cheer the heart with a glass of good wine, to caress the sleek head of a child.

Of these moments of your life, which are the least known but which were, perhaps, the sweetest to you, there is some trace in your writings, but none in the books written about you. Will you, then, permit a poet just once to see in you not only the monumental genius, the martyr of his own and others' passions, the creator of three superposed worlds, the judge of the human race, the lover of God, but also the happy mortal, the offspring of sun and earth, the man humanly human?

THE DANTE OF THE LEGENDS

OETIZING moderns, whose imaginations soar the higher the more they themselves wallow in the mire, have spread abroad the idea of a Dante wholly great; at every moment of his life proud, upright, heroic—a Dante who regards with a Michaelangelesque frown the great ones of the earth and even the saints in heaven; a Dante wholly majestic and awe-inspiring; a Dante à la Carlyle, an incarnation perfect and entire of the Hero as Poet. I do not wish indeed to suggest that the Dante thus pictured is false, but I claim the right to doubt if it is the only true Dante.

Arguments for thus fashioning a Dante *alla dantesca* are at hand by the hundred. The *Divina Commedia* alone would be more than sufficient. One who has written a work like that with a comprehension so vast and so new of the historic in life and of the profound moral demands of a religious faith taken seriously—and taken with such sincerity that it is compelling even to-day on us who are distant and disinterested readers—such a man could not have had a small mind and a common spirit.

But the prolific phrase-makers of our day (whom Dante, if he returned to life, would treat, I hope, as Cervantes treated the bachelor-of-arts)[1] forget, in the over-stressed exuberance of their exordiums and perorations, two simple truths which a very elementary knowledge of history teaches to anyone who can see an inch before his nose. The first is that a man, even a very

[1] Samson Carrasco in *Don Quixote*, Part II, Chap. II. ff.—Trans.

excellent man, is never all of one piece and one colour; so that side by side with great achievements are to be found the falterings of weakness. We should not take advantage of this fact, as certain so-called doctors of medicine have done, to explain a genius by his defects, but neither is there need to forget or disregard the defects when we are concerned not to illustrate the work, but to write all the pages of a man's life. The other truth, which derives from the first, is that to picture a man of genius always in a statue-like attitude of severity and solemnity is a stupidity equal to the opposite one of the expert psychiatrists who study the great only in the spasms of epilepsy.

At first, we experience surprise and a feeling of repulsion and disenchantment. Then, on reconsidering and re-examining the question, we see that it is better thus, and that thus it had to be. The great are great just because, in the midst of common life and in spite of the hindrances of the flesh and of their own baseness, they have succeeded in expressing and in creating something which surpasses themselves and their time. The hero, in spite of his valet's opinion, is a hero even in his dressing-gown.

On this account, I attribute to the surviving legends about Dante much more value than is granted them by the zealous advocates of the 'critical' or 'historical method.' Not all these pleasantries and tales are likely to be true, but writers who have discussed them up to the present have shown themselves over-fastidious, being prejudiced always by the superhuman image of the poet to which we referred a moment ago. To be sure, the Dante derived from these tales is different—and in some instances shockingly different—from the Dante that we may call 'official' and sacrosanct. Some of the traits are those of the historical Dante; others appear coarsened and exaggerated; many new ones are added, not all of which do him credit.

We knew already that Dante was proud, and in the traditions we find some traits of arrogance side by side with instances of his intense application to study and of his remarkable readiness of wit. But besides the confirmations, there are also revelations, and not all conform to the idea which we have of him. This other Dante, the non-historical Dante, was not a well-bred person. He was not ashamed to ill-treat anyone who failed in respect toward him, to abuse anyone who did not answer to suit him or who annoyed or offended him. He himself was highly sensitive, but he took pleasure in deriding others. Up to this point the tradition is probable, if not actually true. But worse follows. He did not disdain to be a tale-bearer; on occasion, he pilfered; he was not ashamed to vie in scurrility with Gonnella, the jester, to throw compliments to the girls in the streets, to consort with prostitutes, to amuse himself with plays on words, and to show himself greedy of tit-bits.

And this is not all. We always see him in the legends in situations which are ridiculous or humiliating for a man such as he was. We learn that he was set to train cats. We see him on intimate terms with buffoons; derided for his low stature and for his greediness at table; soundly thrashed; sought as adviser in the matter of seducing a woman; suddenly dumb at the beginning of a discourse through previous over-confidence; and, finally, once suspected of heresy.[1] Quite different from the perfect Dante of the heroic biography with a face stern and frowning, like an ancient Roman mask.

But up to what point may we accept as true the gossiping, irreverent legend?

Dantologists have never taken very seriously this little Dante—the 'stuff that buffoons are made of,' to quote Farinelli—and they have always preferred Alighieri the Great. Who would think them wrong? But the less decorative Alighieri is not to be thrown away without examination, and the anecdotes told about him are not all to be rejected. At times there is more flavour of life in the legend than in the authentic historical documents, which are not always impartial and clear.

In regard to these anecdotes Moore[2] states that the 'great majority' of them were told of other men before they were told of Dante. This is not true. Of the forty-five legendary motifs or themes which I have collected, only six are to be found in texts earlier than the time of Dante; two are related also of contemporaries; six are told of persons who lived somewhat later: that is, of the forty-five, only fourteen, at most, are suspect. Where is Moore's 'large majority'?

That of the remaining thirty the most are either false or doubtful is quite probable, not to say certain; but that all are false or doubtful I firmly deny. Some are told by men who lived shortly after Dante and held him in respect and admiration—Boccaccio, Petrarch,

[1] These legends with their variants are collected in *La Leggenda di Dante* by G. Papini. Lanciano, Carabba, 1910. The present chapter is, in part, the preface to that collection.

[2] E. Moore, *Dante and his Early Biographers*. London, 1890, p. 167.

Benevenuto da Imola. Others were handed down by oral
tradition, losing in the process exactness in the details
but not all the truth. Some of the stories are in harmony with the character of Alighieri as we know it from
his writings; as, for example, those that illustrate for
us the 'bread that tastes of salt'; and if others put
before us a Dante that does not correspond precisely to
the lithograph described by the Carlylean phrase-makers,
there is no need for us to lose our tempers and become
angry. If the righteous sin seventy-seven times a day,
according to the proverb, is it altogether impossible
that an austere man should be guilty of trifling, or a
hero of pettiness?

Legends exaggerate, expand, disfigure; but they rarely
create. From every bubble, which seems a nothingness,
we derive a drop of water; and from a mass of traditions
we can obtain with patience a speck of truth.

Finally, there needs to be done for Dante what
Socrates did for philosophy: he should be brought down
from heaven to earth. We have raised, with the best
intentions, a statue larger than life. It is time to revive
the real man as he was in life; not indeed in order to
debase him—that which is eternally great in him resists
every such effort of little men like ourselves—but in
order to understand him better. A giant such as Dante
has no need of high heels, of stilts, of embellishments.

The entire truth is due to the genius, as it is to the
hero. And Dante, who spoke the most bitter truths to
the living and the dead, cannot complain if we refuse
to hide his less worthy traits. His weaknesses and his
defects make him seem nearer to us, make him our
brother; a brother immeasurably greater, but fashioned,

nevertheless, of the same earthly clay of which we ourselves are made. And because of this acknowledged
brotherhood we feel that we love him better. We
venerate the saints, but we embrace and forgive our
brothers.

In every man, whether great or small, there is mingled,
as the poet said, fire and filth. The very great men are
those who, like Dante, have known how to expel the
ignoble elements or to consume them in the fire so as
to make the flame burn more brightly.

HEBREW, ETRUSCAN, ROMAN

ANTE is a world in little, and also, by fore-shortening, a people: a people not altogether homogeneous and concordant. I see in him besides the Florentine of the thirteenth century, a Hebrew prophet, an Etruscan priest, and a Roman imperialist.

He was nourished, as all Christians were and ought to be, on the Bible; but I suspect that he was more in sympathy with the Old Testament than the New. In the Old Testament he must have felt himself akin to the prophets. That inner force which compelled him to admonish, to warn, to threaten, to foretell punishments as well as to announce salvation—all this expressed in symbolic language which was often harsh but inspired—allies Dante with the greatest prophets of Israel. Even in his political letters he has a figurative style, an emphasis, an impetuosity of movement which recall the violent denunciations of Isaiah and Jeremiah.

From Etruria he has derived, unconsciously, the two great themes of his masterpiece—a preoccupation with coming events and with the life after death. The Etruscan religion, so far as we understand it from their figurative art, which must serve us in lieu of documents and a sacred text, gave more importance than any other ancient religion to the myths of the dead in the under-world and to the divinities of the Hereafter. In the Etruscan religion there are more demons, and more fearful ones, than in the Hellenic and the Roman.

Certain paintings in Etruscan tombs are anticipatory illustrations of Dante's Hell. Moreover, the Etruscans made of prophecy a real and exact science, haruspicy; and as soothsayers and diviners they were always held in repute and were consulted until the early centuries of the Empire. Destroyed as a nation, they survived for centuries as privileged prophets. Thus in Dante we often find besides the fulminating prophet of the Hebraic type, something of the haruspex who is not content with general predictions but aims at a precision almost mathematical. It may be said that numerical precision with regard to the future is found in the Book of Daniel and in the *Apocalypse*; but the fact that Dante imitated them may be traced to an obscure survival of the Etruscan prophetic consciousness, unless we wish to seek a nearer source in the calculations of Joachim of Flora.[1]

Like the Roman of ancient times, Dante has the twofold instinct of justice and political unity. He unites in himself the two adversaries—Cato, the man of rectitude, and Cæsar, the founder of the Empire. He speaks of Rome as of his true fatherland, and feels that it is still necessary to gather all the peoples and countries of the world under the banner of Rome. He is a jurist with a passion for liberty, and yet resigns

[1] Joachim of Flora (d. 1202) was Abbot of Flora in Calabria. The most famous of his prophetic treatises was his comment on the *Apocalypse*. He proclaimed the doctrine of the three world-ages, and maintained that the dispensation of the Father and of the Son would be followed by that of the Holy Spirit, the precise date of whose coming he announced as 1260. (See the article 'Joachim,' *Enc. Brit.*) Readers of Dante will recall the reference in *Par.* XII, 140–141 to the Calabrian abbot 'endowed with prophetic spirit.' There are numerous references in this volume to his prophecies and to his followers, the Joachimists.—Trans.

himself to seeing a Teutonic prince take the throne of Augustus if only the great Roman unity may be reestablished on the earth.

Some have said of Dante that above all else he bears the stamp of the Germanic mind. The Germans and their admirers, like Houston Chamberlain, are united in maintaining that in aspect, family-descent, and genius Dante is a pure Teuton. There is in him, undoubtedly, a moral earnestness which is to be found in the portrait of the German which admirers of the Teutonic type are accustomed to paint. But earnestness is not, so far as I know, a monopoly of the Nordics. We find a deep moral earnestness in the Hebrew prophets and in the Romans of the great periods.

And so, to return to Dante, I see as actuating causes in his mind the three things discussed in this chapter. I find in him a Daniel without the lions, a Tarchon without Tages,[1] a Cato who did not commit suicide.

---

[1] Tages was a mysterious being who instructed Tarchon, the leader of the Etruscans, in the art of the haruspices.—Trans.

DANTE'S DUALISM

ᏅN the treacherous thickets of literature there is
a race of huntsmen who go beating the bush
night and day, trying to drive into the open
the inconsistencies of great men. People of this sort
do not understand, in the heat of the chase, that
real contradictions are found more often in mediocre
minds, and that in the case of the great we ought to
take account of the vastness of soul and intellect which
gathers within itself opinions and tendencies apparently
contradictory, but actually concurrent and comple-
mentary. In little minds, contrasting ideas live together
with difficulty and must of necessity come to blows; and
in the outcome remain definitely contradictory. But in
vigorous minds, more active and more ample, contrasting ideas work together to produce a richer vision;
and, in achieving harmonious results, arrive at a
higher synthesis which annuls, while it justifies, their
opposition.

Thus it is with Dante. From a distance he
appears a monolith all of a colour; but those who
penetrate within find that he is made of different
marbles brought from different places. Or, rather,
let us say that instead of a monolith we face an
edifice of many styles of architecture to which unity
is given by the burning imprint of his spontaneous genius. As with every great man, Dante is
like a many-sided pillar, and his bust is that of
a herm.

Whoever sees in him only the Thomist[1] or only the Ghibelline, sees but a part of the truth. Dante. is outside the fixed categories, above incidental divisions, beyond the unyielding *yea* and *nay*. In him there is everything: the wisdom of the East, the Greek *logos*, the Christian *caritas*, the Roman *civilitas*. He venerates Aristotle and follows St Thomas, but he does not hesitate to levy upon the Arabians and the Jews. He feeds upon the Old and New Testaments, but does not scorn to make use of Moslem tradition.[2]

In the general principles of his theological belief he is a follower of St Thomas, but he is also profoundly influenced by St Augustine, St Bernard, St Bonaventure, by the mystic Victorines,[3] and the apocalyptic Joachimists.

Dante was, at heart, an Augustinian and a Platonist; intellectually, an Aristotelian–Thomist; and his poetry verges now toward one, now toward the other. He is too messianic and mystic to be called a rationalist; and, at the same time, he has too much intellectualism and civism to be called a purely contemplative mind.

He is an Aristotelian and a Thomist—this has been said often enough, but he makes St Thomas praise the 'invidious truths' of the Averroist philosopher, Siger of Brabante; and makes St Bonaventure, adversary of the Spiritual Joachimists, praise that same Joachim of Flora whom Aquinas himself did not hold in favour.

[1] Follower of St Thomas Aquinas, the great scholastic philosopher and theologian of the thirteenth century.—Trans.

[2] I do not accept in its entirety the exaggerated thesis of Asín Palacios, *La Escatología musulmana en la Divina Commedia* (Madrid, E. Maestre, 1919), but some of the comparisons are certainly worth considering.

[3] Followers of Hugh of St Victor, in Paris.

In Dante lived the man of earlier times, the citizen of Rome who dreamed of Empire; but at the same time he is the messianic disciple of St John and of the Calabrian abbot, who expects from the Veltro, from the Holy Spirit, the spiritual renewal of the world.[1]

Dante is undoubtedly a Christian, although not a perfect Christian—and who except the saints could pretend to be a true Christian?—and he is a Catholic Christian, an enemy of heresy; yet he preserves in his heart a deep affection for the pagan philosophers, cites Cicero as on an equality with the Gospel, and provides for the salvation not only of Trajan, in homage to Gregory the Great, but also of Cato, enemy of the Empire, of Statius, through an unlikely and unverified conversion, and finally, thanks to a half-verse of Virgil's, of the very obscure Rhipeus.[2]

Dante does not choose between the Church and the Empire. He accepts the Church provided it reforms. He desires the Empire provided it fulfils its function. He does not wish that the Emperor should become the master of the Pope, nor that the Pope should usurp the mission of the Emperor. And he brings together these two great powers, which had been for so long a time in opposition, and equalizes them in a higher purpose which transcends them both—the service of suffering humanity, the triumph of peace.

Among the religious orders which held the field in his day and contended for control over the souls of men,

---

[1] For the identity of the Veltro with the Holy Spirit, see Chap. 43 of this volume.

[2] Rhipeus, iustissimus unus
Qui fuit in Teucris et servantissimus aequi.—*Aeneid*, II, 426–427.

Dante takes his seat as a supreme judge who brings together and reconciles the opposed. St Bonaventure, the Franciscan, eulogizes St Dominic, 'harsh to his foes'; and St Thomas, the Dominican, sings the praises of St Francis, who, in strict accord with the Gospel, preached and practised love toward one's enemies. Both Dominicans and Franciscans, Dante seems to say, serve the faith of Christ and the welfare of Christianity; the one order combating heresy which threatens the indispensable unity; the other setting the example of poverty, so desirable at a time when the greed of prelates had alienated many souls from the true Church.

Everyone remembers what admiration Dante has for Julius Cæsar and in what terrible jaws Cæsar's assassins are crushed.[1] Yet the same Dante places the poor Curio[2] in hell for no other fault than that of stifling all hesitation in the mind of Cæsar when he delayed to cross the Rubicon; and in the *Convivio*[3] and the *Purgatorio*[4] he glorifies the younger Cato who committed suicide rather than obey Cæsar. Dante, then, who glorifies the Empire, condemns the man who assisted in the founding of the Empire, and extols him who opposed the establishing of the Empire. This seems a clear contradiction, but the contradiction, when well examined, disappears. In Curio, instigator of civil war, Dante sees one who spoke through evil passions and for private gain.[5] In Cato of Utica, who openly

[1] *Inf.* XXXIV, 61–67.   [2] *Inf.* XXVIII, 94–102.
[3] *Conv.* IV, v, 16; vi, 10; xxviii, 13–19.
[4] *Purg.* I, 31–109.
[5] According to contemporary sources, Cæsar paid the debts of Curio, who, for this reason, became Cæsar's adherent.

opposed Cæsar, he sees one who is redeemed by his love of justice and of Rome—a love so strong as to make him prefer loss of life to loss of liberty. And perhaps in his heart Cæsar himself esteemed Cato more than Curio.

Lastly, for Dante, woman is not only the almost divine Beatrice who draws him toward God. She is also the gentlewoman who makes pretence of love and serves him as a convenient screen; she is the 'pitiful lady' who compassionates him and whom he rewards with respectful affection; she is Pargoletta or Violetta, the Little Maid or the Violet, who gives him occasion for charming and musical songs; or she may be the wild and rebellious Pietra of the stony heart, whom he would like to grasp by the hair and drag with him into 'hot hell.' [1]

Other antitheses and paradoxes could be pointed out in Dante's work, but I should not be justified in calling them contradictions. Multifarious aspects are the right of those who have a rich inner life; and to show a double aspect does not mean in every case to be either insincere or forgetful. Still less so when, as happens with Dante, the apparent dualisms are resolved into a synthesis which surmounts them. Dante is neither wholly pagan nor wholly Christian; but he was unwilling to renounce entirely the heritage of the ancients. Even more he distinguished the human needs of the contemporary civil life from the ultimate goal to which the soul of man is destined. Each one of us desires salvation and the joy of everlasting life; but meanwhile, since we are here

---

[1] The references, which students of Dante's minor works will recognize, are to the *Vita Nuova* and to names which occur in the *Rime*.—Trans.

below, we must live with one another in the best possible way. We must follow, first of all, the Gospel and the saints; but in our desire for peace and justice during our enforced earthly habitation we need not throw away either Aristotle or Cicero. Holding these desires and beliefs, Dante was neither wholly Guelph nor wholly Ghibelline. If the Pope leads us, or ought to lead us, to the peace of heaven, the Emperor is better qualified to secure peace on earth.

Faith—and faith, too, in revelations of the future—is the very essence of the Christian. But we cannot renounce the aid of reason, which is a gift from God. And we do no wrong if, after having followed St Bernard or Joachim, we go to school to Aristotle and Seneca. St Thomas, it is true, has constructed a wonderful edifice wherein reason demonstrates to the intellect the solidity of faith; but if certain useful truths are found in St Augustine or in Hugh of St Victor, or even in Pier Giovanni Olivi[1] and Ubertino da Casale,[2] why reject them? St Thomas is the fortified tower where we can barricade ourselves, but the others are eagles or doves which fly above the highest ramparts.

Was Dante conscious of this duality within himself? Or did these different attitudes of mind succeed one another at intervals as time went on, without his even being aware of their contradictions?

[1] Pier Giovanni Olivi (d. 1298) was a Franciscan, leader of the Spirituals, and a teacher at Sta. Croce in Florence, where, possibly, Dante listened to his lectures. v. Davidssohn, *Firenze ai Tempi di Dante.* Florence, Bemporad, 1929, pp. 223–224.—Trans.

[2] Ubertino followed Pier Giovanni as leader of the Spirituals. There is an interesting reference to him in *Par.* XII, 124.—Trans.

I believe that the synthesis of these contrary elements was brought about by the natural unifying power of his genius, nourished as it was by so great and varied a culture; and that through his complete universality, which brought into intimate contact past, present, and future, he could rightly offer himself, in the *Commedia*, as the symbol of the whole human race.

THE THREE GREAT PARADOXES

*L*IKE every great work, Dante's is an answer. It is the expression of a desire to supply a lack, a deficiency, a want, in the ordinary temporal existence. An unbearable sense of mediocrity is the point of departure for attaining to greatness. To the humbleness of their lot the heroes of the intellect reply with the greatness of their work. Therefore we must keep in mind three paradoxes in the character of Dante.

Reacting to the wretchedness of his ruined life, Dante answers with his immeasurable pride, his consciousness of being almost a supreme master of men, an adviser of emperors, a judge of pontiffs, a herald of the designs of God.

To his natural sensitiveness, almost feminine, correspond, by contrast and revulsion, the boldness of his conceptions, the rashness of his designs, the audacity of his aims and words.

To his deep and persistent sensuality—sometimes running over into licence—he reacts by turning again to an earlier poetic motif and magnifying it until it becomes almost the spiritual deification of the Beloved. The eternal sensualist makes of his Lady almost a counterpart of Our Lady.

The poor mendicant exile conceives of himself as an intermediary between earth and heaven. Timorous even to the point of weeping, he becomes the intrepid and pitiless chastiser of men. The slave of sex in adoration exalts the transfigured woman to the side of the Blessed Virgin. All of Dante's work, in its character and in its dominant ideas, is an instinctive and splendid compensation for his sufferings and his weaknesses.

In truth, every great quality derives from its opposite. The mediocre remains mediocre for ever. But from the coward can come forth the hero; from the humbled, the dominating; from the criminal, the saint. The man of the middle class always remains middle class; but the man of the people may become dictator or emperor.

The soul, brought low and hemmed in by circumstance, will rise, create for itself another environment, restore the equilibrium between fate and aspirations, reply with a victorious *Yes* to all the *Noes* of life. He who stands in the middle is content. He who has been condemned to the depths, wishes to spring up to the very summit.

Pride is almost always humiliation which has been overcome, an attempt to escape from the mediocrity of life.

Boldness is fear surmounted, the outbreak of the timid who have cast off their chains, the ferocity of the wrathful lamb.

Platonism is sensuousness transformed and purified, the effort to change the appetite for carnal pleasure into spiritual adoration.

Without these paradoxes, which are the beginning of every real victory over self, we could not succeed in understanding the greatness of Dante and his work.

35

The really great man is not he who is born great, and who through a fatal facility loses his native powers, but rather he who wins his greatness in spite of everything and everybody, against the trammels of his own nature, against every adversity.

THE MODERNITY OF DANTE

OVER every considerable period of the brief history of human thought there presides a supreme genius who sums it up and represents it. For indolent minds, antiquity is Homer, the Renaissance is Shakespeare. Romanticism is Goethe, Modernism is Dostoievski. To Dante belong, as fief or empire, the Middle Ages. In the notorious darkness of the Middle Ages covering a world expectant of the pagan mistral which would sweep away that darkness, there was seen, all at once, in the midst of Italy, a tiny lamp, a lantern, a torch, a pyre, even—as some think— a small volcano; and this light, a little smoky to tell the truth, was called Alighieri.

According to common opinion, Dante might be a megatherium or a dinosaur preserved, at least as a fossil skeleton, at the close of those dark ages which extend from the splendours of Romulus Augustulus to the glories of Cæsar Borgia.

The thoughts and the faith of Dante, which were as flesh and blood to him, are now dust and ashes because Catholicism (according to the epigones of the slayers of Christ) is no more than a badly embalmed corpse still standing upright, perhaps through the effect of devilish injections. But there survive, so they say, of this mediæval monster called Dante, some precious fragments of poetry. Art, and art alone, has been able to preserve an anachronistic document of the infantile conceptions of an epoch past and gone.

Dante, to use the accepted phrase, summarizes and closes the Middle Ages. He is a monument, but of a city in ruins, of a civilization fallen to pieces; and the monument is saved only because of the beauty of certain capitals, of a group of bas-reliefs, of a few arches, of three or four pinnacles. But Dante, as a whole, belongs to a world entirely dead. He is at once the cathedral and the sepulchre of the Middle Ages.

The truth, as I see it, is absolutely different. Without any rhetorical trickery, we can speak of the modernity of Dante.

Of course, not everything in him is alive and modern, just as not all of Tolstoi, who lived in our own time, is alive and modern. Nevertheless, there are certain substantial elements of the Dantesque spirit so modern as to be, even to-day, among the hopes and ideals for whose fulfilment we still look to the future.

I shall say nothing of Catholicism and of Catholic philosophy. In spite of all the hasty grave-diggers, there are still some people in the world who believe firmly in the kingdom of Christ and in His law; and there are still to be found—and not only among the clergy and the seminary-teachers—ardent Thomists and Scotists and sincere admirers of St Bernard and St Bonaventure. The wise ones will say that thinkers holding such beliefs have been superseded for centuries, and that they form no integral part of the stream of modern culture. Let us leave these wise folk to wade in the stream until the moment, fast approaching, when they drown.

Let us turn our gaze rather to those modern Catholics and, in general, to all Christians who feel keenly the necessity for not limiting their religious life to mere devotional mechanics. In all these people we find, here in the well-advanced twentieth century, the same aspirations and hopes as in Dante. Let me mention two of them.

First of all, an aversion to the prominence of the political side in the life of the Church, and to any intermingling of economic activity and priestly function. Modern Catholics are as hostile as Alighieri was to the politician-priest and to the man-of-business-priest. They are convinced that the Church is, in its essence, a spiritual society with spiritual aims, and that therefore it must avoid, so far as social obligations and historical changes permit, all meddling, direct or indirect, in political affairs. This means that priests ought not to belong to any political party or take part in the government of a country, or share in the struggles between factions or classes, unless they are acting as peace-makers. Their mission is moral and spiritual only; they are called to direct the faithful to the betterment of their souls and to eternal salvation, not to administer states.

Priesthood deals only with divine things, and politics is one of the most earthly among all earthly things, and one of the furthest from the evangelic ideal. The priest must be neither a prince nor a minister of princes, nor in any way a partaker in the civil government of states. Cæsar is one thing and Peter is another. In the Catholic Church there is one king only, Jesus Christ. All emperors, kings, presidents, and ministers are subject, if they are Christians, to the moral authority of the Church which can, in given cases, blame and condemn their actions, but cannot and ought not to associate itself with them to govern the human races.

The Church is a teacher. She teaches all men.(and, therefore, men in political life) to be perfect so as to merit peace on earth and bliss in heaven. This is the mission assigned to her by her divine Founder. If in some periods of her history there were abbots who were feudal lords, popes who wished to direct the politics of this or that country, cardinals who were ministers of monarchs, that same history teaches us that from all this the Church received more harm than good. Neither the Reformation nor Encyclopedism would have resulted as they did if all the members of the Church had remained faithful to their purely spiritual duties. By the very necessity of the case, the Church has a policy of her own which is not policy in the usual political sense of the word, but is rather a search for the best way of living among different states and within them. It is a protective policy, not a directive policy. And what else than this did Dante mean when he hurled himself against the popes of his time, who instead of consecrating all their efforts to the perfecting of souls in the requirements of the Gospel and to the pacifying of a disordered world, sided with this or that king, sought alliances and temporal advantages, and by so doing helped to increase immeasurably the fratricidal wars and the divisions between country and country?

Dante was no less severe against the covetousness of the clergy and the frenzied pursuit of riches, all too frequent among the prelates. It is not possible for the Church, as an institution, to preserve absolutely the principle of evangelic poverty (even the disciples had their cashier), but it is most unfortunate for the prestige of the faith that the heads of the Church and, in general, the priests and the monks, should show themselves eager to acquire worldly goods. The Canon Law, in fact, forbids priests to engage in trade or banking, and in these matters very great progress has been made since the time of Dante. But it needed the creation of the Mendicant Orders, the aggressive action of the Reformation, and the hard lesson of more modern experiences to bring about such a result.

And in another aspect of his Catholicism Dante is very modern. He was expecting, as we shall see later, the advent of the Third Person of the Trinity who would drive back to hell every form of concupiscence and of evil covetousness. He was, in fact, although beneath 'the veil of strange verses,' a thoughtful and independent disciple of Joachim of Flora and of the Spirituals. This expectation of the Paraclete is, even in modern times, more alive among Catholic writers than is generally supposed: it is sufficient to instance Léon Bloy.[1]

Even to-day there are those who, remembering Christ's promise in the gospel of St John, expect the third Revelation, the coming of the Comforter, the Epiphany of the Holy Spirit. This expectation is not based, like that of the Joachimists, on fantastic calculations; nor does it give rise among Catholics to heretical communities. It is a vague expectation, more a hope than a belief; and in those who accept it there is no

---

[1] This expectation appears in almost all the works of Léon Bloy, especially in *L'Ame de Napoléon*. Indications of a desire for a new Revelation appear also in De Maistre and Huysmans.

inclination to separate themselves from the Church or to refuse the least part of its dogmatic teaching.

The attitude of these Catholics, then, is very similar to that of Dante, who never intended, even in his messianic prophecies, to separate himself from Catholic discipline.

This is not the place to ask how far the hope of a future and explicit manifestation of the Holy Spirit may be in conformity with the teaching of the Church. Here we are speaking of the modernity of Dante, not of his orthodoxy. Moreover, if there were in him some shadow of heterodoxy, the fact would remain that such shadows have not disappeared entirely from the modern world, and that even on this point he could be considered, whether for good or ill, alive in the world of thought to-day.

Dante's modernity reveals itself, however rash such a statement may appear, also in his fundamental political concept.

As everyone knows, this concept was the restoration of the Empire. Many think that in Dante it means a literary nostalgia for the greatness of Rome, and still more a desire for an authority sufficiently strong and wide to blunt the unwise desires of the papacy for temporal power, and to establish in Europe, and especially in Italy, order, concord, and justice. Although warranted by memories of ancient times and by the political circumstances of that time, torn as it was by strife and fatal divisions, this imperialistic concept of Dante's came to be considered a Utopia, and it is now looked upon as a mere historical relic of mediæval thought. It is a point in proof that at the period of the

Risorgimento many Italians, without quite understanding Dante's ideals, saw in him above all the prophet of national unity and not what he really was, the militant theorist of the imperial idea. The formation of national states which was begun in the Middle Ages and has been protracted, we may say, to our own day, has created a state of mind contrary to the conception of a universal authority such as Alighieri desired. As a partisan of the Empire, he came to be regarded as a Utopian even in his own century, which was moving toward the autonomy of the communes and the division of the governing power; and in our time, as an advocate of the Empire, Dante is regarded as an honourable fossil.

Actually the painful experience of these last years warns us that the creation of national states has been a necessary but not a definitive stage in the organization of the world. The dissolution of mediæval Christianity and the flourishing of nationalism and separatism have brought the nations to carnage and misery. 'The little threshing-floor which makes us so ferocious' is now at length so small in our eyes, and the peoples who inhabit it so connected and bound together by all the forms of modern life, intellectual and economic, that already many are turning in thought, without being quite aware of it, to the mediæval Utopia, to the Utopia of Dante. Once more we seek for unity, though by other ways than Dante's. We are discovering that Europe, or rather all the human race, is destined to disasters always more and more terrible, if it does not achieve the reconstruction of a great political union, which may not be precisely the Roman Empire, but which shall, at any rate, be a multiform organism governed by a single body of laws and by one supreme authority.

The very countries where nationalism is strongest are aware that the present political units are too small to deal with the new conditions of life; and we speak once more of Empire, not because we are moved by nostalgic fancies but because we are driven by urgent spiritual and economic needs.

The problem is to see if this unification will be brought about by means of conquest on the part of one state more powerful than the others, or by means of a voluntary accord which, at the beginning, might consist of a loyal federation. Will unity be imposed by force, or will it come about through spontaneous and analogous desires?

The political unity of the civilized world, of which Dante dreamed, was undertaken in the sixteenth century by the Flemish-Spaniard, Charles V, who handed over Rome to be sacked by the Lutherans, and who in the end abdicated. It was again undertaken in the opening years of the nineteenth century by a gallicized Italian who took the Pope prisoner, and who later died defeated and a prisoner himself. Every other attempt at hegemony—economic on the part of England, military on the part of Germany—has failed in these last years. To-day the attempt is being made to achieve the necessary unity by means of agreements between the nations: by customs unions, continental leagues, a League of Nations.

We speak for the moment only of proposals, of hopes, of tentative approaches. But that Dante is not to-day a stranger among us is shown by the fact that men are beginning to think, just as he did, that in order to put an end to the perilous rivalries of states and to establish a higher form of justice which shall be exercised also for the peoples menaced or sacrificed, the most certain method would be the political unity of at least Europe.

Such a unity would not be the Empire in Dante's sense, but the substance is the same and the end is identical. Dante, then, was not merely a dreamer about the past; he was a seer of the future.

The final proof of the modernity of Dante is in his poetry, that is, in the modes of his literary art. He is accused of an excessive fondness for the use of symbols and of obscure allusions. But has not modern poetry from Mallarmé and Rimbaud onward found once more in the natural universe a forest of symbols almost supernatural? It is said that Dante sometimes creates strange new words, that he does not avoid even plays on words or deliberate alliteration. But do we not find the same thing in *Work in Progress*, the most recent book of James Joyce, who is considered by sophisticated readers the most modern of modern writers?

It is said that Dante was at fault, from the point of view of the latest æsthetics, in wishing to express in poetry that which is foreign to the very nature of poetry, namely, theological truths and abstract thoughts. But has not Paul Claudel, the greatest modern Catholic poet, expressed in verse some of the most mystic dogmas of the Church? And Paul Valéry, the poet who is the latest passion of our *literati*, has he not energetically defended the right of poetry to convey and transmit the most complicated processes of thought?

Also as artist, then, Dante has not been 'superseded';

45

on the contrary, he is able to take his place beside and above the most recent innovators of poetical technique.[1] In the days of ingenuous realism and of scholastic rhetoric, the art of Dante would have seemed gothic, archaic, artificial. Our modern age has ended by returning to him and acknowledging him right.

And, finally, we may say that to-day Dante is more intimately and profoundly alive through our understanding of him than he has ever been since his own times: he is more modern than many moderns, more alive than many who are dead but think themselves alive.

[1] Even the latest among the literary schools of Europe, Super-realism, names Dante among its possible predecessors: 'bon nombre de poètes pourraient passer pour surréalistes, à commencer par Dante. . . .' André Breton, *Manifeste du Surréalisme*. Paris, Kra, 1924, pp. 42–43.

BOOK TWO

Life

THE ORPHAN

OCCACCIO, the writer of *novelle*, tells us in his *Life of Dante* that Dante's mother, being with child, dreamed of giving birth in a meadow to a son who, feeding on laurel-berries, became first a shepherd and then a peacock. This, according to modern interpretation, would have foreshadowed a pastoral poet and a coxcomb.

Although Dante wrote two eclogues in which he appears under the name of Tityrus, he assumed the guise of a shepherd only for a moment, a little while before his death; and granting that he was unduly proud, still no one can imagine him given up to ostentatious display.

Let us then leave the oneirology to the story-teller, and see rather what true omen presaged the coming of Dante. He was born, it seems certain, at the end of May 1265, and was conceived, therefore, at the end of August 1264. And precisely in that month of August there began to blaze in the sky one of those stars which have so often accompanied extraordinary events.

It is no teller of tales who recounts it, but a sober chronicler, Giovanni Villani. 'In the year of Our Lord 1264, in the month of August, there appeared in the sky a comet-star with great rays and a tail; which, rising from the east with great light until it reached the heavens overhead, [sank] toward the west: its tail was dazzling and it lasted three months, that is, until the end of November.'[1]

[1] Villani, *Cron.* VI, xci.

It was, of course, a mere coincidence; but such co-incidences are observed only at the birth or the death of great men; Cæsar,[1] for example, or Dante. It is not fitting that we should recall with reference to a mortal, however great he may be, the star seen in the east by the three Wise Men in the days of the most mysterious birth that the earth has witnessed.

Brunetto Latini, who delighted in astrology, drew from Dante's horoscope, some years later, the prophecy of his future glory. And on this occasion, at least, the astrologer was not mistaken; but the poet bought his greatness and immortality at the heavy price of misfortunes and disasters.

His first misfortune was to be left an orphan while still a child, bereft of both father and mother. His mother, Madonna Gabriella (probably of the Abati family), died when Dante was not more than five or six years old.[2] His father, Alighiero, died before the sixth of August, 1277.[3] When about twelve years old, Dante was left alone with a stepmother.

The biographers have not given sufficient prominence to this early orphanhood of Dante, which left traces in him even until his last years. We know little of his father, and that little is not such as to make him appear a man of much intelligence. The son never mentions him, and when Forese Donati recalls him in one of the famous sonnets of the *Tenzone*,[4] the son in his reply

[1] For the comet which appeared at the time of Cæsar's death, see Suetonius, LXXXVIII.

[2] Zingarelli, *Dante*. Milan, Vallardi, 1931, p. 89 (2nd ed.).

[3] *Ibid.*, p. 91.

[4] For the allusion to the father and for the entire *Tenzone*, see the learned and acute investigation of M. Barbi, *Studi Danteschi*, IX, 5–149; XVI, 69–103. See also Chap. 14 of this volume.

makes no defence of his father. It would appear from these sonnets that there rests on the memory of the dead Alighiero some unavenged shame, we cannot say what, it may be of usury or heresy. His name never appears in the Florentine annals of that stormy period, and from the scanty documents that mention him, we learn only that he loaned money. Probably he was a money-lender in a small way, and not such a man as the son could take pride in, either for quality of mind or for importance of position.

To his mother Dante makes a single allusion. It is when he applies to himself through Virgil's lips the famous words which in the Gospel are addressed to Christ:

Benedetta colei che in te s'incinse ! [1]

Blessed is the womb that bare thee !

But a boy who lost his mother in his fifth or sixth year cannot have very vivid memories of her. There remains, however, the lasting, unsatisfied longing for the mother's caress. Dante lost his mother too early for him to have enjoyed her tenderness, and in his father he found neither guide nor protector.

Although his longing for the maternal affection which he had scarcely experienced may have been the more acute, he must also have felt deeply the desire for the counsel and support of a real father. Even after the orphan has become a youth and a man, he will always be conscious of the unsatisfied hunger which he suffered in his loneliness as boy and as adolescent. Deprived before his time of real parents, he will feel the constant need to create for himself with his imagination another

[1] *Inf.* VIII, 45. Cf. Luke xi, 27.

51

father and another mother. The orphan does not accept his orphanhood with indifference. He has an over-whelming desire to hear himself called son. In the *Commedia*, in the poem which is a mirror of four worlds but which is at the same time the poet's fragmentary autobiography, symbolic but authentic, he is able to satisfy, perhaps without conscious intention, that filial longing. He represents those whom he admires and loves as calling him by the beloved name of son. Brunetto Latini repeatedly calls him 'my son';[1] as do Statius,[2] Cacciaguida,[3] and even Adam[4] and St Peter.[5] His beloved Virgil calls him 'son,' 'dear son,' 'my dear son' many times,[6] and once also 'sweet son.'[7] And, further, Dante represents Virgil as a father in the act of saving his son and holding him close to his breast:

> portandosene me sovra 'l suo petto
> come suo figlio, non come compagno.[8]

Bearing me along upon his breast as his own son, not as a companion.

It seems that this orphan, now a man, is never tired of hearing himself called by that affectionate name which he could have heard from his own parents for so brief a time. And he is not satisfied with being merely called son; he wishes to think that he has found a new father and a new mother. The first who could have seemed to him a truer father than the dead Alighiero was Brunetto

[1] *Inf.* XV, 31, 37. [2] *Purg.* XXV, 35, 58.
[3] *Par.* XV, 52; XVII, 94. [4] *Par.* XXVI, 115.
[5] *Par.* XXVII, 64.
[6] Figlio: *Inf.* VII, 115; *Purg.* XXVII, 35, 128. Figliolo: *Inf.* VII, 61; VIII, 67; *Purg.* VIII, 88; XVII, 92. Figliol mio: *Inf.* III, 121; XI, 16; *Purg.* IV, 46; XXVII, 20.
[7] *Purg.* III, 66. [8] *Inf.* XXIII, 50–51.

Latini, whose 'dear, benign, paternal image'[1] he recalls
although he meets Brunetto in a place of shame. But
nearer to his heart, though unknown to him on earth,
was his ancestor, Cacciaguida, whom he meets in the
light of Paradise, and to whom he says frankly and
openly, 'You are my father. . . .'[2] My real father, he
seems to say, I knew but little and he was of little worth;
but I can call you my father, you who were a knight, an
honoured offspring of the Roman seed, a martyr for
the faith, a Florentine neither decadent nor corrupt;
you, a blessed soul in heaven; you, the first plant of my
stock; in you I see myself and rejoice.

But he who in the mind of Dante more completely
fills the place of the lost and perhaps little loved father
is Virgil. In the *Commedia* and elsewhere, Dante gives
him many names, but the one which most willingly
comes from his pen is *padre*, father. Nor does he call
him simply father, but in the fullness of his affection
he adds other words which make even more tender
that name which he finds so beautiful to speak: 'sweet
father,' 'dear, sweet father,' 'my more than father,'
'my true father,' 'sweetest father.'[3] He gives that
name to some others, but to no one else with such
insistence and tenderness.

So great is Dante's affection for Virgil that he sees in
him not only a father but even a mother. When the
poet, in the eighth circle of the Inferno, is threatened
by demons, he says:

[1] *Inf.* XV, 83.   [2] *Par.* XVI, 16.
[3] Padre: *Purg.* XIII, 34. Dolce padre: *Inf.* VIII, 110; *Purg.* IV, 44; XV, 25,
124; XVII, 82; XXIII, 13; XXV, 17; XXVII, 52. Dolce padre caro: *Purg.*
XVIII, 13. Più che padre: *Purg.* XXIII, 4. Padre verace: *Purg.* XVIII, 7.
Dolcissimo padre: *Purg.* XXX, 50.

> Lo duca mio di subito mi prese,
> come la madre ch'al romore è desta,
> e vede presso a sè le fiamme accese,
> che prende il figlio e fugge. . . .[1]

My leader suddenly took me as a mother who, wakened by the noise and seeing near her the burning flames, gathers up her son and flees.

When in the Earthly Paradise Dante stands trembling at the unexpected sight of Beatrice, he feels the need of turning quickly to Virgil:

> Volsimi alla sinistra col rispitto
> col quale il fantolin corre alla mamma,
> quando ha paura, o quando elli è afflitto,
> per dicere a Virgilio. . . .[2]

I turned to the left as confidently as a little child runs to his mother when he is frightened, or when he is hurt, to say to Virgil . . .

But she who takes the place of the lost and lamented mother in Dante's thirsting heart is no other than Beatrice. He receives her reproofs as those of a mother who is angry but kind and loving.

> Così la madre al figlio par superba,
> com'ella parve a me. . . .[3]

As a mother seems haughty to her son, so she seemed to me.

Dante, the mature, unsparing Dante, who is not ashamed to compare himself to a little child, receives her reproofs as if they were those of a mother:

> Quali i fanciulli, vergognando, muti,
> con li occhi a terra stannosi, ascoltando
> e sè riconoscendo e ripentuti,
> tal mi stav'io. . . .[4]

As children ashamed and silent stand with their eyes upon the ground, listening and contrite and repentant, so was I standing.

---

[1] *Inf.* XXIII, 37–40. [2] *Purg.* XXX, 43–46.
[3] *Purg.* XXX, 79–80. [4] *Purg.* XXXI, 64–67.

At the beginning of his ascent to Paradise, Dante speaks ingenuous words, whereupon Beatrice

> . . . appresso d'un pio sospiro,
> li occhi drizzò ver me con quel sembiante
> che madre fa sovra figlio deliro.[1]

. . . with a pitying sigh, directed her eyes towards me with that look which a mother turns on her delirious child.

Dante is suddenly disturbed by the great cry of the blessed souls and quickly looks toward Beatrice:

> oppresso di stupore, alla mia guida
> mi volsi, come parvol che ricorre
> sempre colà dove più si confida;
> e quella, come madre che soccorre
> subito al figlio palido e anelo
> con la sua voce, che 'l suol ben disporre,
> mi disse. . . .[2]

Oppressed with wonder, I turned to my guide like a little child who always runs thither for help where his trust is greatest; and she, like a mother who quickly soothes her pale and breathless son with her voice which is wont to comfort him, said to me . . .

Beatrice, then, is not only the beloved maiden, the heavenly all-but-goddess, the symbol of Divine Wisdom, but in the poem and in the poet's fancy she is also the mother who saves and who reproves, the gentle substitute for Madonna Gabriella. Dante's love for Beatrice, which in the *Vita Nuova* is Platonic adoration and in the *Commedia* is theological veneration, appears at moments to be filial love. She could not be his bride on earth: in heaven, together with the Virgin, she shall be a mother. The unloved orphan, the exiled Hippolytus who had to endure a stepmother in his home, felt throughout his life the nostalgic longing of his lonely

---

[1] *Par.* I, 100–102. [2] *Par.* XXII, 1–7.

childhood; and he has represented himself, even when almost old, in the aspect of an infant and a little child. He has found a compensation for the sadness of his orphanhood in new kinships transfigured by his inspired imagination and by the divine sweetness of his poetry. But we must always remember that Dante was not loved enough in the early part of his life—and perhaps he never was.

9

UNRESPONSIVE BEATRICE

THE most significant event in the boyhood and youth of Dante was his meeting with Beatrice and his love for her. No other fact of his life had more influence or importance in his work.

A poet may be permitted at this point to ask a question which would seem trivial or ridiculous in a man of learning: what were Beatrice's sentiments toward Dante? did she pity him, or did she even fail to understand him?

I speak of the Beatrice real and alive, the Beatrice of flesh and blood, dressed in white and crimson, the legitimate daughter of Folco Portinari and of Cilia Caponsacchi; the Beatrice who was the second wife of Simone dei Bardi; not of that symbol which she became in the mind of Dante, first taking shape in the *Vita Nuova*, becoming well-defined in the *Convivio*, and all-controlling in the *Commedia*.

Dante has lifted her above the human, but in life and reality she was human, entirely human, perhaps too human. The poet has transfigured her, and we all rejoice in this creation of his or we discourse learnedly about it; but, in the first place, there was in the city of Florence a Beatrice, daughter and wife, who was born in 1266 and died in June 1290; a Beatrice corporeal, terrestrial, and visible, who would have existed even if Dante had not loved her, even if Dante had not sung her, even if Dante had not exalted her in the Paradise of his mind to a place approximating that of the Madonna.

That this child, this married girl, had all the marvellous qualities which Dante discovered in her and described in phrases suited only to the great saints, to the Mother of Christ, or to Christ Himself, we permit ourselves to doubt, indeed we must doubt it. Supreme poets, with their kindling imaginations and with the strength of their emotions, create a reality which is more real to us than the actual and historical, but they cannot annihilate the actual and historical. It may be inferior or uglier, but it existed and must be taken into account. To recall it to our memories, especially in order to show the manner of the transfiguration, is neither forbidden nor wrong.

What, then, would the historical and concrete little Beatrice have thought of that very timid lover of hers who transformed himself so often into a most ardent singer of her praises? We know, or think we know, what Dante felt for Beatrice during her life and after her death; but we do not take the trouble to know, or at least to comprehend, what Beatrice felt for Dante. It is, of course, Dante who most concerns us, Dante and his passion, fruitful of art and of ecstasy. But the life of each one of us is in some degree a reflection of the attitudes and responses of other beings who come in contact with our life and who for good or ill, for a brief or a long period, make a part of it. Beatrice, in short, has always been studied as 'object' of the poet Dante. Perhaps it is time now to consider Dante, even though hastily, as 'object' of Beatrice.

We all agree that Dante loved, adored, deified Beatrice. But what did Beatrice think of Dante? How did she receive his love? Did she love him in return? or did she laugh at him?

We must be content with the few references to her behaviour which Dante makes in the *Vita Nuova*. They are very few. Dante speaks at length of Beatrice, but his purpose is to tell of the virtues which he saw in her, of the strange effect which these had on him, and of the visions, apparitions, and hallucinations which presented her to his mind. Of her life and of her sentiments he says almost nothing, but sufficient, at least, to enable us to risk a few reasonable guesses.

The first meeting of Dante and Beatrice, when each was nine years old, does not count; Dante alone is inspired with love. He becomes disturbed by this 'youngest of the angels' without her even being aware of it. At the second meeting, when he is eighteen years old and she has completed her seventeenth year, Beatrice makes the first step: 'passing through a street she turned her eyes toward the spot where I stood greatly abashed, and with ineffable courtesy she saluted me most modestly.'[1]

Although Dante has written several pages and a sonnet or two on the almost supernatural effect of this salutation, the account does not imply on the part of Beatrice any response to his love. She was attended by two ladies older than herself, and she saluted him out of courtesy.

At that time, that is, in 1283, Beatrice was already married to Simone dei Bardi. This seems clear from the fact that in the first sonnet Dante calls her 'Madonna,' a title which was given to married women;[2]

[1] *V.N.* III, 1.
[2] It becomes clear from other evidence than the title of 'Madonna' that Beatrice was loved by Dante at least for a time after her marriage, since Folco's will, in which his daughter's position appears as that of a married woman, is

and it is unthinkable that this 'angel,' a compound of all the virtues human and divine, could harbour the idea of a forbidden love, even though it were Platonic.

But Dante, as we know from the *Vita Nuova*, pretended to love other women, and of one woman especially he professed himself the admirer and wrote rhymes in her honour so that many talked of it. 'And for this reason, that is, because of this false rumour which gave me the unmerited fame of a man fallen into evil-doing, that most gentle lady . . . passing along where I was, denied me her most gracious salutation.' [1]

Dante goes on to explain, through 'a youth clothed in very white raiment,' the reason for Beatrice's denying him her salutation. 'Our Beatrice,' says the youth, 'has heard from certain persons who spoke of you, that the lady whom I named to you . . . received from you some harm; and therefore this most gentle lady, who is opposed to all things harmful, refused to salute you, fearing lest it might be harmful.' [2]

An explanation rather over-subtle and not quite convincing. Almost all the commentators explain the last phrase as meaning that Beatrice fears lest Dante may cause annoyance or harm also to her. But in this case, would she have said *noiosa*? It is possible, on the other hand, to give these words another and quite opposite meaning. Beatrice feared, by saluting Dante who was troubling another woman with his attentions, to trouble him, to cause him annoyance, *noia*. And from this one could allege a certain jealousy on the part of

---

dated 15 January, 1288. Therefore Beatrice must have been married at the latest in 1287.

[1] *V.N.* X, 2.   [2] *V.N.* XII, 6.

60

Beatrice, who (according to a statement in the same chapter) was aware of the poet's love: 'In truth your secret must have become somewhat revealed to her through long observation of your condition.' Now that Dante follows another woman and writes for this other 'little things in rhyme,' Beatrice, almost as a return blow or in revenge, punishes him: she no longer salutes him. But jealousy, as the anatomists of the heart know, is not always a proof of love; often it is a proof of the contrary. In Beatrice, there may have been in place of love, which was not there and could not be, a certain feminine satisfaction in the devotion of this youth who was obscure and poor and probably not even good-looking, but who had an intense nature and manifest talent. Learning that he had taken to writing verses for other ladies, she may have felt vexation, disappointment, anger, but not jealousy. But it may well be that the reason of her not saluting him is that which Love gives to Dante: If another pleases you, I do not wish to be troublesome to you by saluting you as I did formerly.

There may be also the wish to prove his constancy: If my salute used to fill you with happiness, as I know it did, my refusing to salute you should fill you with pain; thus I will assure myself whether you still love me, or if you have, in truth, changed. Or else: If your love (whether feigned or not) gives offence to another, who does not love you, I do not wish to give you annoyance with my salutation in case you have ceased to love me.

However we look at it, there is not apparent in Beatrice the least return of his love either when she salutes him or when she does not. A woman might be pleased, through vanity, that a youth should swoon for love of her without her having any tender feeling for him. But this self-love is the opposite of true love.

But the clear and unmistakable proof that Beatrice cared nothing for Dante is found in the famous wedding-scene. The poet is conducted by one of his friends, perhaps Guido Cavalcanti, to a marriage feast. There, suddenly, he sees Beatrice and the usual effects follow: pallor, faintness, trembling, and so on. Of this the ladies become aware, and 'whispering together with this most gentle lady they mocked' Dante.[1] It is not credible that they ridiculed him while they were talking to Beatrice without her joining in the ridicule, because a little later Dante, who has returned to his house to the 'chamber of tears,' thinks within himself, 'If this lady knew of my condition, I do not think that she would thus mock at me.'[2]

But just a little before this he had said that she knew his secret. Therefore she ridiculed Dante, knowing very well what his condition was. If a woman has the least bit of affection for a man, she does not acquiesce in laughing at, ridiculing, making fun of, in short, in mocking at that man before his own face and in the presence of others. Neither would she do it if she had even a little pity for him. She might, through shyness, keep silent while others derided him, but she would not take part in the derision, as Beatrice so heartlessly did that day.

And after all why should Beatrice have loved Dante? That meagre youth of low stature, emaciated by his

[1] *V.N.* XIV, 7.　　　　[2] *V.N.* XIV, 9.

study and by the strength of his emotional nature, of a family neither illustrious nor rich, and not yet famous in his own name for his writings, expressing himself with ardour when he wrote, but shamefaced and tongue-tied in her presence—such a person was not likely to kindle the heart of a woman already married, who was too young and too lacking in delicate perceptions to be able to understand the divine quality of his art and to foresee the future greatness and fame of the young poet who sang her praises. At times she may have felt a certain pleasure in the incense of the sonnets and *ballate*; but often, I think, she would have smiled at his ingenuousness and jested about it with her well-born friends behind the poor young poet's back.

Some time after this episode, the mocking laugh was changed to a lament for the death of her father,[1] nor do we know if Beatrice ever saluted Dante again before her own death, which occurred five months after that of her father.[2] And from the moment of her death she, who did not know love or did not wish to love, was loved and glorified as no other woman has ever been except Mary the Virgin.

[1] *V.N.* XXII, 2, 3. '. . . this lady was full of bitter grief and wept piteously.'

[2] Folco Portinari died 31 December, 1289, and his daughter Beatrice, 1 June, 1290.

10

'THE DEAR, BENIGN, PATERNAL IMAGE'

ANTE'S first real teacher was undoubtedly Brunetto Latini. It has been debated far and wide whether he was a teacher in the customary professional sense, but such discussions are useless. Brunetto the notary, secretary to the commune of Florence, ambassador, writer, and statesman, did not make a business of teaching, nor give public and private lessons at fixed hours and for a salary. He had, nevertheless, a passion for teaching, as we learn from his writings; and often, when the occasion was suitable, he must have lingered to talk with the young Florentines who showed a love for science or literature, and who promised well. One of these was Dante.

When they first met, and where and when they conversed together and on what subjects, we do not know, and it is a waste of time to try to find out.

The fact is that, in the *Inferno*, Dante is still deeply moved as he recalls the 'dear, paternal image' of Brunetto, and that Brunetto, in turn, calls Dante 'son.' But there is only one reference to the teaching of the master: 'you taught me,' says Dante, 'how a man makes himself eternal,' how he achieves enduring fame. For those times Brunetto was a man of varied if not sound learning, but he had no individual system or art to transmit to his disciples. His greatest work, *Li Livres dou Trésor*, *The Treasury of Knowledge*, which he commends to Dante, is one of the many mediæval medleys of varied erudition. He compiled his *Trésor* at

Paris, in a language not his own, pillaging without risk Pliny, Solinus, St Ambrose, Isidore of Seville, Palladius, Aristotle, Cicero, John of Viterbo, Daudé de Prades, and others. He adds nothing of his own but mistakes.[1] His *Rhetoric* is a paraphrase in Italian of the first book of Cicero's *De Inventione*. As to his compositions in Tuscan verse, it is better not to speak. Brunetto may have been a good lawyer and a good compiler of political letters, but he was certainly not a poet nor, to tell the truth, even a tolerable versifier. His *Tesoretto* is a long-winded poem of 2944 washed-out septenary verses, flabby and tiresome, which must have stirred pity in Dante. This is the way Brunetto tells the story of the creation:

Omai a ciò ritorno	I now come to the time that God
Che Dio fece lo giorno,	made the day and the pleasant light,
E la luce gioconda,	and He created heaven and earth and
E cielo e terra ed onda	water and air.
E l'aire creao.	And He fashioned the angels, each
E li angeli fermao	one separately and all out of nothing.
Ciascun partitamente	Then the second day, by His great
E tutto di neente.	power, He established the firmament.
Poi la seconda dia	And the third, so it seems, He set
Per la sua gran balìa	apart the sea and divided the land. . . .
Stabilio 'l fermamento.	
E 'l terzo, ciò mi pare,	
Specificò lo mare	
E la terra divise. . . .[2]	

A man who wrote such verses could not be teacher of the art of poetry to the future author of the *Divina Commedia*. And those who venture to suggest that the *Tesoretto* was the forerunner and perhaps the inspiration

[1] Ch. V. Langlois, *La Connaissance de la nature et du monde d'après des écrits français à l'usage des laïcs*. Paris, Hachette, 1927, pp. 340–342.
[2] *Il Tesoretto e il Favolello*, ed. B. Wiese. Strasbourg, Heitz, p. 29, vv. 427–441.

of the *Commedia*—owing to certain resemblances in the initial outline—show that they do not know where art dwells. There remains, however, the weighty testimony of Dante and his openly declared gratitude. Brunetto taught the young man, or the boy, in what way a man makes himself eternal, famous through the centuries. Brunetto was not a church-goer, nor even, I think, a religious man; and he was not able to point out to Dante the ways by which, in truth, a man makes himself eternal, that is, renders himself worthy of that blessed eternity which is found in Paradise. The notary and diplomatist had a great love, ill-requited, for poetry and literature, and he must have kindled in the adolescent mind of Alighieri a vision of the men of earlier times who were still alive in the world because of their works and the renown which recommends them and illumines them. Although Brunetto was a man of action—as diplomatist, if not as warrior or merchant—he felt, nevertheless, that his chief strength was in the art of using words; and that by means of the well-chosen and well-placed word a man could make his influence and fame endure for many centuries. He gave to Dante, therefore, the passion, the dream, the desire to achieve fame through the art of words among those 'who will call this time ancient'—the art which leads not only to literary but to civil renown. Brunetto was a little like the sophists of ancient Greece; he maintained that eloquence and adroit discourse were necessary weapons for carving a way in the government of the city and the state. A proof that the Florentines remembered him as a teacher of the relations which exist between rhetoric and the art of governing is to be found in the closing words

of the death-notice, often cited, which Giovanni
Villani includes in his chronicle: Brunetto 'was the
beginner and master in refining the Florentines and in
making them skilful and correct in speech, and in
teaching them how to guide and rule our republic
according to the art of politics.'[1] We should not
forget that, although throughout his life Dante desired
the poet's crown, he also had the ambition, until the
death of Henry VII (1313), to be a statesman.

Brunetto's influence on Dante, therefore, was both
parallel to and different from that which Guido
Cavalcanti exercised on his young friend. For Guido,
the poetry of love was a mark of the noble and gentle
soul and a means of purifying it. To serve the Lady
in verse meant to raise himself above the sensuous,
shopkeeping crowd, and to make himself citizen of a
noble and ideal republic of the Platonic pattern.
Brunetto, on the other hand, directed Dante to glory,
to that worldly renown which the poet will come to
despise[2] precisely because it is not sufficiently lasting,
sufficiently 'eternal,' but which, at the same time, he
will long for all his life, and long for in its two greatest
forms, renown as a poet and as a statesman. And for
this reason it pleased the writer of the Commedia, by
way of recompense, to 'make eternal' the master who
first made him conscious of this thirst in his soul.

But how can we reconcile the affectionate gratitude
expressed by Dante with the public, though posthumous,
denunciation of sodomy which he makes at the very
moment of his glorification of the master? For Brunetto
is accused of this Socratic vice by no other voice or

[1] *Cron.* VIII, x.   [2] *Purg.* XI, 100–117.

tradition save that of Dante; and to many it seems un-
fitting and unworthy of Alighieri that he alone should
have defamed in this way his first and dearest teacher,
the one to whom, according to his own words, he
owed so much; for whom, on his own confession, he
wished a longer life; whom he always recalls with filial
sorrow.

Almost all readers of the *Commedia* are certain that the
sodomites are placed in that circle of the Inferno where
we find Brunetto; and their belief is not shaken by the
fact, undoubtedly disturbing, that except for Dante's
denunciation we have no proof that Brunetto's companions were guilty of this unclean sin. Of Priscian, who
was among them, there is a tradition that he was an
unfrocked monk; Francesco d'Accorso was reputed a
usurer; Andrea dei Mozzi was a gouty and foolish
preacher.[1] We may ask whether those may not be right
who see in this circle not sodomites but contemners of
divine laws.[2]

For the sin of 'violence against God' the proofs against
Brunetto are not lacking. Giovanni Villani called him
'a worldly man' (*mondano uomo*); and Latini himself in
the *Tesoretto* confessed, 'You well know that we are
considered a little worldly.'[3] And *mondano*, in the
language of that time, meant the opposite of *spirituale*,
religious.

---

[1] Andrea dei Mozzi was apparently transferred to Vicenza for political not
moral reasons. Cf. P. E. Palandri, *Annuario Dantesco*, 1929 (Florence, 1931),
pp. 91–118.

[2] The first to raise doubts on this question was Merlo in *Cultura*, V, 1884,
pp. 774–784. See also A. Padula, *B. Latini e il Pataffio*. Milan, Rome, Naples:
Albrighi and Segati, 1921.

[3] vv. 2560–2561.

Moreover, Brunetto, who in the *Trésor* condemns sodomy[1] severely—and this he could scarcely have done had he himself been guilty—makes in the *Tesoretto* an open confession of his slight respect for God and His Church: '. . . I have been a wicked sinner, since for my Creator I had no care; nor had I any reverence for Holy Church, but rather have I offended her in word and deed.'[2]

It will be said that Brunetto could make confession of his impiety, of which he says he is repentant, but that he would have been ashamed to confess to the vice of Sodom, which was punished severely by Florentine law. But, we may ask, was there not the Inquisition to punish offences against Holy Church? And why should he have repeated three times in voluminous works, in French and in Italian, his severe censure against the sodomites?

It seems a little strange that if Dante did indeed believe his master guilty of such a sin, he should treat him like a father and have himself called son by Brunetto. Brunetto, born about 1220, could not have known Dante until after 1280, and at this time the master was sixty years old and the disciple little more than fifteen. There would rise in the minds of readers of the *Commedia* rather unpleasant conjectures as to how Dante came to know Brunetto's secret vice. Brunetto, moreover, is represented by Filippo Villani as a man full of raillery and jests,[3]—qualities which are more the attributes of a Voltairian *avant la lettre* than of a homosexual.

[1] v. *Trésor*, ed. Chabaille, p. 300 and pp. 379–381. The condemnation is repeated in the *Tesoretto*, vv. 2859–2864.

[2] vv. 2522–2529.

[3] 'Fuit Brunectus scurrilis', etc. in M. Scherillo, *Alcuni capitoli della biografia di Dante*. Torino, Loescher, 1896, p. 151. Villani refers also to *libidinis aculeos*, but the 'libido' is not necessarily sodomitic.

In any case, even if Brunetto's sin were not what most readers believe on the declaration solely of Dante, there would remain guilt and disgrace no less serious. But to Dante's mind the sins of heresy seemed less iniquitous than other sins: we need cite only Farinata degli Uberti, well known as an epicurean, and Frederic II, whom he places with Farinata but without the accompaniment of harsh words; and indeed in another place in the *Inferno*, Dante says that Frederic is 'worthy of honour,' *d'onor sì degno*.[1]

Dante, it appears, looked upon free-thinking as a grave fault but not such as to destroy greatness of soul or even reputation. The effects of sodomy are quite different. Dante could have condemned Brunetto as an unbeliever with justice, but without plunging him into the filth of a sin which belittles and debases him. Placing Brunetto near to Capaneus and Farinata, majestic spectres of pride and irreverence, does not associate him with the corrupters of youth. To make him a sodomite would be too great a cruelty against the master and would place the poet himself under suspicion—the favourite disciple of an unseemly plotter against the chastity of boys.

But all these fine-spun arguments avail little against Dante's precise accounts of the partitioning of the damned in the seventh circle; and we are forced to conclude that the troop of those moving along in the place where poor Brunetto is seen is indeed composed of sodomites.[2]

[1] *Inf.* XIII, 75.
[2] Cf. *Inf.* XI, 16–90 and XIV, 19–27. Those who are continually moving must necessarily be the sinners against nature.

We do not know what reasons led the poet thus to be the pitiless executioner of a man respected and loved; nor does it help us to inquire in what way the disciple came to a knowledge of his master's repulsive sin. One thing, however, is certain: to Dante alone the compiler of the *Tesoro* owes the worst and the best of his fame.

_____

*C*HE friendship between Dante and Guido Cavalcanti appears to have been foreordained by the
underlying similarity of their fates. The life
of Cavalcanti is, in certain aspects, almost a prototype
of Alighieri's.

Each was bound to a Beatrice. Guido was the husband
of the one, a daughter of Farinata degli Uberti; Dante
was the worshipper of the other, a daughter of Folco
Portinari. Both Guido and Dante were condemned to
exile at the demand of factions of citizens. Both died
of the same illness, malarial fever, which Guido con-
tracted at Sarzana, and Dante on his return from Venice
to Ravenna.

Although, in the *Inferno*, the father of Guido declares
the two friends equal in 'loftiness of genius'—and much
may be conceded to a father in torment—the differences
are many and great. Guido was a sceptic and perhaps an
epicurean,[1] Dante was a believer, even if not always
orthodox; and a Christian, even if not always perfect.
Guido was a poet, but of the second or third rank;
Dante was one of the noblest and most powerful poets

[1] See the well-known evidence of Boccaccio (*Decameron*, VI, 9).
I recognize the objections raised by Parodi (*Bull. della Soc. Dant.* XXII, 1915,
pp. 37–47), but they do not convince me because (1) the fact that an idea is found
attributed to several persons does not prove that it is true only of the first;
(2) Boccaccio had been told by his father and other old men about things that
had occurred in Florence in their time, and he must have known certain things
better than we do; (3) if Guido's 'disdain' refers, as Barbi and others think, to
Beatrice (symbol of Divine Wisdom), we have an implicit confirmation from
Dante himself that Guido was irreligious.

that humanity has known in six millenniums of literature. Guido was studious, at least in the periods of
leisure left by his roving love-affairs and his political
quarrels, but studious in the manner of the gentlemanly
dilettante who wishes to include among his other
luxuries a little poetry and philosophy. Dante, on the
other hand, from the period of his youth had kept fore-
most in his thoughts the desire to acquire universal
knowledge, and he became one of the most profoundly
and individually learned men of his time.

There were other differences also between the two
friends, external but no less important. Guido was older
than Dante by eight or nine years, perhaps more;[1] and
at that age a seniority of ten or fifteen years makes a
great difference. Guido belonged to a noble and
wealthy family, and could flaunt himself in many ways,
while Dante was of a family much less prominent and
powerful; and after his father's death, and long before
his exile, he had to struggle against the restrictions imposed by a genteel poverty. And, finally, Guido was a
man much more violent and rash than Dante; he tried, as
we know, to kill Corso Donati, and by Corso's partisans
he was stoned and wounded in the hand.[2]

Guido, let us add, could not have had a very easy
temper. Villani says that he was 'sensitive and easily
angered' (*tenero e stizoso*);[3] and Corso Donati, his enemy,
nicknamed him *Cavicchia*, which means, according to
the dictionary, a tactless and obstinate man.[4] It would

[1] Guido was born certainly before 1259, and the date has been placed by
many at about 1250.
[2] Dino Compagni, *Cron.* I, xx.   [3] Villani, *Cron.* VIII, xlii.
[4] D. Compagni, *Cron.* I, xx. For *Cavicchia*, see the note by Del Lungo. For
the meaning of *Cavicchia*, see also D. G. Rossetti, *Dante and his Circle*, Intro. to
Part I, note on quotation from Compagni.—Trans.

seem from this that Guido was irritable and prone to take offence.

Nor was his manner of life without blemish, if we can believe a sonnet addressed to him by his brother-in-law, Lapo degli Uberti, in which there are clear allusions to unnatural offences.[1] Taken altogether it must have been convenient for Dante to represent his journey to the Inferno as beginning some months before the death of Guido, thus avoiding the necessity of placing his friend either among the heretics or among the sodomites.

For these reasons I do not believe that the friendship between the two poets was so deep and intimate as most readers suppose. Dante, it is true, often calls Guido 'first of my friends'; but when we recall that the friendship began in 1283 when Dante was scarcely eighteen years old, we may infer that 'first' is to be understood in its usual sense of first in point of time, and not in the sense of 'greatest' or 'dearest,' which is the usual interpretation.

There can be friendships—especially among men of letters—which are apparently staunch and which are really the response to a certain intellectual sympathy; but they may be accompanied in the depths of the heart by a mixture of intolerance, jealousy, and even hatred. I do not say that this was the case with Cavalcanti and Alighieri, but we may infer that their friendship had two phases: one from 1285 to 1292,[2] characterized by

[1] It accuses Guido of having spoken in one of his poems about a shepherdess when, as a matter of fact, he had been seen in the 'wood' with a 'fair-haired, short-coated lacquey.' v. also Davidsohn, *Firenze ai tempi di Dante*. Florence, Bemporad, 1929, pp. 333–334.

[2] I do not set down this date at random. In 1292 Dante was absorbed in his philosophical and religious studies (*Conv.* II, xii, 7), and Guido left Florence with the intention of making a pilgrimage to Compostella.

fresh, eager, and affectionate intimacy; the other, from
1293 to the death of Guido in 1300, colder and perhaps
troubled by some discord or misunderstanding. If the
famous sonnet of reproof, *Io vegno 'l giorno a te*, is really
Guido's, it seems to me that there are clear indications
of a dissension between the two. The second quatrain
reads: Much company was wont to displease you; you
always avoided dull people. Of me you spoke so kindly
that I gathered up and cherished all your verses. ·

We can understand the 'dull people' to be those
'philosophizing' and 'religious' men whom Dante had
begun to frequent and whom Guido, a gentleman of
pagan spirit by family tradition and natural disposition,
did not find to his liking. Whoever was occupied with
philosophy in those days was either a friar or a priest;
and the boundaries between philosophy and religion were
not as yet quite distinct. Guido, poet of love and no
friend to Latin, to scholasticism, or to friars, could not
look kindly on Dante's plunge into those studies and
into that mystic and monkish company. In the third
line of the quatrain just quoted there appears a certain
sadness on Guido's part because Dante does not speak
of him so affectionately as in the past: 'di me *parlavi* sì
coralmente,' you *used* to speak of me so affectionately;
you used to, but do so no longer.

And there remains the telling fact that on 24 June,
1390, Dante joined the other Priors in banishing Guido
from Florence. It is all very well to say that Dante could
do no less, and that in disregarding the claims of friendship for the sake of peace and justice he gave proof also
on this occasion of his upright mind and his civic
honesty. But if Guido had actually been at that time

the first, the best, of his friends, would Dante have voted to send him into exile? Would he not have opposed that decision with all the vigorous eloquence of his affection? Besides, his term of office as Prior had almost expired (Guido had to leave Florence at the end of June 1300, and Dante would have gone out of office on 15 August), and he could have asked for a delay in the sentence. Or he could have resigned.

I maintain, then, that the harmony and intimacy which had existed in the early years between the two poets of the White party had for some years ceased to exist; and it is not impossible that there lay underneath, with one or the other, a grain of envy.[1]

In the *Commedia*, as everyone knows, Dante mentions Guido only twice, and on both occasions to praise and to disparage him in the same breath. In the first instance (*Inf*. X, 61–63), Dante recognizes Guido's 'loftiness of genius,' *altezza d'ingegno*, but quickly adds that Guido disdained Beatrice, that is, that he scorned the science of divine things, Theology, which for Dante is superior to everything else.[2] The 'disdain' can also be taken as alluding to Guido's scant admiration for the real Beatrice in whom he could not, perhaps, see all the wonderful beauty and excellence which Dante discovered in her. In that famous terzina Dante seems to say to Guido's father: Your son did not love the knowledge of the faith, Theology, and did not make himself

---

[1] Dante says to Sapia (*Purg*. XIII, 133–135) that he will stay only a short time in the circle of the envious, but confesses that he has on a few occasions experienced the feeling of envy.

[2] I believe, as do the authoritative Dantists (D'Ancona, Rajna, Barbi, Zenatti, Bianchi, and others), that the famous 'disdain' of Guido (*Inf*. X, 61–63) refers to Beatrice and not to Virgil.

worthy to be brought before her in the Earthly and in the Celestial Paradise. To me, on the other hand, Virgil was sent in order that I might ascend to her where she stands transfigured and triumphant.

In the other famous passage (*Purg.* XI, 97–99) Dante affirms through the lips of Oderisi that Cavalcanti has taken away from Guinizelli 'the glory of our language'— of our language, he says, not of poetry—but immediately adds

> . . . e forse è nato
> chi l'uno e l'altro caccerà del nido.

And perhaps he is born who shall drive from the nest both the one and the other.

Many believe that in this future victor Dante sees himself, and—granted his pride—there is nothing incredible in this boast. He drove Cavalcanti from his real nest, from his city, and now with the *Commedia* he is certain of driving him from the nest of poetical glory. But if, as certain writers maintain, Dante wished to allude to others than these or to some undetermined person yet to come, the fact remains that Guido Cavalcanti will be driven from the nest, or, as we say to-day, surpassed.

In the mind of Dante, as we see, two almost contradictory states of feeling alternate when he recalls the first friend of his youth. He acknowledges Guido's worth and immediately after, by implication, disparages and humbles him: Guido did not lift his mind to things divine, he is not worthy to mount toward heaven, and on earth there is someone already born who will deprive him of his poetical primacy.

We need not be surprised at this confusion of

77

opposite feelings which modern psychologists call ·
ambivalency. It is common enough among us, and
whoever studies himself deeply will easily discover it in
himself too. Hatred and love, veneration and envy,
attraction and fear, are pairs of sentiments which are
opposed but often inseparable. In this strange way the
human heart is•put together, and Dante, however great,
was human.

THE SOLDIER POET

ANTE is perhaps the only Italian poet who ever fought in a real pitched battle. When he was twenty-four, 11 June, 1289, he was at Certomondo (or Campaldino), where the Guelphs and the Ghibellines faced each other in a bloody fight. At the head of the Guelphs was Florence; at the head of the Ghibellines was Arezzo and its bishop. The army which moved out from Florence numbered about 12,000 men; that from Arezzo was somewhat smaller, but confident of victory. The Guelphs, however, were victorious; but the battle was exceedingly fierce and hard-fought. When the ranks were broken, the Ghibellines 'were put to flight and killed: the regular Florentine soldiers, who were accustomed to routs, slaughtered the fleeing Aretines; and the auxiliaries had no pity.'[1] The Aretine forces lost 1700 dead and more than 2000 prisoners.[2]

Among the Florentine horsemen who sustained the first attack of the Aretines and who were thereby unhorsed and thrown into confusion, was Dante. Later, he recounted in one of his letters, now lost, the part which he had taken in that battle. He said (according to Leonardo Bruni, who had the letter before him) that he was no 'novice in arms' at Campaldino, 'where he experienced great fear, but, in the end, the greatest joy because of the varied fortunes of that battle.'[3]

[1] D. Compagni, *Cron.* I, x.   [2] Villani, *Cron.* VII, cxxxi.
[3] Solerti, *Vite di Dante.* Milan, Vallardi, p. 100.

79

It is almost certain that he took part also in the incursions which the victorious army made that summer into the country around Arezzo, and even under the walls of the enemy-city. In the rapid and joyful movement of the lines which open Canto XXII of the *Inferno*, we seem still to feel the gay confidence of the young soldier:

> Io vidi già cavalier muover campo,
> e cominciare stormo e far lor mostra,
> e tal volta partir per loro scampo;
> corridor vidi per la terra vostra,
> o Aretini. . . .

In former times I have seen horsemen moving camp, and joining battle and making their muster, and at times retiring to escape; and I have seen them making forays through your land, O Aretines. . . .

Dante's military experience did not end at Campaldino. He undoubtedly took part the same year, 1289, in the war against Pisa and in the capture of the castle of Caprona:

> così vid'io già temer li fanti
> ch'uscivan patteggiati di Caprona
> veggendo sè tra nemici cotanti.[1]

Thus I saw the foot-soldiers, who were coming out from Caprona under terms of surrender, afraid at seeing themselves among so many enemies.

And with this impressive sight end, so far as we know, Dante's military experiences. He took part in these affairs as a matter of party loyalty or civic duty, certainly not for the pleasure of fighting or for military glory, because often in his writings he shows himself opposed to war of every sort.

But it is no unusual thing to find a young poet present at a battle. Everyone recalls Æschylus at Marathon,

[1] *Inf.* XXI, 94–96.

Cervantes at Lepanto, Tolstoi at Sebastopol. But it does not happen often. Poets in all countries are men who have more love for studies and the quiet of the countryside than for the bloody tumult of battle.

Horace fought valiantly with Brutus at Philippi, but when he saw things going badly, he ran away, even leaving his shield behind him.[1] No famous Italian poet after Dante, from Petrarch to Manzoni, took part in battles. We must get to Foscolo, Mameli, and D'Annunzio to find in our history examples of soldier-poets.

Dante, then, is the only one for many centuries who fought in a battle. We may be certain that he fought bravely and that at least one of the 1700 slain was killed by him. At the very time that Dante was writing harmonious rhymes for the still living Beatrice, he stained his hands with blood.

What must he have felt on that hot and sultry day of June, in view of La Verna of the Stigmata, when he saw himself assailed by shouting foes, by horsemen in armour; when he was thrown, perhaps, by having his horse killed, and confused by the furious onslaught of the Aretines? And with what thoughts did he, the courteous lover, the melancholy maker of rhymes, raise his sword to wound and to kill?

There have been poets and writers who killed— Villon, Ben Jonson, Chiabrera, Baretti[2]; but in these

---

[1] Horace, *Odes*, II, vii, 9 ff.

[2] The episodes here referred to in the lives of François Villon, Ben Jonson, and Gabriello Chiabrera are known to most English readers. The story of Baretti's trial for murder may be read in Boswell's *Johnson*. Among the witnesses for Baretti were Dr. Johnson, Sir Joshua Reynolds, Edmund Burke, David Garrick, and Oliver Goldsmith. 'Never,' says Boswell, 'did such a

instances it was a case of homicide committed for private reasons. Dante killed in battle in an honourable cause; but as we read his sentences of condemnation in the *Commedia*, we wonder whether Dante too, sword in hand, may not have sent a soul before its time to that world of the dead.

And perhaps we know also the name of his victim: Buonconte di Montefeltro. The hypothesis is not mine; it is that of a careful and serious Dante scholar, Nicola Zingarelli. Let us turn to the terzina where Dante addresses Buonconte:

> E io a lui: Qual forza o qual ventura
> ti traviò sì fuor di Campaldino,
> che non si seppe mai tua sepultura ? [1]

> And I to him: What violence or what chance carried you so far from Campaldino that your burial-place was never found ?

Zingarelli, commenting on this passage, writes: 'In that question is summed up all the vain searching on the field of battle and around it for the body of Buonconte . . . and perhaps the question revealed to him just who it was had given him that stab in the throat.' [2]

And it was indeed strange that of all the illustrious men who fell at Campaldino only Buonconte, who fought on the opposite side, arouses Dante's interest and leads him to recount the episode in detail and almost, we may say, with tenderness. It is even more strange that Dante, in order to send Buonconte to Purgatory,

---

constellation of genius enlighten the aweful Sessions-House.' *v.* Boswell's *Life of Johnson*, ed. Birkbeck Hill. Oxford, Clar. Press, 1887 ; II, pp. 96 ff.—Trans.

[1] *Purg.* V, 91–93.
[2] Zingarelli, *Dante.* Milan, Vallardi, 1931, p. 259.

on the way to ultimate salvation, invents all the famous
story of the storm, the flooding of the river, the struggle
between the angel and the demon over the body. The
storm itself is certainly no invention, because on the day
of the battle 'the sky was covered with clouds,'[1] but all
the rest of the story is something that no one could have
known either in the natural or the supernatural part.
Dante must have imagined it for himself, driven by something which resembles remorse.

We must suppose that Dante, knowing that he had
himself killed Montefeltro, invented that final adventure
compounded of human, divine, and diabolic elements,
in order to give to the dead knight some recompense for
his wretched end. Dante must many times have recalled
that fierce battle of his youth and the killing of Montefeltro; recalled it not indeed with real remorse, since
Montefeltro had been killed in just warfare, but with
compassionate regret, increased by the mysterious dis-
appearance of the body. And then he thought of reward-
ing the noble victim of partisan warfare and of saving
his soul, at least in the poem and in intention, in order
to make amends for the violent separation of soul from
body so many years before. And Canto V of the
Purgatorio, which closes with the gentle prayer of Pia, is,
as it were, the funeral oration over the slain pronounced
by the slayer.

[1] D. Compagni, *Cron.* I, x (ed. Del Lungo, p. 41).

THE OX AND THE EAGLE

N the years which intervened between the date of the first sonnet, 1283, and the death of the first friend, 1300, Dante was influenced by four men: a patrician, a notary, and two friars—Guido Cavalcanti, Brunetto Latini, Remigio Girolami, and Pier Giovanni Olivi: a gentleman who was a gentle poet, a compiler who was a mediocre poet, a Dominican philosopher who was an execrable poet, a Franciscan philosopher suspected of apocalyptical heresy.

Two poets and two philosophers. And they have nothing in common except their connection with France. Guido lived for a time in Provence and admired the troubadours; Brunetto lived in Paris and wrote his greatest work in the *langue d'oïl*; Fra Remigio was a student and licentiate at Paris, where he had as master St Thomas Aquinas; Olivi was really French, having been born at Serignan, and his true name was Pierre Jean Olieu.

Dante was encouraged by Guido in the study of the new philosophical love-poetry. He was strengthened by Brunetto in his natural desire for the renown which comes from public office and especially from study and letters. But he was influenced in a very different way from this by the two friars.

Fra Remigio Girolami (1235–1319), recalled from Paris, while still a deacon, to lecture in theology at Sta. Maria Novella in Florence, became one of the important members of the Dominican order of Preachers in Italy.

84

In 1294 and in 1313 he was prior of Sta. Maria Novella, and in 1309–10 he was Provincial of the Roman Province.

He was a famous preacher and had in his audience princes and kings. He composed funeral panegyrics by the dozen, usually rubbish. He wrote sermons, prologues, verses, expositions, and treatises on an infinitude of subjects, and did not disdain to cite either the old pagan writings or the romances of chivalry. In his sermons he does not always show good taste: there is an excess of punning and of fantastic comparisons. In his more considered works, though he is learned and subtle, he does not display any marked traces of original thought.

Nevertheless, he was a man of vast learning and of lively talent. Dante had read his writings and remembered them so well that the beginning of the *Convivio* is an almost literal translation of a prologue on science written by Remigio;[1] and a part of the invective of St Peter in the *Paradiso* echoes an idea developed by Fra Remigio in his commentary on the *Song of Songs*.[2]

But in Florence, Girolami represented, first of all, the new scholastic philosophy; that is, he represented his master, St Thomas Aquinas. Aquinas had come to Florence, and to Sta. Maria Novella, in June 1272; and Dante, who at that time had completed his seventh year, may have seen him. But the most illustrious follower

---

[1] G. Salvadori, *Sulla vita giovanile di Dante*. Rome, Soc. Ed. Dante Alighieri, 1906, p. 109.

[2] Cf. the commentary on the Canticle (Bibl. Laurenziana, Conv. 362, fol. 109r) and *Par.* XXVII, 40 ff. For this and other parallels, *v.* Busnelli, *Studi Danteschi*, XII, 108–9.

and apostle whom the 'great mute ox of Sicily'[1] had at that time in Tuscany, was Fra Remigio, and it is quite probable that it was he who first made known to the young Alighieri the two great works of Aquinas, *Summa Theologiæ* and *Summa Catholicæ Fidei contra Gentiles*. In so far as Dante's mind is Thomistic, it is due, at least in its beginnings, to the energetic lecturer at Sta. Maria Novella.

The second of the two most celebrated schools then in Florence conducted by religious orders was that of the Franciscans at Santa Croce. There during Dante's youth two famous Franciscans taught and preached, Pier Giovanni Olivi and Ubertino da Casale, both of whom belonged to the group of the Spirituals (initially followers of Joachim of Flora). Pier Giovanni taught at Santa Croce from 1287 to 1289, when Dante was between twenty-two and twenty-four years old. It is almost certain that Dante listened to the lectures of Pier Giovanni, if indeed he did not know him.[2] At any rate, he read some of the Franciscan's writings, for traces of Pier Giovanni's thought are found in the *Commedia*.

Pier Giovanni was among those who saw in the prophecies of Joachim of Flora the prediction of the Franciscan age; and in the new order represented by the Spirituals, who practised absolute poverty as opposed to the corrupt luxury of Rome, he saw the beginning of the new reign of the Holy Spirit, longed for and foretold

---

[1] The phrase quoted does not mean that St Thomas was born in the island of Sicily, as an English reader might readily suppose. His birthplace was Aquino, between Rome and Naples, in territory which then formed part of the Kingdom of the Two Sicilies.—Trans.

[2] R. Davidsohn, *Gesch. von Florenz*. Berlin, 1908, II, 2, p. 275. U. Cosmo, *Giorn. Dant.*, VI, pp. 112 ff. F. Sarri, *Studi Francescani*, XI (1925, pp. 115 ff.).

with exactness and certainty by the Abbot Joachim. We shall see later what a deep impression was left on the mind of Alighieri by the bold theories of Olivi, who in these same years converted to Spiritual Franciscanism his colleague, Ubertino da Casale, who had come to Santa Croce a little later than himself. The writings of Olivi were condemned, and before his death he abjured his errors; but there remained, both in Italy and in France, many followers of his teachings, some professed, some secret. Among the latter, as we shall prove in another part of this book, was Dante Alighieri. If in its background and structure the *Commedia* is theological, Thomistic,[1] its prophetic inspiration, expressed in symbolic form, is derived, through Olivi, from Joachim.

We cannot imagine two minds more in contrast than those of the two famous friars who influenced the mental development of the young Dante. Fra Remigio Giro-lami, the Dominican scholastic and Thomist, diligently studious of diverse cultures and indulgent to the profane writers; and Pier Giovanni Olivi, the Franciscan visionary and half-heretic, who cared for nothing except the interpretation of the Scriptures and the imminent spiritual revolution of the world.

Through the Dominican, Dante came in contact with St Thomas Aquinas, and through St Thomas with Albertus Magnus and Aristotle. Through the Franciscan, Dante became permeated with the message of St Francis and the mysticism of St Bonaventure and

[1] Not Thomistic solely. See, for example, B. Nardi, *Saggi di Filosofia Dantesca*. Soc. Dante Alighieri, 1930. Manichean elements have been pointed out by L. Tondelli, *Mani. Rapporti con Bardesane, S. Agostino, Dante*. Milan, Vita e Pensiero, 1932.

thus found his way to Joachim, the seer of San Giovanni in Fiore, and through him to the heretic Montanus and the visionary of Patmos. On the one side, the good Brother Thomas, whom his contemporaries in derision called the 'dumb ox of Sicily;' on the other, St John, the Eagle, the first announcer of the Paraclete and of the Eternal Gospel. And confronting each other in the mind of Dante, under the guidance of the two eloquent teachers, were the two fires kindled in southern Italy to illuminate the last great period of the Middle Ages— St Thomas Aquinas and Joachim of Flora: the Builder and the Dreamer; the wise architect and the inspired Prophet; the conscientious Rationalist and the reasoning Utopian. The one represented Science with all the majesty of his well-constructed systems; the other represented Mysticism with all the splendour of his prophecies of a new earth of the free and the perfect.

Which had the deeper influence on the spirit of Dante, the Ox or the Eagle? It is difficult to say. Certainly both influenced him. Dante was at one and the same time a scientific theologian and a prophet in expectation of radical changes. St Thomas taught him to build with order and wisdom the three-part temple of his poem; but in the centre of that temple is a tabernacle covered with mystic emblems which encloses a flame kindled with sparks that come from Joachim, from Pier Giovanni Olivi, and from Ubertino da Casale. Dante, in the vastness of his mind, succeeded in reconciling the antitheses of the two giants, and was at one and the same time follower of St Thomas and of Joachim, disciple of the Ox and continuator of the Eagle.

THE SCANDAL

ON the lives of almost all famous men there is a scandal—or what appears such to enemies, to the envious, to the ignoble. In the life of Alighieri the greatest scandal, in the eyes of devoted Dantomaniacs, is the poetical dispute, *la tenzone*, between Dante and Forese Donati.

The *Tenzone* consists of six sonnets full of insults and offence: three written by Dante against Forese, three by Forese against Dante. It appears that Dante began the sequence in a sonnet ridiculing his friend; Forese, however, had the last word. The poems were exchanged in one of the years between 1290, the year of the death of Beatrice, and 1296, the date of Forese's death.

Of Forese we know very little, and no other rhymes of his are extant. He was a son of Simone Donati, a brother of the insolent Corso Donati who tried to lord it over Florence and was killed in 1308, a brother also of Piccarda who is one of the first souls met by Dante in the *Paradiso*. Forese's wife was a certain Nella, and by her he had a daughter. Dante speaks of him in the *Commedia*, and the only point on which the *Tenzone* and the poem are in accord is on the subject of Forese's excessive gluttony.

What led to the unseemly bickering in these half-joking, half-spiteful sonnets is not known, and to guess at it is futile. Not all the insulting allusions tossed back and forth between the two so-called friends are entirely clear, but as much as is understood does no honour to either of them.[1]

Dante accuses Forese not only of being a great eater but also a bad husband because he is a night-walker, and a night-walker because he is a thief, and although a thief, of being so deeply in debt that he is likely to end in prison. Dante adds that Forese has a scarred face, that he is a bastard and is perhaps guilty of adultery with his sisters-in-law.

Forese, in his turn, accuses Dante of being the son of a father who, because of some mysterious sin, does not find peace even in the tomb; of living on charity and at the expense of asylums meant for the poor; of being a coward who does not avenge the injuries done to his father; and of becoming a friend to the man who thrashes him.

How much truth there may be in these violent and disgusting accusations is not easy to say. Some, perhaps; the gluttony of Forese for which he is punished in the *Purgatorio*,[2] and the lack of desire on the part of Dante to exact vengeance on behalf of injured relatives.[3] For all the rest, documents and proofs are lacking, and it is probable that in the excitement of the recriminations both men invented charges or at least exaggerated them. It matters little to us to know what sort of man Forese may have been—apart from the light thrown on the sort

---

[1] The merit of having cleared up the difficulties in the *Tenzone* belongs especially to M. Barbi. See his learned and penetrating exposition in *Studi Danteschi*, IX, pp. 5–149. I find unconvincing the argument advanced by D. Guerri, that the *Tenzone* is a jest of the first years of the fifteenth century. v. *La corrente popolare nel Rinascimento*. Florence, Sansoni, 1931, pp. 104–148. On this book v. M. Barbi, *Studi Danteschi*, XVI, pp. 69–103.

[2] *Purg.* XXIII, 40 ff.

[3] *Inf.* XXIX, 18–36.

of friends that Dante chose; but it matters very much to know if the reproaches cast at Dante are based on truth. That his father, Alighiero, was a money-lender is shown by documents, and the distance between money-lender and usurer is not great. It is unlikely, however, that Dante had recourse to the institutions for the poor or that he solicited aid from the Donati, although it is known that he was forced to contract debts even before his exile. That he was not a coward is clear from his conduct at Campaldino; but, on the other hand, the reproof of Geri del Bello, one of his unavenged kinsmen, would suggest that Dante had neglected to avenge, according to the usage of those times, some insult or injury done to his father.

But that Dante did not take too seriously the contumelies and calumnies of Forese is proved by the way in which he speaks of his dead kinsman in the *Purgatorio*. He recalls, covertly, the *Tenzone* and perhaps the not irreproachable life which they had led together:

> . . . Se tu riduci a mente
> qual fosti meco, e qual io teco fui,
> ancor fia grave il memorar presente.[1]

If you call to mind what you were with me, and what I was with you, even now the memory may be a grief.

These memories, then, were not held in honour by either one of them. But Dante, a little while before, had said to him:

> la faccia tua, ch'io lagrimai già morta.[2]

Your face which once I wept for dead.

Dante, then, had wept for Forese's death in July 1296; which means that after the *Tenzone* they had been better

---

[1] *Purg.* XXIII, 115–117.   [2] *Purg.* XXIII, 55.

friends than before. And Dante makes Forese speak of his widow, Nella, in words of deep and reverent affection —of that wife whom Dante had facetiously represented as alone in her bed and coughing, basely neglected by her husband. It almost seems that in that episode of the *Purgatorio* Dante had wished to write the recantation of the *Tenzone*. And Forese is one of the few to whom the poet names Beatrice and Virgil. A great honour.

In any case, for those who imagine a Dante always austere, unbending in his philosophical gravity, and absorbed every day of his life in the contemplation of terrestrial angels and angels of the empyrean, the *Tenzone* is deeply offensive. For in these sonnets the lachrymose and metaphysical poet, soon after the death of Beatrice and perhaps during the very time in which he was writing the *Vita Nuova*, goes to loggerheads with a glutton who is notorious also as a thief, and uses and receives words which suggest a vulgar manner of life rather than the exalted world of visions and contemplation in which we like to think that the young poet had placed his permanent habitation. What makes it worse is that Dante was really the first to stir up the unseemly wrangle and to give to the other, more irascible, man an excuse for rolling him in the mud. To find oneself in the presence of a Dante who in fear of his adversary, though only for a brawling joke, has filled his wallet with the same material that Thais was plunged into and that made Cambronne famous; a Dante who lives at the expense of relatives and takes a beating tamely,—this Dante is such a spectacle as to make every good Dantomaniac of strict observance shudder with horror. Add to this also an implicit lessening of genius; for the sonnets of the coarse glutton are not inferior either in wit or style to those of the already recognized poet.

But if we remember that the two disputants are Florentines, and especially that they are Florentines of the thirteenth century, the surprise and distaste will diminish. A true Florentine can renounce all and endure all. He can give up his coat and his dinner; he can submit to the direst poverty and to the misgovernment of the powerful. But even if he were at the point of death he cannot forgo his pungent wit, his biting jest, his sarcastic retort, his mockery. Nor does he find it contrary to his taste to annoy his best friend with words of raillery and derision, to take advantage of comical or embarrassing aspects which present themselves, unfortunately, in every man.[1] And if the victim is himself a Florentine, we may know where the affair began but not where it will end. A dispute begun in jest may become a violent attack continued in earnest. Even to-day Florentine boys, at the first word of ridicule, retort with aspersions against the father and the mother of the jester, exactly as Forese did and as Dante, in his turn, did. And scornful words, like blows, do not promote peace. One word leads to another, and whoever does not wish to be outdone, makes extravagant statements or invents facts. But after a few hours, or a few days, or a few months, those who, to judge from what they said, were most bitter enemies, now find themselves drinking together and resuming their former peaceful relations. The outburst is over, the score is even, the words were but words,

---

[1] On this trait of the Florentines see the discourse entitled *Firenze*, given by G. Papini, 1 May, 1932, in Palazzo Vecchio (Florence, Casa Editrice Nemi, 1932).

and each one knew and knows just what they amounted to.

Thus it was, as I see it, with Dante and Forese. They were still young, they were Florentines, of fluent and biting speech. They were amused, they were angry, they became reconciled. And Dante would not have been averse, in the interval between a poem in the *dolce stil nuovo* and a disputation in philosophy, to an exchange of fisticuffs—in sonnet-form.

15

IN THE PRESENCE OF THE POPE

*L*ET the truth be told, and the whole truth, even when it is about Dante. The part which he took in civic affairs from 1295 to 1300 was of little importance. In the suspicious and factious democracy of the Commune one man could not legally hold continuous authority in public affairs. Only an armed ruffian, like Corso Donati, or a foreigner invested with authority by the Pope, like Charles of Valois, could attempt or, at certain moments, succeed in exercising a true, directive hegemony.

There were six or seven councils, including both major and minor, which kept watch over one another and took turns impeding one another; and, in addition, there was a parliament which assembled them all every two months. Thus between magistrates and councillors there were hundreds of rectors: the Podestà, the Captain of the People, the Consuls of the Guilds, the Ancients, the Priors of the Guilds, and so on. The most important office was, in theory, that of the Priors; but they were six in number and remained in office only two months. We can imagine how pre-eminent and lasting the influence of any one of them would be.

Dante was Prior from 15 June to 15 August, 1300; but previously, in 1295 or 1296 and perhaps afterwards also, he took part in several of the many councils which were held then in Florence, and we have record of his presence at six councils in 1301. Some of the opinions expressed by Alighieri on these occasions are recorded,

95

but only two have any importance:—on 15 March, 1301, he opposed the grant of a subsidy to Charles of Anjou; and on 19 June, 1301, he was opposed to their continuing the service of one hundred soldiers maintained by Florence for Pope Boniface on the borders of Tuscany. Neither time, according to history, did his advice prevail; but his opposition to the controlling hand of the Pope was later one of the prime causes of his exile from Florence.

In 1300, before he became one of the Priors, two duties were entrusted to him: the first, in April, was to oversee the widening of the street of San Procolo; the second, in May, was to undertake an embassy to the town of San Gemignano. The biographers have talked much about the importance of these two extraordinary appointments, but an examination of the documents reduces them to very little. The widening of the street was a matter of some importance to Dante who owned two bits of land and a small house near by; but in itself it was a matter of small account. The embassy to San Gemignano consisted merely in carrying a request to that commune to send someone to represent them at the election of a captain for the Guelph League of Tuscany.

In short, from 1295 to 1301, Dante was only one of many citizens—hundreds of citizens—who in those confused and disorderly years took part in the many councils of the commune. One notable office, and only one, he held at the end—and it was the last: the embassy to Pope Boniface VIII.

In October 1301, when Charles of Valois, summoned by the Pope to re-establish peace in Tuscany, approached Florence, the new Florentine Signoria decided to send three ambassadors to Rome to the papal Court to oppose the intrigues of the Black Guelphs, who were well-disposed toward Charles. Those selected were Maso Minerbetti, Corazza da Signa, and Dante Alighieri. The precise date of their leaving Florence and of their arrival in Rome is unknown; but thanks to the spirited and vivid prose of Compagni we know how Boniface received them. 'The ambassadors having arrived in Rome, the Pope received them alone in his private apartments, and said to them secretly, Why are you so obstinate? Humble yourselves before me. I tell you truly that I have no other intention than to bring about your peace. Two of you return home, and if you secure obedience to my will, you shall have my blessing.'[1]

The great Pope did not go round about or resort to subterfuges: Humble yourselves; obey. He did not regard the men before him as the ambassadors of a free commune; he treated them as rebellious servants or stubborn vassals. The pontifical court was full of Florentines, and Boniface knew very well what were the sentiments and the opinions of those who stood before him, but especially of one of them: of that man of medium stature, with the protruding lower lip, maker of rhymes for love of women, but, at the same time, adversary of kings and popes.

Boniface sent back to Florence the two weaker and less steadfast men, but kept at his court, almost as a pledge and hostage, the third ambassador, the more formidable and eloquent Dante.

Probably Dante had already seen the haughty Pope the year before, when he had come to Rome for the Jubilee;

[1] D. Compagni, *Cronica*, II, iv (ed. Del Lungo, p. 139).

but this was the first and the last time that he stood
before Boniface, close to him, face to face. What impression must this audience have made upon him who
even then was dreaming of the advent of the Third
Kingdom against the unfaithful and simoniacal Church,
and who was hoping perhaps, in accord with the belief
of the Spirituals, that an emperor would come to subdue
it? What did he think of those brief and arrogant words
—Humble yourselves to me; let my will be obeyed?

Did Dante say anything in reply? Or did he close his
lips in disdainful silence, more eloquent than words?
And on that day of audience in October or November,
1301, was there born in Dante his lasting anger against
the Pope whom, through 'reverence for the supreme
keys,' he will call the 'new Christ,' but whom he will
describe also as 'prince of the new Pharisees,'[1] as
usurper of the seat of St Peter, as him 'who has made a
sewer of my cemetery'[2]; and for whom he will prepare
a hole in the region of the simonists?[3]

This embassy to Rome is one of the most solemn
moments in the life of Dante and, indeed, in the history
of that century. The Pope and the poet are face to face,
adversaries. Two of the greatest minds of that age, very
much alike in their unbending pride, very unlike in
everything else.

Both are strong and great: Boniface because of his
exalted office, the abundance of his wealth, and the
alliance with princes; but only for the moment. Before
two years have passed, he will be seized and treated like a
criminal, his palace sacked, his person outraged, and he

---

[1] *Inf.* XXVII, 85.   [2] *Par.* XXVII, 22–26.
[3] *Inf.* XIX, 52–57.

POPE BONIFACE VIII

Statue in the Cathedral, Florence. Work of the School of
Arnolfo, fourteenth century. [*Photo: Alinari.*]

will die a month later, consumed by madness.[1] Dante, apparently, is powerless, because he represents a party on the eve of defeat and is, at the moment, in the hands of the Pope. But his strength, hidden as yet, lies wholly in his heart and mind, in the power of his art and of his words; and to him, not to Boniface, belongs the future.

Brothers only in pride, in everything they were antagonists: worthy, however, of standing face to face and of measuring and judging each other. Two colossi: the successor of Peter and the heir of Virgil; the one already meditating his edict, *Unam Sanctam*, the other the future author of the *De Monarchia*; the Pope who wished to command kings and emperors, and the Poet who will judge relentlessly, from on high, not only kings and emperors but popes as well.

Both are Utopians, but preoccupied by opposite Utopias; by Utopias drawing to an end, but very much alive still in Boniface and Dante, more than in any other men. In Boniface it is the theocratic Utopia, which ends, we may say, with him. In Dante it is the imperial Utopia and that of the Eternal Gospel, which will scarcely survive the poet's century. Boniface was dreaming of the Pope as the lord of the world, who would have the *plenitudo potestatis* and set it *super reges et regna*. Dante was speculating upon a new revelation, upon the advent of the Holy Spirit which should render useless both popes and kings; and meanwhile he placed his hopes in a lord of the temporal world, an heir to the Roman Empire. It was Boniface who had induced Celestine V, the 'angelic pope' of the Joachimite Spirituals, to

[1] G. Villani, VIII, lxiii ('tutto si rodea come rabbioso'). Grief produced a strange malady so that he gnawed at himself as if he were mad.

abdicate; it was he who had smiled at the 'fatuous men' who expected the end of the world. Dante was a friend and disciple of the Joachimists and the Spirituals, and in his poem he will write with the same pen about the infamy of Boniface and the glory of Joachim of Flora.

Both Boniface and Dante felt themselves possessed and inspired by God: the one as pontiff, the other as poet. But Boniface, a man of action, of finance, of law, despised the poet in Dante; and Dante did not recognize in the simoniacal and traitorous Cardinal Caetani any divine quality. They could not understand and still less esteem each other. Boniface, shrewd and learned in canon law, recognized only the authority of written law, the power of armed force, the power of wealth. Dante, poet and philosopher, Platonist and mystic, admitted no other legitimacy and sovereignty than that of the spirit, and these only in their highest forms. Boniface, man of the Campagna, had preserved in his manner and speech something of the cynical hardness of the marauding feudal vassals, and seemed, at moments, but a rough man of the people wearing the papal crown. Dante was the polished and cultured townsman, the courteous gentleman, the scholar and artist.

Nor did they resemble each other in appearance. Boniface, at that time, was an old man of sixty-six years, but tall and robust. Dante had passed by only a year the 'middle point on the journey of our life'; he was of medium height, but already a little stooping and thin through his long devotion to study. Both, however, had broad foreheads, a stern expression, and brilliant, piercing eyes.

In spite of so many contrasts a similar fate awaits

them. In 1302 Dante will be accused of barratry and rebellion, and condemned, if taken, to be burned alive. In 1303 the assembly of Paris, convoked by Philip the Fair, will accuse Boniface of heresy, of simony, of practising the black arts, of robbery, of incest, and of sodomy. Unjust accusations in both cases, but they deprived Dante of his country for ever and cut short Boniface's dreams and his life before his time.

Perhaps no other pope was hated so far and wide as Boniface VIII. The Franciscan Spirituals hated him; the surviving adherents of Celestine, the Ghibellines, and the powerful Colonna family hated him; the King of France, the despoiled noblemen, and the hard-pressed subjects hated him. And these innumerable hatreds, which only superiority could excite and keep alive, give to Boniface an air of grandeur almost titanic.

But no hatred was so fatal to him as that of the poets. He had against him the two greatest poets of his time: Jacopone da Todi and Dante. He injured both. It was due to Boniface that Jacopone lay in prison from 1298 to 1303. It was due to Boniface that Dante lived an exile from his birthplace from 1301 until his death. Both poets had their revenge; and the evil renown of Boniface through the centuries is due, in great part, to what they wrote about him. Messer Ludovico Ariosto was not altogether wrong when he advised the great ones of the earth to keep the goodwill of the poets.

In those days of 1301 Boniface did not imagine or foresee that his Florentine half-prisoner would one day mark him for the pits of hell, and that the poet would have him condemned from the heights of Paradise by the mouth of St Peter himself. If the Pope could have imagined any such thing, Dante would never have got away alive from his hands. The terrible Pope had killed many enemies, his own and the Church's, and would not have hesitated at one more. And the world would have gone without the *Divina Commedia*. Luckily, Boniface had greater power of will than of imagination, and Dante was saved. On 4 November, Charles of Valois entered Florence, and the news must have reached Rome quickly. Dante understood that his every hope was ended; and he succeeded, we do not know how, in disappearing from the papal court and returning to Tuscany.

16

FIRE AGAINST FIRE

THE reward which Dante received for all that he had done, from 1295 on, for the good of his country was accorded in the fashion common to tyrannical democracies: banishment, pillaging of houses, confiscation of property, sentence of death. They wished, they tried to destroy him utterly. They deprived him of the sight of his native city, his *patria*—which is half his life to a man of feeling. He was separated from his family, reduced to poverty and beggary—which is death itself to noble minds. He was loaded with infamy, given the name of barrator, falsifier, thief, simonist. Finally, he was threatened with the destruction of his body. In every possible way they intended to put an end to Dante. When you take away from a man his native place, his wife and children, his livelihood, his honour and good name—what remains to him? A disdainful spirit in a fragile body. That is still too much. The soul must be divided from the body; the body must be consumed by fire.

To us, so far removed in time, these things astound and horrify. We, who know Dante as the triumphant Blacks in November 1301 did not and could not know him, and see in him the poet-prophet of the *Commedia*, are inclined, in our turn, to condemn unjustly Boniface, Cante de' Gabrielli (the podestà of Florence who pronounced the sentence of banishment), and all their accomplices and helpers.

But we must remind ourselves that Dante, at that time,

appeared in the eyes of most people as only one of many Florentines who had taken a small part in the government of the city, and as one of the many who wrote love-poems for real or imaginary women. No halo then surrounded the head of the proscribed. And we must remember especially that in those turbulent and cruel times every political party which got possession of a city was forced and indeed compelled to banish or destroy the representatives of the opposite party. The Blacks had the advantage, thanks to Boniface and Charles of Valois; and all those who had not sided with them and had created opposition to the Pope and the French had to be banished or suppressed.

Let us note also that Dante was condemned together with others, and that the accusations in the formal sentence are not *ad personam*, but collective. Several times the text repeats the expression, 'they or any one of them,' *ipsi vel eorum aliquis*. It is not stated, then, that Dante himself was actually charged with having given or taken money from wrongful motives; but the general tone of the sentence is such as to make us suppose that, in the opinion of the judges, no one of the condemned had transgressed because he loved his country, but rather because he thirsted for gold.

Let us add also that Dante had given some occasion to his adversaries for accusing him. Not of peculation, certainly, in which perhaps no one believed then and in which to-day no one could believe; but there remained the fact that Dante had failed to oppose the bad government and the atrocities of the Whites in the city of Pistoia in 1301, when, although he was no longer one of the Priors, he had often been called in to the councils and would have had opportunity, had he chosen, to oppose those shameful deeds. Moreover, the charge of his being opposed to Boniface was true: an accusation which might have brought him honour among the Whites, the Ghibellines, and posterity, but which, of necessity, was held a crime by the party enjoying the protection of Boniface.

The history of those centuries is full of similar injustices and condemnations. Dante himself, in 1300, had signed a sentence of banishment; and it is certain that if the Whites had been triumphant in 1302 or 1303, and Dante had returned with them to Florence, there would have been slaughters, sentences of death, infamous accusations, and confiscations at the expense of the Blacks.

For two or three years after his banishment Dante did not give up the hope of re-entering Florence in triumph. On 8 June, 1302, we find him at the meeting of the exiles at San Godenzo; in 1303, at Forlì to aid the undertaking of the Whites against Florence; in 1313 he was urging the Emperor, Henry VII, to besiege and punish the city. From 1304 to the coming of Henry, Dante kept aloof from the other exiles and tried to win his return to his country by peaceable ways, through his eloquence and the fame of his writings; but every attempt failed because he was not willing to return in humility as a penitent. He still hoped, naïve dreamer that he was, to re-enter Florence in triumph, summoned thither by her citizens, and in the glory of their acclaim, to receive the poet's crown.

But Dante was never the man to remain in accord with parties. In consequence, he was threatened with death not only by those within the city, but also by those without. The evidence of the *Ottimo Commento* and, in particular, a clear allusion made by Brunetto Latini,[1] show that his companions in misfortune, either because they found themselves in difficulties through having followed his advice, or for other reasons, began to hate him and tried, possibly, to kill him. No other meaning can be attached to the words of the old master:

> La tua fortuna tanto onor ti serba,
> che l'una parte e l'altra avranno fame
> di te; ma lungi fia dal becco l'erba.

Your fortune reserves such honour for you that the one party and the other shall have hunger for you. But the grass shall be far from the goat.

The words of Cacciaguida convey the same meaning:

> E quel che più ti graverà le spalle,
> sarà la compagnia malvagia e scempia
> con la qual tu cadrai in questa valle;
> che tutta ingrata, tutta matta ed empia,
> si farà contra te; ma, poco appresso,
> ella, non tu, n'avrà rossa la tempia.[2]

And that which will weigh heaviest upon your shoulders will be the wicked and foolish company with which you will fall into this valley: which all ungrateful, mad, and pitiless, will set itself against you; but, soon after, it, not you, will have the forehead red.

It was, then, because of this threat of death that Dante made a party of himself alone, that is, established that superior party of which he was the commander and the only soldier. And, henceforth, he remained outside and above parties. At the coming of Henry, Dante did not speak and write as a Ghibelline, but as the enemy of every division and disorder, as a seeker for peace, for the unity of Italy and of all Christian countries under the

---

[1] *Inf.* XV, 70–72. [2] *Par.* XVII, 61–66.

leadership of one who would re-establish the Roman Empire.

The beginning of Dante's misfortunes lay in his having belonged, or in having appeared to belong, to one of the factions of the Guelph party; and as a White Guelph he was included in the sentences of 1302. There were two sentences: the one of 27 January, comparatively mild; the other of 10 March, much more severe. In the first, Dante was condemned, together with three others, to pay a fine of 5000 gold florins, to stay outside the borders of Tuscany for two years, and to lose what we to-day call civil rights. Dante did not think even for a moment either of appearing or of paying. It would have been an acknowledgment of the truth of the accusations, and he knew besides that not even the accusers honestly believed in those accusations. To them it was a matter of putting outside the law a political adversary who might become dangerous; and no humiliation on his part would have availed to remove their suspicions and save himself from future persecution.

In the second sentence, Dante together with fourteen others was condemned to death. The manner of the execution was specified: if any one of them fell into the hands of the commune, he should be burned alive. There was to be no mere display of power, no half-measures; he should be burned in the fire until he was dead: *talis perveniens igne comburatur sic quod moriatur*. The same death which later overtook Cecco d'Ascoli and Savonarola.[1]

---

[1] Cecco, or Francesco, Stabili da Ascoli was burned as a heretic in Florence, in 1327.

The great Dominican was burned in 1498, when Alexander VI was pope.—Trans.

But Dante contrived not to be taken, and Boniface failed where later Alexander VI succeeded. But the thought of the fire must have remained stamped into Dante's mind, and it may have been one of the unconscious motives which drove him, a little later, to begin the *Inferno*; everlasting fire against promised and threatened fire. The Hebraic principle of an eye for an eye was not wholly dead in the prophetic soul of Dante. He did not disturb himself to cast into the fire of hell Messer Cante de' Gabrielli d'Agobbio, mere executor of others' commands and vendettas, who had no special resentment against Dante; but he knew, and so wrote it, that the true author of his disaster was Pope Boniface. He says it clearly in the words of Cacciaguida, when he speaks of his exile:

> Questo si vuole e questo già si cerca,
> e tosto verrà fatto a chi ciò pensa
> là dove Cristo tutto dì si merca.[1]

This is willed, this is already sought for, and soon will be accomplished by him who plots it there where every day Christ is bargained for.

To Boniface, then, belongs the guilt of having condemned Dante to death by fire; and Dante in turn, as equal to equal, as prophet against pontiff, condemns Boniface to be consumed by everlasting fire. In the vision of 1300, a place for Boniface is already prepared in the pits of the simonists. And in the written poem, in the eager question of Nicholas III, we seem to hear the frenzied impatience of the avenging poet:

> . . . Se' tu già costì ritto,
> se' tu già costì ritto, Bonifazio? [2]

Are you already standing there? Are you already standing there, Boniface?

---

[1] *Par.* XVII, 49–51.   [2] *Inf.* XIX, 52–53.

But when Dante wrote these lines, 11 October, 1303, had already passed. Boniface had died of madness in Rome, and the visitor to the Inferno was certain that the fire was already burning the legs of the simoniacal pope. It was not the fire which ends with death, like that with which Dante was threatened, but fire everlasting, that fire which still illumines with its sinister gleam the figure of the haughty pontiff.

17

THE GREAT PILGRIM

*F*OR almost twenty years the life of Dante was that of a pilgrim—not a pilgrim of love, nor a pilgrim to Rome for religion's sake; not even a wanderer for pleasure or variety. He was a pilgrim of necessity. At the beginning of the *Convivio* he laments having gone 'through almost every part to which our language extends, a wanderer, almost a beggar. . . .'[1] But we must take account of the *almost*'s which appear twice among so few words: almost every part, almost a beggar. Dante did not see all Italy, nor did he live 'begging his livelihood bit by bit.'

Certain biographies convey the idea that from the time of his exile, Dante devoted himself to making a tour of Italy. His merely naming a city, a district, a mountain, is regarded as certain proof of his sojourn here, or at least of his passage. Some biographers, finding Italy too limited a field for Dante's roving mania, have sent him beyond the Alps, into France, Flanders, Germany, Switzerland, and finally 'over seas' to Oxford. But even the journey to Paris, which has in its favour the testimony of Villani and Boccaccio and seems indisputable to many, is far from being certain or probable. The proofs are too few and the reasons against it too weighty.[2]

But he certainly traversed Italy from the Alps to Rome;

[1] *Convivio*, I, iii, 4.

[2] The fundamental book on this subject is *Dante e la Francia*, by A. Farinelli (Milan, Hoepli, 1908, I, pp. 91–134).

Also M. Barbi thinks the journey to Paris 'scarcely probable' (*Enc. It.*, XII, 330).

and from undeniable references in his writings, or from documents, or from legitimate inferences, we know to what places he went or where he stayed. In Tuscany—Lunigiana, the Casentino, Arezzo, Siena, Pisa, Lucca; and beyond Tuscany—Forlı, Bologna, Verona, Mantua, Venice, Ravenna, and perhaps Genoa and Milan. As for his journeys to convents—San Benedetto dell' Alpe, Fonte Avellana, the monastery of Corvo—these are suppositions more or less supported by evidence, except the last, which is almost certainly a fable.

We picture him going on horseback across hills and rivers, silent, with knitted brows; sometimes in the company of noblemen or of merchants, sometimes quite alone, uncertain of the roads and of the halting-places. There is undoubtedly autobiographic reminiscence in that passage of the *Convivio* where Dante recalls the uncertainties of the wayfarer: 'And just as a pilgrim who goes along a road where he has never been before, and thinks that every house which he sees in the distance may be the inn, and finding it not so, turns his faith to the next one, and so from house to house until he comes to the inn. . . .'[1]

But this wandering from castle to castle and from town to town could not always have been unhappy, because Dante, according to his own words, was curious about new things:

> Li occhi miei ch'a mirare eran contenti
> per veder novitadi ond'e' son vaghi.[2]

My eyes which were intent on gazing in order to see novel sights of which they are desirous.

---

[1] *Conv.* IV, xii. 15.   [2] *Purg.* X, 103–104.

Fanciful inferences, however, about places where he sojourned or passed are less important to us than to know what his life was in those years. An unhappy life, undoubtedly, but rather that of a courtier than a mendicant. This is not mere conjecture, but an opinion supported by the expert authority of Michele Barbi. 'The position of Dante,' he says, 'when he had separated himself from his companions in exile, was almost that of a courtier. To hasten here and there, where there were noblemen reputed liberal toward men of wit and learning or even of pleasant disposition, so that the court felt honoured by their presence and made use of them in affairs of importance, or found amusement from their talents in daily life; to live, therefore, among a throng of people coming and going, people of different natures, different in taste and understanding, varying from persons of knowledge and political experience to buffoons. And usually these last were not the least welcome or the least liberally rewarded or the first to be dismissed.'[1]

A life often embarrassing and humiliating. Not indeed that among courtiers there were not persons both honoured and honourable, like that Marco Lombardo immortalized by Dante; but their position was always that of temporary servitors who depended on the humours and caprices of the prince, and had to propitiate him with their accomplishments, good or bad, in order to obtain protection and means of subsistence. Add to this the promiscuous intercourse with people of every sort and kind who gathered at the most abundant tables and had need to be tolerant of others and to bring

[1] *Enc. It.*, XII, 329.

themselves into favour. Of this troubled life among noblemen far from noble, among strolling players and buffoons, there are echoes in the legends about Dante, and probably not all the legends are without foundation in truth. Dante was not a man given to jocularity; on the contrary, he was easily moved to reproof and scorn; while noblemen have commonly preferred those who made them laugh to those who made them think. And we can well believe that Dante was obliged to remove himself from one of those courts because he had become too much disgusted with the buffoons who enjoyed a greater degree of the patron's favour than he did.

In short, Dante was not a true courtier. Nor was he a true beggar, since in some sort he served his protectors; but neither was he a free man. Whoever understands the dignity of self-respect and knows the pride of the poet, can imagine what must have been Dante's sufferings during those enforced wanderings.

But at least, we ask, they made use of him in affairs of importance? It seems not. The only duties entrusted to Dante about which we are certain, are the conclusion of the peace between the Malaspina and the bishop of Luni, and the embassy to Venice on behalf of Guido Novello—missions disproportionate to the greatness of the man. They bring to mind the story of the painter Menighella who induced Michelangelo to draw a St Roque or a St Anthony destined to be daubed with colour for the delectation of peasants. The greatest men can accept certain tasks through necessity or goodwill, but not without a secret bitterness.

Dante, therefore, who had to maintain himself and his sons, was obliged very often to appeal to the generosity of the noblemen who received him. Traces of these requests, which must have cost his pride so dear, remain even in the *Commedia*. In the *Purgatorio*, when he meets Currado Malaspina, he speaks in high praise of Malaspina's descendants:

> e io vi giuro, s'io di sopra vada,
> che vostra gente onrata non si sfregia
> del pregio della borsa e della spada.[1]

And I swear to you, so may my journey on high be accomplished, that your honoured race does not disgrace its reputation of the purse and the sword.

It was a receipt of the grateful poet for hospitality received. Although this reference to the purse seems out of place in the poem of Christian salvation, there is another of the same sort in the words of Cacciaguida which praise Can Grande della Scala, one of Dante's protectors, for a liberality past or desired:

> A lui t'aspetta ed a' suoi benefici;
> per lui fia trasmutata molta gente,
> cambiando condizion ricchi e mendici.[2]

Look to him and to his benefits. By him shall many people be transformed, rich and poor changing condition.

The meaning seems to be: You shall go almost a beggar, but the lord of Verona, Can Grande della Scala, will by his liberality change your condition, and will make rich you who had been poor. A prophecy which was never realized for the poet, but it gave rise perhaps to the calumny that he was one of the many flatterers who hung about noblemen's courts in those days. There is an echo of this in a sonnet attributed incorrectly to Cino da Pistoia, where Dante, together with Manoello

[1] *Purg.* VIII, 127–129.   [2] *Par.* XVII, 88–90.

Giudeo, is placed in the Inferno in the region of the flatterers.[1]

In reality, as the poor poet was neither a mendicant nor a mountebank, neither was he a servile toady of the powerful; but through his pressing need he had to bring himself to praise those little worthy of his homage. His life as a 'man of the court' must have been painful and sometimes detestable; but on the whole he was something half-way between the gentleman-companion and the diplomatist, between the secretary and the counsellor.

But in other and far higher ways than these already spoken of, Dante was a pilgrim. Before his exile he had gone in 1300 to Rome for the Jubilee announced by Boniface VIII, and it is precisely this year which he selected as the fictitious date of that pilgrimage to the Empyrean which forms the *Divina Commedia*. He mentions other travellers, *pellegrini*, who like himself were going to Rome;[2] but he wished to be *romeo*, a religious pilgrim to Rome, in order to mount to that more splendid Rome which is Paradise.

His first master, Brunetto, had gone on a pilgrimage to Campostella; and his first friend, Guido, had set out from Florence to go there. But Dante aspired to a very different pilgrimage—not indeed to Rome 'to see our Veronica,' or to Campostella to pray at the tomb of St James; but a pilgrimage toward those heavens where he could speak with the Apostle and see, face to face, the true image of Christ.

---

[1] Part of this sonnet, written after the death of Dante, may be found in Zingarelli, *Dante*, p. 670.
[2] *V.N.*, XL ; *Par.* XXXI, 130 ff.

The Middle Ages are full of pilgrims. Down every road pass the Christians who are journeying toward Spain or Rome or the Holy Land. Alighieri, greater than all other pilgrims, imagines and describes an ideal and sacred pilgrimage which leads him across the darkness of the Inferno and the mountain-ledges of Purgatory to the City of Light and Beatitude, to the feet of the Trinity. The other pilgrims go to venerate tombs and sepulchres; Dante ascends on the wings of poetry even to the living God. The *Commedia* is the wonderful itinerary of the most wonderful pilgrimage which any Christian ever made before death.

IN THE PRESENCE OF THE EMPEROR

ANTE kissed the feet of only two men—Boniface, the Pope, and Henry, the Emperor. He knelt before Boniface in 1301, when he was sent to Rome as ambassador; before Henry in 1311 or 1312, perhaps at Milan, perhaps at Pisa. Dante paid homage to the Pope in observance of ceremonial usage; to the Emperor through motives of eager devotion.

He kissed the feet of the human being who had most greatly stirred his wrath, and of that other who had roused his highest hopes—the simoniacal pontiff and the peace-making king. Both, not long after the kiss bestowed by Dante, flickered out wretchedly.

Dante has left an account of his homage to the Emperor, in his famous letter to Henry: 'ego qui scribo . . . velut decet imperatoriam maiestatem benignissimum vidi et clementissimum te audivi, cum pedes tuos manus meae tractarunt et labia mea debitum persolverunt.'[1]

Who was this man whose feet one of the proudest men of all time did not disdain to kiss? He had been, up to a little while before, the count of a small domain not much larger than the modern Luxembourg. He was elected king of Germany in 1308, and crowned emperor at Aix-la-Chapelle in 1309. He descended into Italy in October 1310, and was crowned with the iron crown at Milan, 6 January, 1311. When Dante saw him he must

---

[1] *Epis.* VII. I who write . . . saw thee most benignant and heard thee most merciful, as befits imperial majesty, when my hands touched thy feet and my lips paid their due tribute.—Trans.

have been nearly forty years old. He was of medium height, like the poet, and had a squint in one eye.

Among the many German emperors after Charlemagne who came down into Italy, Henry VII was one of the most unfortunate. His father had been killed in battle in 1288, leaving him an orphan of tender years; his brother Waleran died in Italy at the siege of Brescia, and his wife Marguerite at Genoa. He himself, within less than three years from the time he crossed the Alps, died of fever at Buonconvento. He had come to restore harmony between Guelphs and Ghibellines, and both parties were dissatisfied with him: many abandoned him, many betrayed him. He had come to make peace, and many cities rebelled against him; some, like Florence, closed their gates in his face and answered his messengers with insulting words. He had come to be crowned by the Pope in St Peter's, and when he reached Rome he had to fight his way in, taking a part of the city by armed force; and, finally, only through a popular uprising did he succeed in being crowned, and even then not in St Peter's but in the church of St John Lateran; and by three cardinals, not by the Pope. He had come to re-establish the authority of the Empire against the leader of the Guelphs, King Robert of Naples; and in order to gratify the Pope, Clement V, he had to grant a year's truce to Robert. When finally he started to make war in earnest, he was stopped for ever by death.

His undertaking was a lamentable failure. He exhausted men and German money in vain; he diminished still further the prestige of the imperial name; he did not succeed in subduing the centres of the Guelph resistance, Naples and Florence; he delayed too long in regions and in enterprises of little importance; and he left affairs in Italy in a worse condition than he had found them. Henry was a Utopian who, plunged into the midst of harsh and complex realities, did not know how to be an aid to his friends or a vexation to his enemies.

The city which did him the most harm and brought about his greatest humiliation was Florence. The man who more than all others believed in him as saviour and avenger was Dante, an exile from Florence. In the duel between the city and its greatest citizen, the city conquered. The gold of Florence, and her skilful management, accomplished more against the poor Emperor than the army of the King of Naples did. Dante saw the situation clearly when he passionately urged Henry to move against the fox and the viper of the Arno, instead of delaying in northern Italy. But when finally, 19 September, 1312, Henry laid siege to Florence, it was too late. He did not dare, or was not able, to invest it vigorously; and on 30 October, apparently through lack of provisions, he was forced to retire without giving battle. A Florentine, Betto Brunelleschi, had already on an earlier occasion answered the imperial ambassadors that 'the Florentines would never lower their horns for any lord,' and this time it was true. The fox of Dante knew how to be the bull, taking its stand behind wall and moat in order to repulse the idealistic Emperor. During the siege the Emperor stayed at the monastery of San Salvi, a few paces from the city; but he was not accompanied by the Florentine Dante, who, although he had incited the Emperor to chastise the city, had not wished to fight against his own birthplace and men of his own blood.

In 1310, when Alighieri first knew that Henry was

about to descend into Italy, his joy was great. Italy would once more become the garden of the Empire, the authority of the Pope would be blunted, peace would be restored between city and city, between citizen and citizen; he himself would be able to see once more, 'with other fleece,' his 'beautiful church of St John.'

Not content with prostrating himself at the Emperor's feet, Dante addressed a passionate letter to the kings, princes, and people of Italy; another, very eloquent, to Henry himself; and a third, full of threats and fury, to the 'most wicked Florentines within the walls.' And at the same time he wrote the *De Monarchia*, a logical defence of universal monarchy and virtually a reply to the *Unam Sanctam*, the famous Bull of Boniface.

But his ardent words and his impassioned support availed little or nothing. We do not know what Henry and Dante said to each other at their first and perhaps only meeting. It is unlikely that the Emperor understood fully the greatness of the man who knelt before him. Not because Henry was a barbarian; he had been educated at the French court, he spoke French well, and he did not despise talent and ability. Nor was he the uncouth mediæval Teuton such as we imagine. He was, on the contrary, more Gallic than Germanic, both in his culture and his interests.[1] But probably he did not read the Italian vernacular, and Dante must have seemed to him just one of the many banished Italians who were rushing to him from every part, only more cultured and more sincerely devoted to the imperial cause. Perhaps Henry managed in time to read the *De Monarchia*, but it

[1] In 1294, in consideration of a regular revenue, he had agreed to support French policy.

is certain that he did not know the *Inferno*, completed by that time, nor those cantos of the *Purgatorio* which were already written.

Undoubtedly, in speech as well as by letter, Dante would have denounced to the Emperor the stubborn attitude of Florence and the danger threatening thence, and would have exhorted him to hurl himself without delay against that city. Although he was a dreamer, Dante saw the situation more clearly than Henry. At the beginning of the fourteenth century, Florence held a position like that of England at the beginning of the nineteenth century in the wars against Napoleon. From Florence came the sinews of war, the florins which bought the traitors and strengthened the rebellious; from Florence came the intrigues, the plots, the interested counsels. And taking the world as it was then, Florence was nearer right than Dante. The imperial idea was at an end; and only from the rich and independent middle classes of the cities could the modern states be formed. The idea of Empire was more splendid, and would have saved them many crashes and disasters; but it no longer had a secure foundation in the new society which was just becoming articulate. Christendom was breaking up; the Empire would remain a memory until the coming of Charles V and Napoleon.

Dante's counsel, finally, would have seemed suspect to Henry because he would have thought the exiled Florentine more interested to secure his own repatriation than to aid the Emperor's undertaking. When at length Henry decided to listen to him, it was probably too late.

Meanwhile the poet had taken refuge, it seems, in the Casentino, as guest of the counts of Battifolle, and thence he must have followed the movements of the Emperor. And Henry with his goings here and there, from Milan to Genoa, from Genoa to Pisa, from Pisa to Rome, must have seemed to Dante like a blue-bottle fly that goes blundering about a room among people who wish him dead. And perhaps that little cross-eyed man, who had roused so much reverence and exaltation in Dante's soul, now moved him to pity. At the end of August 1313, when Dante received news of the death of his idol, we may be sure that he wept; and with his tears of compassion for the poor unsuccessful emperor must have mingled his tears of rage.

But Dante would not be unfaithful to Henry even after death. The blame for the disaster, so Dante makes Beatrice say, rests on blind and unwilling Italy.

> 'n quel gran seggio a che tu li occhi tieni
> per la corona che già v'è su posta,
> prima che tu a queste nozze ceni,
>   sederà l'alma, che fia giù agosta,
> dell'alto Arrigo, ch'a drizzare Italia
> verrà in prima ch'ella sia disposta.
>   La cieca cupidigia che v'ammalia
> simili fatti v'ha al fantolino
> che muor per fame e caccia via la balia.[1]

In that great seat on which you fix your gaze because of the crown which is already placed above it, shall sit (before you are summoned to this wedding-feast) the soul, imperial on earth, of the noble Henry, who will come to direct Italy before she is ready. Blind Greed, which lays a spell on you, has made you like the little child who dies of hunger, and yet drives away the nurse.

He whom, alive, Dante had called another Moses, a new David, bridegroom of Italy, and even Lamb of God, becomes now in humbler guise the nurse driven away by the foolish suckling. The admiration has become less

[1] *Par.* XXX, 133–141.

emphatic but more human; the exalted worship becomes filial affection.

The sepulchral monument which Tino di Caniaino carved for the unhappy emperor in the cathedral of Pisa is splendid and noble; but more resplendent and lasting is that which the disappointed Dante raised to him in these lines on the shining, mystic rose, the 'candida rosa,' of Paradise.

THE END OF THE PILGRIMAGE

THE twenty-fourth of August 1313, the date of the death of Henry, marked the end of Dante's earthly hopes. Eight years later, in August or September 1321, the poet himself died, and of the same fever that killed the Emperor.

In 1315 his native Florence once more menaced him with death. As he had not accepted the humiliating conditions of the general pardon offered to the exiles in August of that year, and had not presented himself within the time limit before the vicar of King Robert, he was condemned, together with the other rebels and Ghibellines, to be beheaded. Dante was still dreaming, and would go on dreaming until his death, of a repentant Florence placing on his head in solemn ceremonial the laurel crown of the poets. Florence, however, occupied herself with his head only to decree that it should be severed from his shoulders if he should fall into her hands: *Caput a scapulis amputetur ita quod penitus moriatur.* In 1302 Florence had promised him death by fire; now, instead of the throne of triumph, she offers the headsman's block; instead of flame, steel. Florence had resolved to cut off from herself by every possible means this undesirable son of hers, *unless* he should present himself humbly in San Giovanni as an offering, as a reprieved criminal. And he was unwilling to re-enter San Giovanni except to receive a crown! Between Florence and Dante there is no coming to terms: the city and the citizen are equally obstinate. The poet asks from her the consecration of his glory.

The city demands from the poet his humiliation or his blood.

Since he could not and would not return to Florence, since he did not wish to remain longer at Verona where the gay and miscellaneous court was not to his liking, he had to seek another refuge. He chose Ravenna. Just when he went there and whether he lived there continuously we do not know with certainty. Clearly not before the summer of 1316, when Guido Novello da Polenta succeeded Lambert; and not after January 1320. And in those years he was at Verona again, and at Mantua and Venice.

We do not know if it was Guido Novello who called him to Ravenna, or if the new podestà, a known friend to poetry and to men of talent, limited himself to receiving the poet with kindness. Furthermore, we do not know what members of his family Dante had with him: doubtless his son Pietro who had ecclesiastical benefices at Ravenna; perhaps also his son Jacopo and his daughter Antonia who became a nun at Santa Maria dell' Ulivi, taking the name of Sister Beatrice; and perhaps also his wife, Gemma.

Neither do we know if he taught in the university at Ravenna, or whether he had private pupils or only younger friends who later boasted of having been his disciples. In short, except for his embassy to Venice and his death, we know little or nothing of his last years.

It is probable, however, that at Ravenna he wrote the last cantos of the *Paradiso*, and that the glorification of the eagle was composed in the selfsame place where the Empire began and ended. There has been much talk, apropos of Dante at Ravenna, about the Byzantine records and monuments; but to Dante the Eastern Empire meant little. To him Ravenna was the place which saw the beginning and the end of the true empire, the Roman Empire. Cæsar, the founder, according to Dante, moved from Ravenna to cross the Rubicon:

> Quel che fe' poi ch'elli uscì di Ravenna
> e saltò Rubicon, fu di tal volo,
> che nol seguiterìa lingua nè penna.[1]

> That which [the Imperial Eagle] did when it came forth from Ravenna and leapt the Rubicon, was of so bold a flight that neither tongue nor pen can follow it.

And at Ravenna the last miserable Emperor of the West, Romulus Augustulus, was captured and deposed. At Ravenna also Odoacer was defeated and killed, the first barbarian in Italy who openly took his place in the line of the successors of Cæsar.

Other records at Ravenna, but Christian this time, would have roused Dante's interest: those of the saints Romualdus and Peter Damian whom the poet recalls in the *Paradiso* and in cantos which were almost certainly composed at Ravenna.[2] Peter Damian more than all others must have pleased him because earlier than Dante, in the *Liber Gomorrhianus* and in other books, he had denounced with Dantesque severity the unclean vices of the prelates and the friars.

But if the melancholy city, the last refuge of the Empire and of Dante, roused memories of a past that was splendid, the reality in those first decades of the fourteenth century was less impressive. The territory

---

[1] *Par.* VI, 61–63.
[2] On the influence of St Peter Damian on Dante, see P. Amaducci, *Nel cielo de' contemplanti*. Rome, Alfieri and Lacroix, n. d.

was small, and the people who inhabited it were not distinguished. Guido da Polenta, the nephew of Francesca da Rimini, was a good soldier and a graceful writer of *ballate*; but he could not compare with Can Grande della Scala. Nor was he sufficiently strong to maintain himself in the government. Exactly a year after Dante's death, in September 1322, he was turned out by Ostasio II, and 'died in exile and disconsolate, in 1330.'[1]

And at this point we must observe that Dante did not bring good luck to those whom he loved and who, in turn, loved him. His mother died a few years after his birth; his father died when Dante was still a youth; his first friend, Guido Cavalcanti, died young; Beatrice died at twenty-six years of age; Can Grande at thirty-eight; Guido Novello, as we have seen, lost, soon after Dante's death, both his rule and his life.

Some have imagined that Dante busied himself in the solitude of Ravenna with the study of theology in the company of the archbishop Rainaldo Concoreggi. But it is impossible that there could have been any intimacy between the two men. Rainaldo had been one of the favourites of Boniface VIII, and when he was rector of the Flaminia at Forlì, he was assaulted in a Ghibelline tumult and severely wounded. It is not possible that the archbishop would have enjoyed conversing with an enemy of Boniface, one who passed for a rabid Ghibelline, and who was a friend of the lord of Verona.

Dante, however, did not lack companions—but what companions! Dino Perini, a shallow-brained young Florentine; Menghino Mezzani, notary and indifferent rhymester; Pietro di messer Giardino, another notary; a

[1] G. L. Passerini, *La Vita di Dante.* Florence, Vallecchi, 1929, p. 340.

physician from Certaldo named Fiduccio de' Milotti; Bernardo Canaccio, who scribbled Latin verses. The greatest poet of his time, and one of the greatest of all times, was reduced to conversing with these provincial would-be intellectuals, who could not comprehend either the loftiness of his wounded soul or the marvel of his poetry. He was writing the cantos of the *Paradiso*, the most perfect and most glorious of the entire poem, and he was surrounded the while by affixers of seals and by fourth-rate poetasters. His sons, as we know from what they have left, were of small mind and of slow understanding. Much has been written about his daughter (Antonia = Beatrice?), who consoled with filial and womanly gentleness the last years of the melancholy father; but it is all an embroidering on nothing. We could imagine with equal justification that this grown-up daughter with her caprices and petty womanish ways greatly wearied the singer of the *Paradiso*.

In short, Dante was an eagle who was forced to content himself with the companionship of sparrows and barnyard fowls. If the story related by Vasari is true, that Giotto, at the suggestion of Alighieri, was called to Ravenna by Guido Novello to fresco a church, then one friend worthy of Dante, at least in the field of art, saw the poet in these last years of his life.

Others, it is true, addressed themselves to him from a distance. But what sort of men were they? The extravagant and overbearing Cecco d'Ascoli, a philosopher suspected of heresy and a clumsy versifier, who afterwards in the *Acerba* had the effrontery to ridicule the *Divina Commedia*. Then there was the humble and obscure teacher of grammar at Bologna, Giovanni del Virgilio, who permitted himself to advise Dante as to themes for new poetical works, and invited him, we do not know by what right or authority, to betake himself to Bologna, there to receive we don't know what laureation or complimentary award.

And Dante, who was thought by everyone to be reserved and churlish, deigned to answer the poetic effusions of the self-important grammarian of Bologna with two eclogues in Latin, and sent him two new cantos of the *Paradiso*; refusing, however, to accept the invitation to go to Bologna.

This was one of the oddest adventures in Dante's life as a poet. Imagine it! Dante in the rôle of shepherd! Dante an Arcadian! If ever there was a poet who had nothing in common with Arcady and pastoral poetry, that poet was Dante. And yet while he was describing in powerful verse the loftiest heights of the Christian Paradise, he travestied himself in the guise of an old shepherd with the name of Tityrus, who converses with other shepherds, milks his ewe, and stretches himself on the grass. It is true that Tityrus is the first name used by the Roman Virgil in his Eclogues; but it creates an incongruous effect to see Dante, the theologian and prophet, schooling himself to take to his lips the pastoral syrinx in order to do honour to one who admired him to be sure, but as a pedagogue would admire from a distance a volcano which casts forth at the same time lava and flowers. And the other shepherds are too inferior to Tityrus (Dante) for the fiction to take on an air of grandeur. Mopsus is Giovanni del Virgilio, Melibœus is the young Dino Perini, Alphesibœus is Master Fiduccio, Iolas is

Guido Novello, and Phyllis, we suppose, is Gemma Donati.

Dante would have found better company in the twisted pine trees of Chiassi above the solitary shores of the Adriatic, or among those saints, emperors, and angels in mosaic, with their enormous, staring eyes, who for centuries had awaited from the walls of San Vitale and of Sant' Apollinare a song which should release them from that enchantment in the sacred stone.

Dante's conversation was now more with the dead than with the living. He must have had a foreboding that the end of the *Commedia* would precede by only a little the end of his life. Alone among men, as he had always been, rejected and proscribed by his fatherland, with no hope of seeing a worthy emperor crowned or of witnessing the victorious descent of the Veltro, he passed his days among visions of the Empyrean and in the melancholy contemplation of that city where the Roman Empire had died ingloriously in 476, and whence the last degenerate heirs of that Empire had been driven out for ever by the barbarian Astolphus in 751.

Ravenna, city of pine trees and the dead,[1] was in a sense predestined to see the end of the last great man who remained loyal to the imperial idea. In 1321, Dante was in his fifty-sixth year. He could not be called old, but his hair was already white and his shoulders more bent than in the days of his early manhood. But perhaps he would have lived longer if it had not pleased Guido Novello to give the poet a token of his goodwill. In 1321 there had been a quarrel between some Ravennese

[1] Many years ago I called the city a sepulchre. v. *Nipoti d'Iddio*. Florence, Vallecchi, 1932, pp. 213–219. The essay on Ravenna dates from 1905.

and Venetian sailors in which two Venetians were killed and several wounded. Venice, having other reasons for starting a quarrel with Ravenna, displayed intentions far from pacific. In consequence, Guido thought it well to send an embassy to the Queen of the Adriatic. Dante was selected, we do not know whether in company with others or alone, to go to Venice. It is believed that while he was returning to Ravenna by land, traversing the region of miasmal marshes between Pomposa and Comacchio, he fell ill of malaria. In a body already exhausted by strong emotions, by mental sufferings, and by study, the fever must have been severe and must have started other ills, because the soul of Dante freed itself from the weary flesh probably on the fourteenth or fifteenth of September. Thus, indirectly, by the fault of two bands of sailors, drunk and bloodthirsty, Dante died before his time, the greatest poet Italy ever had, and one of the twenty or thirty supreme minds which the earth has distilled from the generations of mankind in six thousand years of history.

It is not known who was with him at the last moment: his daughter, perhaps, or his wife; certainly his sons, a friend or two, and a friar to commend his soul.

If in those days of febrile stimulation he looked back upon his life, he must have thought it strange that there at the end he should find in the names of those about him reminders of the three beings who had filled so great a part of his thoughts and imaginings. The daughter, destined to be called Beatrice, if she was not already known by this magic name, brought back the memory of the 'youngest of the angels' in Florence. The professor of Bologna bore in his name the glory of Dante's master and guide, the Roman Virgil. The lord of Ravenna recalled his kinswoman, that Francesca who had moved the poet so profoundly in the whirlwind of the carnal sinners.

But if in the sleeplessness of fever he reviewed one after another the events of his whole existence, from the first springtimes in Florence to this grievous vigil of autumn in Ravenna, a season which he would not live to enjoy, he must have thought that his life had been a series of misfortunes and disillusions. The death of Beatrice, the twofold threat of death hurled by the city which he loved, the humiliating exile, the wandering among people who did not perceive his light, the enforced begging of his bread in courts and castles, the performing of duties that were beneath him as the price of his livelihood, the death of Henry VII, the unfulfilled hope of laureation among the marbles of his 'bel San Giovanni'—these were some of the links in the cruel chain.

One thing, and one only, remained which would redeem with interest all the disappointments and sorrows: the last born child of his genius, the work which, as he must have known, would be his everlasting compensation through the centuries to come. The *Divina Commedia* was finished, the book which inclosed in the most powerful and melodious verse of all our poetry, his revenge, his hopes, his prophecies, his visions of earth and of heaven. He knew with certainty that he had not passed his life uselessly on earth; he knew that men would remember him to eternity; and that the Florentines themselves would beg for his poor body which they had tried to destroy with fire and steel.

The sacred poem which embraced the universe, and guided souls from the dark forest of sin to the mystical rose of the radiant Blessed and to the inscrutable circle of the Trinity, was finished and consigned to immortality. Dante, who was born and who had lived for this, could now die.

BOOK THREE
Soul

DANTE, A SINNER

HAT Dante was a sinner and guilty of many sins, and that he himself admits it in open or in indirect confession, is a truth denied by no one. In the introduction of the *Commedia*, the poet depicts his wandering in the dark forest of evil and sin; and the first two parts of the poem are a progressive purification up to the second forest, the one in the Earthly Paradise, where Beatrice summarizes the accusations against her poet.[1] That Dante was a sinner, like all of us, is not a matter for surprise. He was a man, not an angel; an artist, not a saint.

But in what ways and to what extent did he sin? The flock of modern Dantomaniacs, driven by the romantic habit of making every genius a demi-god, gladly passes over the sins of Dante, and either thinks them less grave than they were, or translates them into adroit euphemisms which lessen them and almost absolve them. Wrath, for example, becomes 'generous disdain'; pride becomes 'natural consciousness of his own greatness,' and so on.

Others, on the contrary, because of their scornful intolerance of that semi-deification attempted by the fanatics, exaggerate the failings of Dante, or think that they have discovered new ones, on the basis of fantastic and insufficient proofs, such as the emotion of the poet before certain of the damned: his pity for Paolo and Francesca, for example, would be taken as an indirect admission of his adultery with a sister-in-law.[2]

[1] *Purg.* XXX, 109–145; XXXI, 1–69.
[2] The most notable of these Devil's advocates was the lunatic Vittorio

This time, however, the truth lies between the two extremes. Dante was not that 'spotless conscience' that his sheep-like worshippers imagine; neither was he the half-blackguard that the others would have him.

We need not put unquestioning trust in the confessions of the poet. When a man judges himself, he almost never judges accurately, either because of that natural self-esteem and leniency illustrated by Christ in the famous parable of the mote and the beam, or because of insufficient self-examination—for introspection is not at all easy even when done in good faith. Therefore, those who interpret the judgements must take into account the man who is making the confession, must note differences in moral sensibility and in the systems of valuation. A saint like Francis of Assisi thinks himself the worst man in the world; a madman like Benvenuto Cellini boasts of having committed murders.

If, for example, in the opening canto of the *Inferno*, the three beasts of the wood typify, as most commentators maintain, luxury (in its mediæval sense), avarice, and pride; and if they symbolize the chief impediments to Dante's salvation, that is, the sins to which he is most addicted, we can say at once that a third of the confession is mistaken. Dante was never avaricious, nor is there a trace of avarice in the records relating to his life. Obviously, only by a misuse of the word can we call avaricious a man who laments his own poverty.

Perhaps, however, some malicious person might say, since Dante received from his father only a meagre

Imbriani. See his article, *I vizi di Dante* (1883) in *Studi letterari e bizzarrie satiriche*, edited by B. Croce. Bari, Laterza, 1907, pp. 359–381. Also *Studi Danteschi*. Florence, Sansoni, 1891, pp. 427 ff.

legacy and very soon after, by reason of his banishment, was forced to incur debts or to beg, he lacked the first condition, and the essential one, for display of avarice. But the imaginary speaker would be mistaken. The miser is not always rich, and sometimes those who have few possessions are very niggardly with those few; and we have no lack of examples of very miserly beggars.

But in order to know by what sins the soul of Dante was tempted or overcome, it is best to pass in review the seven deadly sins of the Christian doctrine. Since we are discussing a Catholic, we may be permitted to measure him by the teachings of the children's catechism. When a poet professes himself a Christian, the fact that he is a great poet is not sufficient excuse for his becoming or remaining a sinner. And in the case of Dante there is the express command of Christ: 'Judge not, that ye be not judged.' Few men have judged others with such assurance and severity as Dante judged them. It is only fair, then, that he should not escape the judgement of others.

The count is quickly made. Of the seven sins of first consequence, three or perhaps four are foreign to Dante. Since he was a man of laborious and sober life, we cannot accuse him of sloth or of gluttony. As for envy, he himself says, at one point in the poem, that he must stand in the circle of the envious, but only for a little time,

> chè poca è l'offesa
> fatta per esser con invidia. . . .[1]

because slight is my offence committed through being envious.

---

[1] *Purg.* XIII, 134–135.

In spite of this definite confession, it seems almost incredible that Dante should have been capable of envy even a very few times. He was too proud to be envious. There is nothing to surprise us in this statement. The truly proud man is so certain of his own superiority that he cannot lower himself to envy those who are, in his own opinion, inferior to him. And pride is not the only sin which saves a man from another sin, sometimes more grave. Luxury and gluttony usually exclude avarice; just as avarice is often a safeguard against gluttony, luxury, and sloth. Pride is not only a counter-poison for envy, but is almost always a weapon against sloth. The proud man covets glory, and Dante himself, in lines that are famous,[1] notes that fame is not acquired in bed. It is this mutual incompatibility of certain sins which makes it impossible to find the instance of a man, however much he may have sinned, who was guilty of all seven.

Dante was guilty of three of them, easily discernible from his works—lust, wrath, and pride. One must admit that these are heavy sins; and if there are gradations of gravity, they are among the gravest that imperil the soul of a Christian.

We could add besides that these three sins associated with Dante are the perfect and exact opposites of the three cardinal virtues of the Christian, and especially of that heroic embodiment of Christianity which was found, in Dante's time, in the genuine Franciscan.

The perfect Christian must take a vow of chastity, and Dante, more than was befitting a moralist and a prophet, yielded to lust.

The virtue most recommended to all Christians is

[1] *Inf.* XXIV, 47–48.

humility, and Dante was not only proud but he often indulged openly in self-praise.

Patience and resignation even in the midst of misfortunes and injuries—the 'perfect joy' so eloquently explained by St Francis to Brother Leo[1]—are the third proof of fortitude and faith demanded of Christians. Dante, on the contrary, was inclined to anger; and he showed, in his life and in his writings, a passion against men, parties, and cities which sometimes reached ferocity. One of the most famous eulogists of St Francis was, however one may regret to say it, a spirit radically anti-Franciscan.

Dante is so really and abundantly great, in spite of his fallible human side, that I should not dare, even if I were able, to act as his accuser or defender. But our Florentine Titan has a right to the truth, which is not always, alas! what it seemed. Perhaps, however, one of his posthumous friends may be permitted to suggest an addition to the judgements already passed, which may succeed in explaining, if not in harmonizing, the undeniable discords of his spirit.

A sin is always a sin whatever its name and form, and all are blameworthy in the sight of God. But from the psychological point of view, if not from the theological, a distinction is possible and justifiable.

There are base and despicable sins characteristic of base and despicable souls, such as gluttony, sloth, envy. There are other sins which more readily dominate souls which are vigorous and noble. Of this last sort, we believe, are the sins of Dante. I do not say that lust is a

---

[1] v. *The Little Flowers of Saint Francis*, translated by T.W. Arnold. London, Dent, Chap. VIII, pp. 25–28.—Trans.

trivial and pardonable sin, but it may be the beginning of love: love of particular, mortal persons, not of the Eternal and Perfect Being; love of the flesh more than of the spirit, love turned away from its true object, love perilous and base. But even in such love there is a beginning of self-forgetfulness, an overcoming of frozen indifference, a spark of fire which can burn in desires more worthy. Where there is love, there is a possibility of purification, and the libertine may raise himself to saintliness. Dante himself has shown to what heights the love of a woman may lead. Where there is love, even ill-placed love, there is always hope of salvation. There is but one real enemy: indifference.

Pride, in its most endurable forms, is desire for glory, for greatness; desire which is blameworthy in an absolute Christian, but which is natural in heroic natures. And in lofty minds, wrath is hatred of injustice and of wrong, a generous anger which the ascetic does not know, but which was and will continue to be the glory of the apostles and the prophets.

21

SELF-PRAISE

WHEN a man is Dante Alighieri and is writing the *Divina Commedia*, the temptations to pride are natural and understandable. Pride, for a Christian, is always a sin even when the greatest poet in the world is in question; before the judgement-seat of God there is no difference between a transcendent genius and a poor and ignorant old woman, when judgement is to be pronounced upon their obedience to the moral law. Dante himself has plunged into the Inferno men of the highest excellence because they were stained with base iniquities. A pre-eminent talent is not a special passport which grants immunity; it is an aggravation of the offence.

But from the human point of view, the pride of a creative genius, if not excusable, may, in a sense, be justified by the loftiness of the work upon which he is engaged. He who has no faith in himself does not create, and from faith in himself he passes easily to an exaggerated consciousness of his own merits and his own powers.

Such pride grows stronger, the more his pre-eminence remains unrecognized and the genius himself is persecuted. There rises in the wounded soul, as by a natural reaction, an irresistible tendency to declare that which is ignored or denied. You do not wish to acknowledge me (he seems to say), but a day will come when you will be compelled to admire me. You drive me out now, but a time will come when you will call me back. I seem to

143

you an obscure suppliant for alms, but I am creating works which will reveal to you what message I carry in my soul.

Something like this must have been in the mind of Dante from the first days of his exile onward, and especially when the *Commedia* was advancing well. The enormous disproportion existing between the genius which he perceived within himself and the inferiority of his earthly lot; the immense distance which stretched between his hopes and his power of expression on the one side, and the opinion which others, even those who knew him intimately, had of him on the other, must necessarily, in accordance with a well-known psychological law, have increased in him the conviction and almost the intoxication of his lonely greatness. No one enjoys so deeply as the slave does the taste of his secret inner liberty. No one feels his innocence so much as the guiltless man unjustly condemned.

Dante's pride, therefore, has in it nothing unnatural, nothing surprising, especially since he repented it, as a Christian, and openly confessed it.

But there is something else which we may find surprising: it is his habit of praising himself and the qualities of his genius more often and more freely than befits so lofty a spirit. A man may be proud and, because of that drop of vanity which is always mixed with pride, take pleasure in the praise of others. But that he himself, on every possible occasion, should write in praise of his own intellect and his own works is a matter less easily understood.

Such is Dante. His habit of self-praise, if it does credit to his frankness, is all the more surprising because it is not common among writers. It is in contrast, moreover, with the very essence of that pride which, when it is complete, does not deign to speak of itself. Let us note, too, that Dante is conscious of the unseemliness of self-praise: 'It would be necessary,' he says, 'for me to speak in praise of myself, a thing which is altogether blameworthy in whoever does it.'[1]

In the *Convivio*, after having said that 'to undervalue oneself is, in itself, blameworthy,' he adds, that 'self-praise is to be avoided like the falling-sickness, inasmuch as we cannot speak any praise of ourselves which would not prove a greater shame to us.'[2]

But even in the same work he forgot his own precept, and forgot it still more in the *Commedia*.

Proofs of this are before our eyes. Dante speaks often of his genius, and at bottom there is nothing wrong about that since the gifts received from God ought not to be hidden. But when he speaks of the 'swiftness' (*celerità*) of his genius,[3] or of his 'excellent' (*eccellente*) ability,[4] or of his 'lofty talent' (*alto ingegno*),[5] and of the 'loftiness of genius' (*altezza d'ingegno*),[6] or of the 'lofty fancy' (*alta fantasia*),[7] or of the 'memory which is unerring' (*mente che non erra*),[8] our amazement is legitimate. And those whom he meets on the threefold journey are represented as dispensing similar praises. He meets Brunetto and immediately puts into the master's mouth the famous words:

[1] *V.N.* XXVIII, 2. [2] *Conv.* I, ii, 7.
[3] *De V.E.* II, i, 1. [4] *De V.E.* II, i, 5.
[5] *Inf.* II, 7. [6] *Inf.* X, 58–59.
[7] *Par.* XXXIII, 142. [8] *Inf.* II, 6.

> . . . Se tu segui tua stella,
> non puoi fallir a glorïoso porto,
> se ben m'accorsi nella vita bella.[1]

If you follow your star, you cannot fail to reach the glorious port, if in the fair life of the world I discerned rightly.

The first discourses of Beatrice to Dante are a wise mixture of praise and blame:

> . . . per larghezza di grazie divine
> . . . .
> questi fu tal nella sua vita nova
> virtualmente, ch'ogni abito destro
> fatto averebbe in lui mirabil prova.[2]

. . . through abundance of divine graces . . . this man was potentially such in his youth that every natural ability would have made excellent proof in him.

Dante, according to the beloved, was endowed with 'good, earthly vigour' (*buon vigor terrestro*), and, according to Cacciaguida, the divine grace was diffused in him beyond measure:

> O sanguis meus, o superinfusa
> gratia Dei, sicut tibi cui
> bis unquam coeli ianua reclusa ?[3]

O my offspring ! O overflowing grace of God ! to whom, as to you, was the gate of Heaven ever opened twice ?

And finally St Peter, after having examined Dante on matters of faith, embraces him three times, 'so much had I pleased him in what I said.'[4]

From his youth onward, Dante was conscious of speaking well and writing well in verse. In the *Convivio* he is not ashamed, besides affirming the great value of

---

[1] *Inf.* XV, 55–57.   [2] *Purg.* XXX, 112, 115–117.
[3] *Par.* XV, 28–30.   [4] *Par.* XXIV, 154.

his comments,[1] to point out the beauty of his canzone which begins *Voi che intendendo il terzo ciel movete*: 'Notice its beauty, which is great whether in its construction, which pertains to the grammarians, or in the ordering of the discourse, which pertains to the rhetoricians, or in the rhythm of its parts, which pertains to the musicians. These qualities in it may be discerned as beautiful by whoever examines it well.'[2]

In the *De Vulgari Eloquentia* he never names himself expressly, but constantly alludes to himself as the friend of Cino, and cites initial lines of his own poetry. He is among those Florentine poets who have recognized the excellence of the Italian vernacular[3] and have rendered it more harmonious and capable of fine distinctions;[4] and who have elevated it so that it has become distinguished, lucid, accurate, refined;[5] and through their use of this idiom they have gained renown.[6] And when he ends his canzone, *Io sento si d'Amor la gran possanza*, he cannot help exclaiming,

> Canzon mia bella, se tu mi somigli
> tu non sarai sdegnosa
> tanto quanto a la tua bontà s'avvene.[7]

My lovely song, if you resemble me, you will not be so disdainful as is fitting for your excellence.

The 'beautiful style' (*lo bello stile*) which has brought him honour makes him worthy to be compared with no less than Homer, Horace, Ovid, Lucan, and Virgil; that is, with the poets whom he most admires.[8] His own

---

[1] *Conv.* I, xiii, 12.   [2] *Conv.* II, xi, 9.
[3] *De V.E.* I, xiii, 3.   [4] *De V.E.* I, x, 4.
[5] *De V.E.* I, xvii, 3.   [6] *De V.E.* I, xvii, 2–6.
[7] *Rime*, XCI, 81–83.   [8] *Inf.* IV, 100–102.

147

poem, as everyone knows, he calls 'consecrated'[1] and
'sacred,'[2] as if in competition with the Sacred Scriptures.
Nor is there reason for taking offence, since he writes
under the dictation of love,[3] and faces seas never crossed
before,[4] so that his account shall be 'vital nourishment'·
for those who follow.[5] Moreover, he does not wish to
be accused of having hidden his talents,[6] and his work
will be so powerful that it will drive the impious and the
liars out of the lists in the sight of the world.[7]

This result is due not only to the natural vigour of his
intellect, but to the long sweat and labour of his studies.[8]
Has he not suffered hunger, cold, and vigils for love of
the Muses?[9] Did he not cherish from his birth the love
of truth?[10]

Justly, then, he expects fame after death.[11] Although
his name as yet makes no great sound,[12] it is he who will
'drive from the nest the one and the other Guido,'[13] and
who will finally be crowned with laurel[14] in the beautiful
church of St John.[15]

Not only is he great in genius and in learning but in
uprightness and nobility of soul. He is one of the only
two just men who were in Florence in 1300,[16] and he
proclaims himself without circumlocution 'a man
preaching justice.'[17] He is four-square to the blows of
fortune,[18] and holds exile an honour[19] because his con-

1 *Par.* XXIII, 62.
2 *Par.* XXV, 1.
3 *Purg.* XXIV, 52–54.
4 *Par.* II, 7.
5 *Par.* XVII, 130–132.
6 *De Mon.* I, i, 3.
7 *De Mon.* III, i, 3.
8 *Epist.* XII, 5.
9 *Purg.* XXIX, 37.
10 *Quæst. de A. et T.*, 3.
11 *Inf.* XVI, 66.
12 *Purg.* XIV, 21.
13 *Purg.* XI, 98–99.
14 *Par.* I, 13–33.
15 *Par.* XXV, 7–9.
16 *Inf.* VI, 73.
17 *Epist.* XII, 7.
18 *Par.* XVII, 24.
19 *Rime*, CIV, 76.

science does not chide him[1] 'under the breastplate of integrity.'[2] He is, in fact, the 'sweet fig' among the 'bitter sorb-apples,'[3] the 'lamb' among the 'wolves,'[4] and resembles that Hippolytus of Athens who was unjustly accused by his stepmother.[5] But he consoles himself by thinking that 'to fall with the good is worthy of praise.'[6] To complete his apologia he does not even omit to remind us of his courage, of the time when he fought valiantly at Campaldino,[7] and of that other time when, in the Baptistery, he saved someone who was on the point of drowning.[8]

No one, I think, will deny the truth of these eulogies on himself and his works which Dante supplies liberally and frequently. Posterity has added greatly to these praises, and what was admiration has long since become open adoration.

But we should reflect that the habit of self-praise, censured by Alighieri himself, is not often met with in the ancient poets, still less in the mediæval and in the modern. We can find apologies *pro domo sua* by men accused of public offences, from Socrates and Cicero to Lorenzino dei Medici and Guerrazzi; but in the verses of a poet we very rarely come upon self-praise. Among politicians and orators the habit is not unusual and causes no surprise. In a great poet, who is besides mediæval and Christian, it is extremely rare and is therefore the more surprising.

We have noted at the beginning of this chapter the

[1] *Inf.* XV, 92. [2] *Inf.* XXVIII, 117.
[3] *Inf.* XV, 65–66. [4] *Par.* XXV, 5.
[5] *Par.* XVII, 46. [6] *Rime*, CIV, 80.
[7] Leonardo Bruni, *Vita di Dante*, p. 100 (ed. Solerti).
[8] *Inf.* XIX, 16–21.

justification which can be brought forward in defence of Alighieri and, in view of natural human feelings, we hold this a sound vindication. There remains, however, a confused sense of dissatisfaction, almost of regret, as if some one had usurped the duty which should have been ours. Does it, we ask, befit a man both great and guiltless to indulge in praises of his genius and his virtue?

22

THE CROWN AND THE MITRE

E could define Dante as the man who wished to be crowned, but wished in vain. With what crown? From explicit allusions it is clear that he yearned for the poets' crown, and wished to receive it in no other spot in the world than Florence. Petrarch, many years after him, was satisfied with the Campidoglio. Alighieri, for a similar coronation, could see only his *bel San Giovanni*.

In reality, Dante seems to aspire to other and different crowns. Whoever reads his works with a mind in harmony with that which inspired them, without too much pausing over the minutiæ of the text, will readily perceive that Dante speaks as if he came in the name of an authority transcending the princes of the earth, both secular and ecclesiastical. He sometimes seems to be an unarmed prophet and a king without a kingdom; but in the disheartening days which make up the history of his time and in the most ecstatic moments of his journey in quest of God, his whole attitude resembles that of a sovereign inspired from on high, one who feels himself above kings and pontiffs. He has the air of being a claimant to the throne in disguise, a lord of the world not yet recognized, but no less legitimate for all that. His secret ideal appears to be that of becoming the right arm and the counsellor of the Emperor of the Earth; the herald and representative of the Lord of Heaven. In a word, Vice-Emperor and Vice-God. The Emperor is not there; and when he appears, he hesitates and blunders. The popes, official vicars of God, are traitors to the Gospel and the Church. Dante, in his temporal reality, is a poor wandering exile, without titles, without fiefs, without investitures, riches, armed followers, or crowns. Nevertheless, he assumes the right to reprove the Emperor, to call the nations to account, to curse and threaten the cities, to rebuke and condemn the popes, to admonish and guide the cardinals, to speak in the name of Italy and of the Christian people.

His epistles and the terzine of the *Commedia* are so explicit that there is no need of minute reasoning to prove that Dante took upon himself this supreme office, or that he frankly usurped the imperial and the papal prerogatives. When was a private citizen ever permitted to address appeals so solemn and so peremptory as those contained in the epistle to the kings, princes, and peoples of Italy? We should suppose it to be written by the Emperor himself or by his chancellor; but that a fugitive of little importance, deprived of whatever office or dignity he may have had, should write such a manifesto in order to recall to their duty or to their obedience the legitimate rulers of Italy and all the Italian cities, would be an incredible thing if it had not actually happened.

The same may be said of the fervent and imperious letter to the Florentines, and of the one in which he points out to the cardinals what they ought to think and do in order that the Church and Rome may not perish. It is true that he makes excuses for his great boldness, and admits that his protesting voice comes from one who is low in station; but the deed belies his declared humility. He alone, the least of Christ's flock, dares apostrophize with bold reprimands the greatest assembly of Christendom. In the same way, the epistle to Henry VII is, in its form, that of a most faithful, reverent, adoring follower; but at bottom it is a distinct reproof and a stern appeal. The letter says in brief: What are you doing there wasting time? Blind that you are, do you not know where the real head of the hydra is? Abandon your vain undertakings in Lombardy and hasten to the destruction of Florence!

With what right, by virtue of what privilege, does Dante, almost like a judge appointed by God, place himself above the lords of the earth? First of all, because he is a poet. He declares openly in the *De Vulgari Eloquentia* that the familiars of the '*volgare illustre*,' those who have written in the ideal or literary Italian, surpass in renown the throng of the powerful. 'Nonne domestici sui, reges, marchiones, comites, et magnates quoslibet fama vincunt?'[1] And as he makes it understood that he is one of the first among these familiars of the *volgare illustre*, it follows logically that he held his fame and glory greatly superior to that of kings.

But it is not a question of fame only. In a passage of the *De Monarchia*[2] he recalls the words of Aristotle that he who has the greater intellect ought to be the ruler. As Dante very often affirms, directly or indirectly, the superiority of his intellect and knowledge, it is not surprising if he believed himself to have every right to exercise authority—spiritual first of all, while awaiting the temporal—over other men. He felt, therefore, the legitimacy of his high mission: to bring back to their

[1] *De V.E.* I, xvii, 5.   [2] *De Mon.* I, iii, 10.

duty the two greatest powers of the earth, the Pope and the Emperor. And in case they failed, to substitute himself for them.

Dante offers himself in order to bring light to the blind and wandering peoples, and in a special way to Italy. As a pilgrim journeying through the three kingdoms of the other world, he intends to represent and typify in himself the entire human race. Dante, a synonym for humanity.

He imagines himself chosen for this pilgrimage, where all men are impersonated by him, through the special intervention of the Mother of God, who will permit him, while still alive, to contemplate the mystery of the Trinity. He proposes, in a way, to write a new gospel intended to complete the redemption of mankind. And therefore he dares to make himself the herald of a new manifestation of the Divinity who comes to save, of that Veltro which, in his conception, is the Holy Spirit. He is not only the pupil of Virgil, he is the successor of the two saint Johns: the Forerunner and the Prophet. Finally, with the beatific vision which concludes the *Paradiso*, he makes himself the equal of the greatest saints.

Is it any marvel if from these heights he considers himself superior to all the popes of his time? As judge of the dead, Dante takes the place of the Pope in exercising the power, assigned to Peter, of binding and loosing. The final judgement on the righteous and the unrighteous belongs to God; the poet anticipates this judgement and forestalls it. Equally with God, he dares to ask an accounting from His vicars on earth, and to substitute for their injustices his own higher justice.

Little by little, from being a judge of popes, he raises himself to the seat of vicar of God—as if he were God's confidant, the executor of His judgements. The poor exile under sentence of death places himself, by his own volition, above the vacant thrones or the thrones ill-occupied, and unites in himself the veiled splendour of the two suns.[1]

Rarely has mortal man dared to pretend to such crowns and, by his manner of speech, to engender the thought that he believed them already placed upon his own head. The modern superman, in comparison, is only a paper-weight in imitation bronze.

When Alighieri is invested by Virgil with complete freedom of will in the famous line,

per ch'io te sovra te corono e mitrio [2]

therefore I crown and mitre you lord of yourself,

his mind selects precisely those two symbols of highest power to which his own secret desire had turned—the crown of the Emperor and the mitre of the Pope.

---

[1] Dante did not have a high opinion of kings: 'ai regi, che son molti, e i buon son rari'—the kings who are many, and the wise are few (*Par.* XIII, 108). See also *Par.* XI, 6 ; XIX, 112–148.

[2] *Purg.* XXVII, 142.

23

FEARS AND TERRORS

*W*AS Dante a bold man or was he, as is usual with those who are meditative and given to study, more excitable than daring? At this late day it is not easy to answer such a question.

As to his physical courage, we know from the letter cited by Leonardo Bruni that at Certomondo Dante at first experienced 'great fear' in the disorder following the assault of the Ghibelline forces, but that later he fought valiantly with the other horsemen until they gained the battle.

We do not know what part he took in the military enterprises in the first period of his exile (1302–1304) before separating himself from the other banished men; but we know from a reference in the *Ottimo Commento* that the wrath of the Whites against their great companion had its origin in the counsels of delay and postponement urged by Dante upon those rabidly impatient men. Those counsels, as it appears, did not obtain the hoped-for result, and it is likely that the 'evil' and 'stupid' men accused Dante of cowardice. Undoubtedly they turned against him with malevolence, as appears from the allusions of Brunetto and Cacciaguida.

But it is difficult, even for a psychologist or a moralist, to distinguish between prudence enlightened by wisdom and hesitation counselled by fear. Usually we judge by the outcome. Desperate decisions are at times the most prudent, while in other cases the apparent cowardice of a Fabius demands more real courage than furious onsets require, and in the end proves itself right.

In the case of Dante, we must remember that, like all poets of genius, he had an extremely acute sensibility and a very powerful imagination. These qualities make poets write, among other things, Divine Comedies; but they induce a susceptibility almost morbid in the presence of the dangerous or the terrible. He who has little imagination goes forward, serene and undisturbed, against all the ambuscades of death. He does not imagine; therefore he does not foresee. But he who has the vivid and creative imagination of the poet has an anticipatory vision of all the possibilities and of all their concrete horror; and if, in spite of this, he shows himself courageous, he has much more merit than another.

If we keep in mind that the *Commedia* is, indirectly, a biographical document—nor should we be far wrong, since a poet involuntarily reveals his ruling thoughts even when he is not speaking of himself—we shall find detailed evidence of all that has been said up to this point. In Dante's works the words '*paura*' (fear), '*tema*' (apprehension), '*sbigottimento*' (dismay), and the like, occur very often, and almost always with reference to the writer himself.

We are not considering here the *Vita Nuova* where the 'fearful spirits,' 'the intoxication of great trembling,' the 'strong fear,' the 'terrible dismay' and similar expressions, refer more than anything else to the effects of love or of the suffering which accompanies it. But in the *Inferno* the fears of Dante are beyond counting. In the first canto alone the word is repeated four times:

the wood 'in memory renews my fear';[1] then 'the fear was quieted a little,'[2] but 'not so that the sight of a lion did not give me fear';[3] and especially the she-wolf 'with the fear which came from the sight of her'[4] made his 'veins and pulses tremble,'[5]

The same thing happens repeatedly in the other cantos. The plain trembles, and 'the memory of that terror still bathes (him) with sweat.'[6] Before the gates of Dis his face has the colour of cowardice.[7] When Virgil invites him to mount upon the shoulders of Geryon, behold his condition:

> Qual'è colui che sì presso ha 'l riprezzo
> della quartana, c'ha già l'unghie smorte,
> e triema tutto pur guardando il rezzo
> tal divenn'io. . . .[8]

> Like one who has the shivering fit of the quartan fever so near that already his nails are blue, and he trembles all over only looking at the shade, such I became. . . .

When he has mounted, his 'fear' was greater than that of Phaëton in flight[9]—'whereat I, all trembling, gripped more closely with my thighs.'[10]

At the first words of Pier della Vigna, he stands 'like a man who is afraid.'[11] In the region of the barrators Virgil calls him and he turns as 'the man . . . whom sudden fear weakens.'[12] When he falls among the demons, he sees them pressing forward so that he 'feared they would not keep the compact.'[13] He sees

[1] *Inf.* I, 6.
[2] *Inf.* I, 19–21.
[3] *Inf.* I, 44–45.
[4] *Inf.* I, 52–53.
[5] *Inf.* I, 90.
[6] *Inf.* III, 131–132.
[7] *Inf.* IX, 1.
[8] *Inf.* XVII, 85–88.
[9] *Inf.* XVII, 106–114.
[10] *Inf.* XVII, 123.
[11] *Inf.* XIII, 45.
[12] *Inf.* XXI, 25–28.
[13] *Inf.* XXI, 92–93.

how they treat one of the damned and his 'heart still trembles with fear at the thought of it.'[1] Descending into the sixth *bolgia*, the poet was thinking that the demons might be planning their revenge, and there rose in his mind such a thought 'that it made the first fear double,'[2] and he confesses a little later that he felt his 'hair already standing on end with fear.'[3] Virgil's mere uneasiness is sufficient to frighten Dante: 'thus my Master frightened me.'[4] The recollection of his first sight of the serpents 'still curdles (his) blood.'[5]

The giants make a no less terrifying impression: 'error fled and fear increased within me.'[6] One of the giants, Ephialtes, shakes himself, and then it is worse than ever: Dante thinks himself dying.

> Allor temett'io più che mai la morte,
> e non v'era mestier più che la dotta,
> s'io non avessi visto le ritorte.[7]

Then I feared death as never before; the dread alone would have killed me if I had not seen the chains [which bound him].

The ice which encloses the traitors frightens him even in the moment of describing it:

> già era, e con paura il metto in metro,
> là dove l'ombre tutte eran coperte,
> e trasparìen come festuca in vetro.[8]

I had reached the place (and with fear I put it into verse), there where the shades were completely covered [with ice] and showed through like a bit of straw in glass.

---

[1] *Inf.* XXII, 31.   [2] *Inf.* XXIII, 12.
[3] *Inf.* XXIII, 19–20.   [4] *Inf.* XXIV, 16.
[5] *Inf.* XXIV, 84.   [6] *Inf.* XXXI, 39.
[7] *Inf.* XXXI, 109–111.   [8] *Inf.* XXXIV, 10–12.

We can imagine his state of mind when he found himself confronting Lucifer!

> Com'io divenni allor gelato e fioco,
> nol dimandar, lettor, ch'i' non lo scrivo,
> però ch'ogni parlar sarebbe poco.
> Io non mori' e non rimasi vivo:
> pensa oggimai per te, s'hai fior d'ingegno,
> qual io divenni, d'uno e d'altro privo.[1]

How frozen and faint I became then, do not ask me, Reader, for I do not write it, since all speech would be useless. I did not die, nor did I remain alive. Think for yourself, if you have aught of wit, what I became, bereft of one and the other.

One would suppose that when Dante had issued forth from the Inferno to climb the airy mountain of Purgatory, comforted by the hope of Heaven and by the presence of the angels, his fears would end. Not at all. Dante is warned that he is about to meet a serpent, and he, 'all frozen with dread,' draws close to 'the trusty shoulders' of the master.[2] He wakes from sleep and becomes pale, 'as a man who, terrified, turns to ice.'[3] He feels an earthquake, and a coldness assails him 'such as is wont to seize him who is going to die.'[4] The sudden voice of an angel makes him start 'as do frightened and untamed beasts.'[5]

Later he tells how he finds himself between two fears:

> . . . io temea il foco
> quinci, e quindi temea cader giuso.[6]

. . . on the one hand I feared the fire, and on the other I was afraid of falling off.

---

[1] *Inf.* XXXIV, 22–27.   [2] *Purg.* VIII, 40–42.
[3] *Purg.* IX, 41–42.   [4] *Purg.* XX, 128–129.
[5] *Purg.* XXIV, 134–135.   [6] *Purg.* XXV, 116–117.

An angel tells him to enter into the fire, and then

> . . . divenni tal, quando lo 'ntesi,
> qual è colui che nella fossa è messo.[1]

. . . I became such, when I heard him, as he who is put [head first and alive] into the pit.

The appearance of Beatrice has an even more marked effect. As soon as he is aware of her, he turns

> . . . col rispitto
> col quale il fantolin corre alla mamma
> quando ha paura o quando elli è afflitto
> per dicere a Virgilio: Men che dramma
> di sangue m'è rimaso che non tremi.[2]

. . . as confidently as a little child runs to its mother when it is frightened or when it is troubled, to say to Virgil, 'Less than a drachm of blood remains in me which does not tremble.'

At Beatrice's reproaches he feels

> confusione e paura insieme miste;[3]

confusion and fear mingled together.

From the beginning of his journey Dante had suffered from fear. Beatrice had made this clear to Virgil when she sent him to Dante's aid:

> . . . è impedito
> sì nel cammin, che volt'è per paura.[4]

. . . he is so hindered on the way that he has turned back for fear.

All the while poor Virgil must continue to reprove Dante for his fears and instil courage into him. 'Your soul is hurt by cowardice,'[5] the kind master says to

---

[1] *Purg.* XXVII, 14–15.   [2] *Purg.* XXX, 43–47.
[3] *Purg.* XXXI, 13.   [4] *Inf.* II, 62–63.
[5] *Inf.* II, 45.

him; 'so that you may free yourself from this fear, I
will tell you why I came.'[1] Virgil asks again:

> perchè tanta viltà nel cuore allette?
> perchè ardire e franchezza non hai?[2]
> . . . .
> ogni viltà convien che qui sia morta.[3]

Why do you cherish such cowardice in your heart? Why have you no
daring and self-confidence? All cowardice must here die.

But nothing avails, and Virgil's reproofs to his
timorous companion go on: 'that pity which you mistake for fear';[4] 'let not your fear harm you';[5] 'fear
not';[6] 'do not be dismayed';[7] 'be not afraid';[8] 'I
would not have you afraid';[9] 'put aside now, put aside
every fear.'[10]

Even Beatrice on one occasion must give him a like
reproof:

> . . . da tema e da vergogna
> voglio che tu omai ti disviluppe.[11]

From fear and shame I wish that you should henceforth free yourself.

Only in Paradise will fear cease, replaced by wonder
and by the feeling that what he is called to contemplate
is beyond the power of words.

It would be arbitrary to assume from all these fears
and terrors of the poet in the *Inferno* and the *Purgatorio*,
that Dante was always subject, even in life, to fear.
The demands of art require that when he finds himself
in a place so terrifying as the Inferno, he should display

---

[1] *Inf.* II, 49–50.　　　　[2] *Inf.* II, 122–123.
[3] *Inf.* III, 15.　　　　　[4] *Inf.* IV, 21.
[5] *Inf.* VII, 5.　　　　　[6] *Inf.* VIII, 104.
[7] *Inf.* VIII, 122.　　　　[8] *Inf.* XXI, 62.
[9] *Inf.* XXI, 133.　　　[10] *Purg.* XXVII, 31.
[11] *Purg.* XXXIII, 31–32.

the natural fear that anyone would experience at the mere thought of such overwhelming sights.

But, on the other hand, the frequency of such terrors and the explicit reproaches for cowardice which are so often addressed to him by Virgil, reveal something. Dante's powerful imagination pictured to him those awful visions of hell as if he were indeed there among them; and his imagination was so vivid that it alone could produce the shudders of fear. But the tongue strikes, so the saying goes, where the tooth aches; and the fact that the poet so often represents himself as timorous and pale, like a person shaking with ague, like a dying man or a dead man, leads us to think that he was more easily disturbed, more fearful, than the Dante whom the well-known myth represents as a man made all of granite.

THE TEARFUL POET

*T*HOSE who know Dante chiefly through the commonplaces of monuments to his memory and orations in his honour naturally think of him as a stern, inflexible colossus, more like Capaneus or Farinata than the youthful lover in the pre-Raphaelite paintings. They believe that in his character of prophetic and denunciatory genius he must be above the elementary emotions of ordinary mortals. They do not imagine, for example, a Dante who laughs; his laugh, if ever he laughed, would sound mocking or loudly contemptuous. They are by this time accustomed to see in him only the tower which never totters, four-square to the blows of fortune. Not indifferent, but imperturbable.

And yet those who have been really acquainted with Dante for a while know very well that his spirit was shaken and disturbed not only by indignation. He shows himself in his writings a sensitive, indeed a hypersensitive man, and sometimes even a sentimental person. Perhaps Dante laughed little, but he was abundantly capable of tears. He could be moved to pity and compassion even to the point of losing consciousness, of fainting.

In proof of this the *Vita Nuova* will suffice. Few books in the world are so drenched with tears as this confession of a lover who annotates his adorations and his languors. There is scarcely a page where he does not speak of lamentations, tremblings, and pallor; there is even a 'chamber of tears,' *la camera delle lagrime*. The mere sight of Beatrice is sufficient to make him swoon; the famous scene of the marriage is a case in point. Through his continual weeping he becomes 'in a little time so frail and weak' that people no longer recognize him. His head 'many times moved like a heavy, lifeless thing,' and his eyes from much weeping were 'so weary that they could no longer give outlet' to his sorrow. His life at this time, if we are to accept the text literally, was all 'painful weeping and anguished sighs,' and he fell asleep 'like a beaten sobbing child.' If we were asked how large a part of the *Vita Nuova* is filled with tears, we should have to answer, At least a fourth.

In the *Rime* appear similar themes:

> se vedi li occhi miei di pianger vaghi
> per novella pietà che 'l cor mi strugge. . . .[1]

If you see my eyes dim with weeping through the fresh sorrow that melts my heart. . . .

The remembrance or the dread of faintness returns:

> . . . io caddi in terra
> per una luce che nel cuor percosse.[2]

. . . I fell to earth because of a light which struck into my heart.

Grief reduces him to such a state that a breath of wind will topple the future four-square tower to earth:

> e de la doglia diverrò sì magro
> de la persona, e 'l viso tanto afflitto
> che qual mi vederà n'avrà pavento.
> E allor non trarrà sì poco vento
> che non mi meni, sì ch'io cadrò freddo.[3]

Through sorrow I shall become so thin of body and my face so lined, that whoever sees me will have fear of me. And then no wind, however slight, will blow that will not buffet me so that I shall fall to earth, bereft of my senses.

---

[1] *Rime*, CV, 1–2.   [2] *Rime*, LXVII, 63–64.   [3] *Rime*, LXVIII, 18–22.

These tears and sighs, however, are but a part of those literary conventions which are found in all love-poetry, ancient and modern: the lover wishes to rouse the compassion of the beloved, and women are especially moved by tears in a man. At that time, Dante was young and his mind was disordered by love; moreover, a certain deliquescence is not unnatural in a poet who has found an incomparable woman and then lost her.

In the *Commedia* as well, written when Dante was no longer young (begun, it is believed, when he was about forty years old), we find fresh instances of his sensibility. Francesca's story makes him weep:

> . . . i tuoi martiri
> a lacrimar mi fanno tristo e pio.[1]

Your sufferings make me sad and compassionate, moving me to tears.

This not sufficing, her story makes him fall in a swoon:

> . . . di pietade
> io venni men così com'io morisse;
> e caddi come corpo morto cade.[2]

Through pity I swooned as if I were dying, and fell as a dead body falls.

We might argue that here also Dante is writing about love, and that the vision of Francesca might well have awakened memories of his youthful sufferings. But even a glutton like Ciacco moves him to tears:

> . . . Ciacco, il tuo affanno
> me pesa sì, ch'a lagrimar m'invita.[3]

Ciacco, your suffering so weighs upon me that it asks my tears.

The suicide of Pier della Vigna[4] makes his heart ache with pity, and the weeping of the soothsayers makes him weep in sympathy.[5]

[1] *Inf.* V, 116–117.   [2] *Inf.* V, 140–142.   [3] *Inf.* VI, 58–59.
[4] *Inf.* XIII, 84.   [5] *Inf.* XX, 25.

Who can forget the great lament in the Earthly Paradise? The bitter-sweet words of Beatrice and the song of the angels move him so deeply that

> lo gel che m'era intorno al cor ristretto,
> spirito e acqua fessi, e con angoscia
> della bocca e delli occhi uscì del petto.[1]

The ice which was bound tight around my heart was changed into breath and water, and issued from my breast with anguish through my lips and eyes.

When Beatrice wounds him with new reproaches

> scoppia' io sott'esso grave carco,
> fuori sgorgando lacrime e sospiri
> e la voce allentò per lo suo varco.[2]

I broke under the heavy load, pouring forth tears and sighs, and my voice faltered in its passage.

We do not mean to imply that Dante's weeping on seeing Beatrice again was not pardonable. After the 'ten years' thirst,' again to contemplate 'the youngest of the angels' who has become almost a goddess, to hear from her the merited and tender reproaches, was an experience to shake and move him. But in Dante as a stern judge of evil, the tears which he sheds for the two adulterers, the glutton, the suicide, and the soothsayers, seem less justified. That Dante should have been brought to weep even over the damned and not be ashamed to confess it, seems to me a significant indication of his extremely sensitive mind.

Tears are not unworthy of a man, even of a very great man. Still more abundant tears drop from the pages of

---

[1] *Purg.* XXX, 97–99. [2] *Purg.* XXXI, 19–21.

St Augustine and of Petrarch.[1] But this sensitiveness of Dante, not sufficiently observed by those who see him only in his granite-like or his volcanic aspect, makes us comprehend better the complexity of his character and understand better certain qualities of his genius. If it contradicts the commonly accepted idea of him, no matter! That he was not always the proud oak tree but was sometimes the weeping-willow, only serves to bring him the closer to our own humanness.

[1] In this connection, see the essay on Petrarch by G. Papini, in *Ritratti Italiani*. Florence, Vallecchi, 1932, p. 38.

DISCONTENT AND NOSTALGIA

THOSE who make it their business to sing praises on all occasions and who, as a natural consequence, see a traitor in anyone who does not believe himself to be living in the best of all possible centuries, will find, I regret to say, that Dante, of all men the most critical, was not wholly pleased either with his own times or with the human race in general.

To him the world appeared to be destitute of every virtue and full of iniquity;[1] all forms of human activity, without exception, were 'insensate cares' which weight the soul. Even priests and kings excited in him pity and disgust.[2]

Nothing pleased him. Nothing was in its proper place. Nothing was what it ought to be. Men are all changeable and unstable,[3] all are sinful.[4] And since the greater part follow the senses and not the reason, it follows that most men are to be considered children,[5] or worse still, unreasoning animals and, as it were, dead men.[6]

Florence, his native city, his little *patria*, seems to him an abode of usurers, of robbers, of madmen. His great *patria*, Italy, 'the corrupt Italian land,' is a ship driven by storms and without a pilot, deserted by him who ought to direct her course, battered by strife, at the

---

[1] *Purg.* XVI, 58–60.
[2] *Par.* XI, 1–9.
[3] *De V.E.* I, ix, 6.
[4] *Conv.* I, iv, 9.
[5] *Conv.* I, iv, 3.
[6] *Conv.* IV, vii, 14–15.

mercy of ambitious and unworthy people; she had been, and ought again to be, her own mistress, and instead she is a slave. Her princes are kites who circle above noisome things;[1] her courts are synonyms for baseness.[2]

It is no better elsewhere. The Catalans are covetous,[3] the French vain,[4] the Germans gluttonous.[5]

The Church, as Dante saw it in his day, was a 'thief' and 'prostitute'; a place where the prelates neglect the Fathers and the Doctors in order to devote themselves to the study of the Decretals; where the preachers, no better than beasts, feed the people idle tales; where the friars think only of eating and enjoying themselves; where all hope for riches and care for nothing else. How could it be otherwise, if the head of the Church is 'the prince of the new Pharisees,'[6] like Boniface VIII; or a traitor and a simoniacal 'shepherd without law,' like Clement V;[7] or a covetous pope like John XXII, who prefers the image of St John on the gold florin to the saints Peter and Paul?[8]

The Empire offered Dante no greater consolation. Rudolph and Albert, kept in Germany by their greed, were without care for Italy;[9] the unfortunate Henry VII, who finally came to put in order 'the garden of the Empire,' delayed in empty ceremonies and futile undertakings, did not dare to attack Florence, and died at Buonconvento without having accomplished anything.

Nothing, in his own time, consoles or encourages Dante: The present is evil, decadent, corrupt, shameful.

[1] *Conv.* VI, vi, 20.   [2] *Conv.* II, x, 8.
[3] *Par.* VIII, 77.   [4] *Inf.* XXIX, 123.
[5] *Inf.* XVII, 21.   [6] *Inf.* XXVII, 85.
[7] *Inf.* XIX, 82–87.   [8] *Par.* XVIII, 130–136.
[9] *Purg.* VI, 97–105.

170

Therefore in his search for comfort he takes refuge in the past and the future.

Like all the poets, he is given to nostalgia; and like all the prophets, to messianism.

Nostalgia for the 'primal age,' which, as 'beautiful as gold,'

> fè savorose con fame le ghiande,
> e nettare con sete ogni ruscello.[1]

With hunger made acorns savoury, and with thirst turned every stream-let to nectar.

Nostalgia for ancient and imperial Rome; nostalgia for the primitive Church, not yet ruined and befouled by the base appetite for riches.

Never, perhaps, did the stern and rugged poet speak in accents of such heart-broken tenderness as when, in the words of Cacciaguida, he evokes from the past the pure and upright Florence of earlier times.

But wistful contemplation of the past could not satisfy a spirit so eager and ambitious as Dante's, which turned in disgust and contempt from the present to an anxious expectation of the future. The *Commedia*, as we shall see more clearly in a later chapter, is in its central idea the announcement of a palingenesis, of a renewal of man and of the world; it is a new Apocalypse, whose protagonist is the Veltro, the DXV, the One sent by God. To-day is darkness, but yesterday the sun was shining and will shine again to-morrow.

Those who disparage and despise the present do not enjoy the approbation of many among their contemporaries; nevertheless, to the observant such were the

---

[1] *Purg.* XXII, 148–150.

great men of the past. Great not because of their bitter arrogance or their desire to oppose the mass of complacent men, but on account of those very qualities which are the foundation of their greatness. The mind of the poet—and, in a measure, every great man is a poet—is infinitely more sensitive than that of the ordinary man, and therefore more susceptible to impressions of the world around him. What seems to the vulgar a pin-prick or the buzzing of a fly, is to the poet a knife-wound or a wind threatening calamity. He who lives and rejoices among filth does not notice the stench which revolts the poet accustomed to breathe the air of Elysian gardens. The poet's mind, more alert and active, sees and discovers those evils which to most men, dulled by habit, seem a regular part of the ordinary course of human affairs. The great man has his eye fixed always on things of supreme worth, and as he judges by this ideal standard, he comes to see reality as it is, a conglomerate of errors, faults, and miseries. Ordinary men, on the other hand, hardened in their habits, embedded in the fecund mud of gross living, are not aware of the shadows and the precipices. They are not happy, but they do not know how to account for the prevalent unhappiness. A poet who is content with the world in which he lives would not be a poet. Even Voltaire, the least poetical of the poets, could not swallow the optimism of Leibnitz, and answered him— as he was well able to answer—with mocking caricature; but he felt the need of answering. And what, finally, is Christianity if not profound dissatisfaction with the existing state of humanity, the longing for primal innocence, the preparation for a new life, whether it be the

Kingdom of Heaven on earth or the Life Eternal in the Empyrean?

All poets, and especially the Christian poets, have felt the need of escaping from the present world and of creating by their art a world of their own. Thus Dante escapes to his own world, the world of the dead, the kingdom of the shades, but of dead more alive than the living, of shades as brilliant as flames in the heavens which form Paradise. To call Dante a pessimist, however, would not be entirely just. As is true of the very greatest, he is beyond both pessimism and optimism. He is not an optimist because he sees with clear insight the evils of the present. He is not a pessimist because he remembers the ancient good and trusts in an even greater future good. He could be called, if anything, nostalgic. Just as in the case of poets less great than he was, he suffered from a double nostalgia: nostalgia for that which was and is no longer; nostalgia for that which will be and is not yet. Dante's true intercourse is not among the living, but among the dead and the unborn. He is contemporary with the earliest and the ultimate ages.

THE CORRUPT LAND OF ITALY

ϿT would be both foolish and stupid to say that Dante did not love Italy greatly. For him Italy was the 'garden of the Empire,' the centre of the world; and from its unification, at least from its spiritual and moral unification, must come a new order of things under a single authority which will establish a lasting peace and just laws for all men.

To moderns, who understand patriotism only when it is expressed in adulation and public ceremonies, and maintain that the good citizen is the man who finds his country always right, Alighieri's love for Italy will scarcely seem loving at all, since, for the most part, it is expressed in censures and reproofs: a savage love made up of clawing and biting more than of smoothing and licking.

Although I am a Florentine and know that Florence was most grievously wounded by the teeth and claws of Dante, yet I believe that his sort of patriotism is the most beneficial in moments of confusion and distress. Such patriotism can injure the fame and fortune of the man who displays it and, for this reason, his action is all the more heroic. The same people who have been rebuked, as Dante rebuked the Florentines, and despised for just reason, will later, with the passing of the generations, end by realizing that those reproofs were not unmerited and that they have helped, at least a little, to improve the nation.

These rebukes are signs of a more genuine love than

the conventional flatteries of the timid and the indifferent. Nor need we assume that Dante was always hurling invectives against his country, whether Italy or Florence. From time to time expressions of affection and longing escape from him, which give the key to the true meaning of his bitter attacks. For no one, perhaps, as for Dante is the familiar saying of the stern pedagogue so true—I punish you because I love you. Precisely because he loves his country tenderly he would wish that she should be better, and to make her better he is forced, almost in spite of himself, to touch the sores with caustic words in order to cure them.

Italy, for example, is 'fair Italy'[1] and the 'noblest region of Europe,'[2] but, at the same time, she is called "the corrupt land,'[3] 'servile,' 'a hostel of woe'; even a 'brothel.'[4]

The same thing is repeated for Florence. Dante loved no other place in the universe so tenderly and so stubbornly as he loved Florence. Florence is his 'noble fatherland,'[5] 'the most beautiful and most famous daughter of Rome';[6] she is 'the great town' on the 'fair river Arno,'[7] 'the place most dear,'[8] 'the lovely sheepfold where a lamb I slept';[9] and if he hears a Florentine speaking, he is constrained to aid him through 'love for his native place';[10] nor is there on earth a place more pleasant than Florence,[11] and because he loved her too much, he suffers exile unjustly.[12]

[1] Inf. XX, 61.
[2] De Mon. II, iii, 16.
[3] Par. IX, 25.
[4] Purg. VI, 76–78.
[5] Inf. X, 26.
[6] Conv. I, iii, 4.
[7] Inf. XXIII, 95.
[8] Par. XVII, 110.
[9] Par. XXV, 5.
[10] Inf. XIV, 1–2.
[11] De V.E. I, vi, 3.
[12] De V.E. I, vi, 3.

He speaks of no other city with such kindness and such poignant regret; and of no other with such severity. Although he is her faithful son, he cannot overlook or hide her sins and her defects. Florence is 'full of envy,'[1] and in addition to envy, of arrogance and avarice.[2] She is 'a nest of wickedness'[3] and 'a dismal forest.'[4] At times the reproof becomes ironical, as in the famous apostrophe which refers to the number of thieves who were then in Florence,[5] to her bad government,[6] and to the capricious instability of her decrees.[7]

The 'ungrateful and malevolent people,'[8] made up of 'Fiesolan beasts'[9] and 'blind folk,[10] is further spoiled by the coming in of peasants and by their commercial greed:

> la gente nova e' subiti guadagni
> orgoglio e dismisura han generata,
> Fiorenza, in te, sì che tu già ten piagni.[11]

The upstart people and their sudden gains have bred arrogance and excess in you, O Florence, so that you are already weeping because of it.

It is this thirst for gold, symbolized by the scattering of the golden florin, which makes Florence deserve to be called 'the city planted' by the Demon.[12]
It is not to be wondered at if Florence

> di giorno in giorno più di ben si spolpa
> e a trista ruina par disposto.[13]

. . . from day to day strips herself more of good and seems bent on dismal ruin.

---

[1] *Inf.* VI, 49–50.   [2] *Inf.* VI, 74–75; XV, 68.
[3] *Inf.* XV, 78.   [4] *Purg.* XIV, 64.
[5] *Inf.* XXVI, 1–6.   [6] *Purg.* XII, 102.
[7] *Purg.* VI, 127 ff.   [8] *Inf.* XV, 61.
[9] *Inf.* XV, 73.   [10] *Inf.* XV, 67.
[11] *Inf.* XVI, 73–75.   [12] *Par.* IX, 127 ff.
[13] *Purg.* XXIV, 80–81.

Not even the women escape his censure,—those 'brazen Florentine women,' who go about displaying for the enticement of men those parts of their bosom which ought to be kept solely for the innocent mouths of their children.[1]

When the 'most wretched progeny of the Fiesolans' offer resistance to Henry VII, Dante's wrath overflows against 'the most wicked Florentines.'[2] Already, in the *Purgatorio*, he had called them 'wolves';[3] but now Florence is a stinking fox, a viper which attacks the breast of its mother, a sickly sheep which contaminates the flock, a woman raging in her madness.[4] And notwithstanding all this, Dante dreamed until the end of his days of no other reward for the long labours of his poem than that of receiving the poet's crown in his never-forgotten, his loved and hated Florence.

Other lands than Tuscany and Italy are not treated more gently. Lucca is full of forgers and barrators,[5] Pistoia is 'a fitting lair' for evil beasts[6] and ought to be burned to ashes so that she may cease her wrongdoing.[7] Pisa, as all know, is the 'reproach of the people' and ought to be sunk beneath the waters,[8] because her inhabitants are

> . . . volpi sì piene di froda,
> che non temono ingegno che le occupi.[9]

> . . . foxes so full of craft that they do not fear to be entrapped by any astuteness.

---

[1] *Purg.* XXIII, 101 ff. [2] *Epist.* VI, 24; VI, 1.
[3] *Purg.* XIV, 50. [4] *Epist.* VII, passim.
[5] *Inf.* XXI, 41–42. [6] *Inf.* XXIV, 125–126.
[7] *Inf.* XXV, 10–12. [8] *Inf.* XXXIII, 79 ff.
[9] *Purg.* XIV, 53–54.

The people of the Casentino are

> . . . brutti porci, più degni di galle
> che d'altro cibo fatto in uman uso.[1]

. . . filthy hogs, more worthy of acorns than of other food made for human use.

The people of Arezzo are curs, 'more disposed to snarl than their power warrants';[2] and those of Siena are a vain people.[3]

Romagna is always at war through the fault of her tyrants,[4] and is now peopled by bastards.[5] Lombardy is so fallen that only some old man keeps the tradition of her ancient worth.[6] Bologna is full of avaricious men and panders.[7] The Neapolitans are traitors,[8] and the Genoese are 'men alien to all morality and full of every corruption' who ought to be wiped out.[9]

Not even Rome escapes this universal condemnation. And here we must distinguish between ancient and modern Rome.

Ancient Rome is the holy city worthy of reverence,[10] and from it the Italians derive the beginning of their civilization.[11] It is so sacred that it becomes, on the lips of Beatrice, a synonym for Paradise.[12] But modern Rome, the Rome of Dante's time, is different. It is less beautiful and splendid than Florence, since the view from Monte Mario is surpassed by that from the Uccel-

---

[1] *Purg.* XIV, 43–44.
[2] *Purg.* XIV, 46–47.
[3] *Inf.* XXIX, 121–123; *Purg.* XIII, 151.
[4] *Inf.* XXVII, 37–38.
[5] *Purg.* XIV, 99.
[6] *Purg.* XVI, 115 ff.
[7] *Inf.* XVIII, 58–63.
[8] *Inf.* XXVIII, 16–17.
[9] *Inf.* XXXIII, 151–153.
[10] *Conv.* IV, v, 20.
[11] *Epist.* XI, 22.
[12] *Purg.* XXXII, 102.

latoio.[1] And what is worse, the modern Romans, in their language and their customs, are unworthy of their fathers: 'We say, then, that the vulgar tongue of the Romans, or rather their wretched jargon, is the ugliest of all the Italian dialects; and this is not to be wondered at since in the corruption of their customs and habits they are the most objectionable of all.'[2]

It appears that not even the majesty of the memories so venerated by Dante was any palliation when he was intent on passing just judgement in accord with truth. So, to summarize his charges, Italy is the first country of the world, but, taking into account the vices and defects of her cities, she is inhabited by the foulest beasts on earth; and if God had listened to Dante's prayers, Pistoia would have been destroyed by fire, Pisa sunk beneath the water, Genoa depopulated, and Florence razed to the ground. So violent in its nature was Dante's love for his, and our, Italy.

In reality he loved Italy in the manner induced by the deplorable times and his own passionate nature. In Rome he saw above all else a symbol—a symbol of the Empire and of the Church, of the two powers which, when they could be brought into harmony, would save the human race. In Italy he saw the garden of the Empire, the consecrated seat of the universal authority which transcends the nations. Dante felt himself a citizen of the world: 'In whatever corner of the earth I may find myself, can I not look upon the sun and the stars? wherever I may be under the expanse of heaven, can I not meditate sweetest truths?'[3]

---

[1] *Par.* XV, 109–110.   [2] *De V.E.* I, xi, 2.
[3] *Epist.* XII, 9. Cf. *De V.E.* I, vi, 3.

But his most impassioned and tender affection was for Florence, especially for the Florence of earlier and uncorrupted times. In the same moment in which he prophesies sufferings and disasters for her, a shade of sadness tempers his ferocity:

> così foss'ei, da che pur esser dee!
> chè più mi graverà, com più m'attempo.[1]

> Would that it had already happened, since happen it must! because the older I grow, the more it will grieve me.

The poet involves in the same affliction his own life, which is passing swiftly away, and his city, which must suffer and make him suffer too. Even in his denunciation he is one with Florence.

[1] *Inf.* XXVI, 11–12.

DANTE AND HIS FELLOW-MEN

WE cannot say that Dante did not love his fellow-men. The *Commedia* has among its other aims that of bringing back the erring to the truth, sinners to the good, unbelievers to the faith, the turbulent to ways of peace. If Dante with fervid impatience desires an emperor who will restore the political unity of the world, it is not only because of his longing for the classical past, his infatuation for certain theories of government, or because his motives are selfish. It is rather because the dissensions and rivalries of states and towns, of parties and communes, the arrogance of the spiritual powers and their quest for temporal benefits, have so disordered the usages of civil life that it is not possible for men to attain in peace their lawful earthly ends or to pursue those other-worldly aims enjoined upon every Christian. There is no more justice in the world, no concord. All, therefore, must suffer. Only the authority of one supreme head, recognized by all, a reverent son of the Church but independent of the Pope, could bring back upon the earth order, peace, and justice. Dante, then, longs for the Emperor because he is moved to pity by the wretched state of mankind. Dante thinks of the good of his brothers, works and writes for them, to better their condition, to save them. He wishes, sincerely, that all were less wicked and unhappy here below, and that all might be made worthy of ultimate beatitude.

Notwithstanding all this, we must admit that in his

works we do not find accents of tenderness for his fellow-men in general. Dante is a Christian, and in his poem he constitutes himself the voluntary lay-apostle of Christianity. He turns with longing to the primitive simplicity and poverty of the Church, but he never surrenders himself to the spontaneous emotion of *caritas*. When he speaks to men or of men, he seems not so much a loving brother as a displeased father or a bad-tempered schoolmaster. His teachings and admonitions to the human race are almost always just, but almost never warmed by the fire of charity, of the charity which reproves but at the same time grieves and pardons. Even when he has in view the good of humanity, Dante is always a little aloof, and easily shows a surly temper. He is a *magister*, a wise guide, an overwrought prophet; he is rarely a sinner who speaks to sinners, a humble man who bears himself humbly among the humble, weeping with those who weep.

He is sometimes moved to compassion, but always under special circumstances and for special beings. He lacks the intense white-heat of St Paul, the universal brotherhood of St Francis. We hear in his words echoes of the *Ethics* of Aristotle and the *Summa* of St Thomas rather than the serene or reverberant phrases of the Gospel. Dante's love is more of the head than the heart, more theological than evangelical.

He has words of warm affection for his *duca* Virgil, for his master Brunetto, for his friend Casella, for his ancestor Cacciaguida; but even toward them he displays that grave dignity which suits an ancient philosopher better than a Christian. Even when he is greatly moved at the torture of another, his emotion more readily expresses itself in hatred for the oppressor than in loving compassion for the victim. Count Ugolino asks him for tears of sympathy: 'And if you weep not now, at what are you used to weep?' But Dante, instead of weeping, waits until the agonized soul has finished his overwhelming story and then invokes the destruction of Pisa and the drowning of all the Pisans: 'May every soul in thee be drowned!' Ugolino asks for tears and Dante, in response, invokes a cataclysm: evil for evil, a vendetta of horror. And then he passes on, satisfied, without addressing another word to the anguished gnawer of the skull.

In Dante's work there are two kinds of love—love for Woman and love for God. Love wholly spiritual for Beatrice, love wrathful and carnal for Pietra. There is also his love for the Virgin Mother and for the Three Persons of the Trinity. But if his love for Beatrice inspires him at times to melodious verse almost tremulous with tenderness, divine love often remains in him more adoration than self-surrender. The prayer of St Bernard to the Virgin is a marvellous supplication in language both poetical and theological, but it is not imbued with that loving and impassioned vehemence which is sometimes found in poets inferior to Dante. He speaks many times of Christ, and always with the greatest reverence and doctrinal correctness; but there is no instance in which he makes us feel that he has suffered with Him, that he has wept in the remembrance of His Passion, that he has laid his head on His bosom, that he has longed to embrace His lacerated body, to kiss His wounds. He calls Christ 'Highest Jove,' 'Lamb of God,' 'Pelican,' even 'the door of the

183

eternal chamber,' and 'abbot of the college'; but all
these appellations come from the brain, not from the
heart. They are abstract or literary formulas, and lack
the force of impassioned ardour. Dante is Christ's
soldier, not His son or His brother. In his love for the
Crucified there is befitting adoration rather than fervent
love. Even when he speaks of the Divine Persons, he
shows himself the rationalist and the scholastic, not the
worshipper whose soul trembles and overflows with
emotion. It is the same when he speaks of men.

Jesus wished to bind together in our hearts love for
the Father who reigns in heaven and love for our
brothers who suffer on earth. He who does not burn
with love for the Father will not easily be moved by
tenderness for his brothers. It is a difficult undertaking
for everyone truly to love his fellow-men. Yet we must
love them in order to respond to the love which God
has for us and to manifest fully, by loving them, the
love which we bear for Him. He who is lukewarm toward God will be cold toward men. He who cannot
suffer with Christ, who suffered for all, will be little apt
to feel compassion for his brothers, who are imperfect
images of Christ.

And yet, Dante loved men, as we have seen. He loved
them somewhat haughtily, more intellectually than
fraternally; but he loved them. And it needs to be said,
in justification of him, that love, even Christian love,
does not consist solely of caresses, embraces, blind in-
dulgence, and gentle words. To love signifies mainly to
obtain what is best for the beloved; and there are good
things procured by means which have at the moment the
look of evil. The stern lessons, the pitiless reproofs, the

bitter invectives can be, according to the times and the particular needs, evidence of the most genuine love if they are inspired by a profound desire to help one's neighbour, to recall him to the vital truths and the right way of salvation. In many cases, love may consist of chiding, of correcting, of reproving, even of scourging with deep-cutting words. What matters is the purity of intention. A false friend may embrace and kiss you in order the better to betray you. Another and a truer friend will cover you with contumely in order to set you back on the right road.

But acerbity does not always secure the desired amendment; we all know that. But neither is it always obtained by honeyed and tearful entreaty. We must take into account the persons concerned, their dispositions, the moment of approach, the circumstances, the causes; and then select in a spirit of brotherliness what the case demands—either the gentle manner or the stinging. But those modern Christians who have the word charity always on their lips, and maintain that charity should be exercised only with affectionate phrases, and who condemn as lacking in charity the vigorous manner so often needed—as if charity imposed an obligation of never saying to the sinner that he has sinned and to the dirty that he has need of washing himself—show that they do not know what charity really is and what true Christianity is in its rich significance.

Dante was one of those Christians who are more disposed to show their affection by reprimands and reproaches than by tender speech and melting tears. This was in accord with his character as it appears in the brief but convincing description of him left by his contem-

185

porary Villani: 'This Dante, because of his learning, was somewhat haughty, reserved, and disdainful. . . .'[1] In the eyes of men he appeared as the sage rather than the devoted friend or the affectionate brother. But to give light to the wandering and the bewildered is also a work of charity.

Although we have noted in him a marked tendency to tears and an almost morbid sensitiveness—more like a woman than a man—Dante was above all an intellectual. And as in all intellectuals, his love for humanity takes forms more theoretical and abstract than warmly human. His conscience assured him that his every effort helped toward the elevation of humanity, and he was content. Why mix with the commonplace, the inferior, the base? Man, seen close at hand, is almost always repugnant. Only saints can overcome the aversion caused by his mediocrity, his baseness, his malevolence. Before having attained a perfection almost divine, it is impossible without the aid of heavenly grace to love all men, one by one, with all the heart. From a distance it is easier. We think of our fellow-men, we do our best for them; but more than this is impossible for those who are not saints. And Dante, alas! was no saint. He was a Christian, but not perfect; and love for our neighbour is the severest test which Christ asks of us. Christianity is beyond question divine precisely because it demands of us that which seems most contrary to human nature. This mingling of affection and resentment which Dante showed toward men is peculiar to those souls, great but not saintly, which feel the demands of love and, at the same time, the impulse of hatred. In connection with

[1] Villani, *Cronica*, IX, 136.

another prophet who loved humanity in the same way, it is fittingly written: 'A ceux qui passent une longue vie difficile, s'interrogeant sur la question de savoir, définitivement, s'il faut aimer les hommes ou les haïr, et se disant qu'il faut régler cela une fois pour toutes, ou aimer éperdument, bêtement, malgré tout, ou s'isoler farouchement et haïr, haïr à tout jamais, la réponse s'impose: l'un et l'autre. Il faut les aimer d'un amour hostile. Les aimer, selon les vers du grand poète Milosz, *d'un vieil amour usé par la pitié, la colère et la solitude.* D'un amour combattu. D'un infatigable amour que la haine viendra sans cesse couper et rajeunir.'[1]

These words seem to have been written for Dante. The love which Dante had for men was of this nature and composition. The distant love of a reserved intellectual, the discriminating love of a proud savant, the almost cruel love of an angry prophet. The uncertain and confused love of one who cannot, however much he may wish it, be a true imitator of Christ.

[1] J. Cassou, *Grandeur et Infamie de Tolstoï.* Paris, Grasset, 1932, pp. 125–126.

28

DANTE'S CRUELTY

ANTE has been universally proclaimed a Christian poet, and for reasons which are obvious the title is rightly his. The *Commedia*, in fact, is a way of perfection, a progress toward God, a flight of a hundred steps by which we may mount from the dark forest to the shining rose.

But if we measure Dante's works by the standard of Christianity, we shall meet with surprises.

The Holy Gospel constantly enjoins gentleness, long-suffering patience, forgiveness. In Dante we find a quick irascibility which often reaches the point of intolerance and sometimes of outright cruelty.

We do not cite as evidence the passage in Boccaccio's *Life of Dante*, because it refers to Dante's political passions, and because we cannot estimate how much truth there may be in this tradition. It may very likely over-emphasize a matter that was of no importance. 'What I regret most to recall in my task of serving his memory,' writes the official biographer, 'is the fact, well known in Romagna, that any gossiping woman or child even, if they were talking of political parties and spoke ill of the Ghibellines, would drive him into such a fury that he would throw stones at them if they did not stop instantly. And he kept this animosity until his death.'[1]

Here we have an instance of simple partisan rage, an outburst so excessive as to make him capable of stoning

[1] G. Boccaccio, *Vita di Dante*, XXV (ed. D. Guerri. Bari, Laterza, 1918. I, 47).

a child. But as if in confirmation, we have explicit confessions of his which reveal a tendency toward a ferocity
so vindictive that it takes no thought for disastrous
consequences.

In the fourth treatise of the *Convivio*, Dante speaks of
the meaning of nobility and considers the question
whether nobility is a quality to be found only in men,
or if it exists also in other creatures and things; and he
asks how we may distinguish the origins of nobility.
Clearly it is not a question likely to rouse the anger of
one who looks upon himself as a philosopher. Nevertheless, Dante bursts all at once into these words: 'If
the opponent means that in other things we understand
nobility to be the goodness of the thing itself, but that
when we speak of nobility in man we mean that there is
no memory of his low origin, we should answer such
stupidity not with words but with a dagger. . . .'[1]
To what other person, especially if he were arguing on
a matter which did not intimately concern either his
honour or his political faith, would it have occurred to
knife his adversary only because that adversary made a
mistake in distinguishing the different kinds of nobility?

More excusable possibly is Dante's savage fantasy in
the presence of the lady Pietra, whom he loved extrava-
gantly but who did not return his love. I do not believe
that in all the other love-lyrics in the world, even in
those inspired by anger, we could find the expression of
desires so atrocious as those in the famous canzone,
Così nel mio parlar voglio esser aspro. '. . . If I had
grasped those lovely tresses which have been whip and
lash for me, seizing them before tierce, I would sport

---

[1] *Conv.* IV, xiv, 11.

with them through vespers and compline. I should not
be kind and pitiful; nay, I should be like the bear when
he gambols. And if Love should use those tresses to
scourge me, I should take my revenge a thousandfold.'[1]

It may be said in defence that when Dante was writing
these lines, he was in a frenzy of love and did not
measure his words; or that he was engaged in a mere
literary exercise and intentionally exaggerated in order
to emphasize the idea of disappointment. But even in
the 'sacred poem,' written for instruction and edification,
we find again this mania of Alighieri's for catching
people by the hair and tearing it out.

Down in the second ring of Cocytus, Dante strikes
with his foot (either by wish, he says, or by destiny or
chance) one of the heads which protrude above the ice.
As the unfortunate soul protests and does not wish to
give his name, the compassionate poet grows angry:

> Allor lo presi per la cuticagna,
> e dissi: El converrà che tu ti nomi,
> o che capel qui su non ti rimagna.[2]

Then I seized him by the nape of his neck and said: You shall tell me
your name, or not a hair shall remain upon you here.

But the damned soul still refuses to speak:

> Io avea già i capelli in mano avvolti,
> e tratti li n'avea più d'una ciocca,
> latrando lui con li occhi in giù raccolti.[3]

I had already twisted his hair in my hand and had torn out more than
one tuft while he, howling, kept his head down.

Then a companion, calling the victim by name,
reveals who he is and Dante looses his hold.

[1] *Rime*, CIII, 66–73.   [2] *Inf.* XXXII, 97–99.
[3] *Inf.* XXXII, 103–105.

It is true that Dante is dealing with a despicable traitor, with that Bocca degli Abati who was the chief cause of the Florentine defeat at Montaperti; but is it quite worthy of a Christian poet to rage in that fashion against a dead man who can still suffer and who is making grievous atonement for his sin?

Dante does not show himself more tender in the Stygian swamp where Filippo Argenti is expiating his arrogance. Dante says to him,

> . . . con piangere e con lutto,
> spirito maladetto, ti rimani.[1]

With weeping and with woe may you remain, curst spirit.

It is because of this pitiless imprecation that Virgil, the gentle Virgil, addresses to Dante the famous encomium:

> . . . Alma sdegnosa,
> benedetta colei che in te s'incinse ! [2]

Disdainful soul, blessed be she who bore you !

We have here an echo of the Bible, but the passage is transferred to an exactly opposite occasion; there it refers to the merciful Jesus, here to the cruel Dante.

The repellent episode does not end at this point. Encouraged by the untimely praise of Virgil, our Christian poet hastens to express a desire which borders on sadism.

> . . . Maestro, molto sarei vago
> di vederlo attuffare in questa broda
> prima che noi uscissimo del lago.[3]

Master, I should like to see him plunged in this hell-broth before we leave the lake.

---

[1] *Inf.* VIII, 37–38.   [2] *Inf.* VIII, 44–45.
[3] *Inf.* VIII, 52–54.

191

And the 'gentle guide' answers in the same tone, competing with Dante in harshness:

> . . . Avante che la proda
> ti si lasci veder, tu sarai sazio :
> di tal disïo convien che tu goda.[1]

> You shall be satisfied before the shore is seen by you ; it is fitting that you should enjoy the fulfilment of such a desire.

The enjoyment promised by Virgil is not delayed:

> Dopo ciò poco vid'io quello strazio
> far di costui alle fangose genti,
> che Dio ancor ne lodo e ne ringrazio.[2]

> Soon after this I saw such a violent rending of him at the hands of the muddy folk that I still praise God for it and thank Him.

Here, unhappily for Dante, we are in complete negation of Christianity; sacrilegious negation, besides, because he would make God Himself a participant. But God is justice, not cruelty. Filippo Argenti is punished for his sins and his punishment will never end. How is it possible that a poet, a Christian, one who ought to be doubly kind, can enjoy seeing an increase in the torment of one who is already suffering without hope? What fearful audacity in his praising and thanking God—Him who was incarnated as the Pardoner—for having granted him such a spectacle!

Let us note that Filippo Argenti is placed among the wrathful and is called by Virgil 'a proud person.'[3] The

---

[1] *Inf.* VIII, 55–57.
[2] *Inf.* VIII, 58–60.
[3] Filippo Argenti appears in one of the stories of the *Decameron*, IX, 8, as 'uomo . . . sdegnoso, iracundo'; a wrathful, choleric man: and when he is angered, 'tutto in se medesimo si rodea,' he eats his heart out with rage.—Trans.

sins of which Filippo was guilty were, it appears, not alien to Dante, who was wrathful and proud himself. As he stood before a brother in sin, he ought to have felt compassion for him and for himself rather than the inhuman desire for Filippo's augmented suffering.

Dante is no more merciful when he is down in Tolomea, where the wretched friar Albergo asks help in opening his eyes sealed by frozen tears:

> . . . . E io non lil' apersi.
> e cortesia fu lui esser villano.[1]

And I did not open them for him. It was a courtesy to be churlish with him.

It is not without significance that Dante has the courage to praise St Dominic because he was 'harsh to enemies.'[2]

We can say in defence of Dante that in his poem he is creating imaginary situations, and that in real life he would act in quite another manner. Very well. But art, equally with dreams, is an indirect confession of the underlying traits of the soul. He who delights in imagining himself cruel shows that he has within himself instincts of cruelty. As art is often a revelation and an outlet for blameworthy sentiments which we do not dare to display in real life, we may suppose that the cruelty which Dante imagined of himself may have been the compensation and the substitute for that actual cruelty which could rarely or never find an outlet in concrete form.

In the *Inferno*, it sometimes happens that Dante

---

[1] *Inf.* XXXIII, 149–150. (It was churlish of Dante not to keep his promise. Cf. 115–117.)

[2] *Par.* XII, 57.

O   193

weeps at sight of the damned. Virgil does not reprove him when he shows pity for Francesca, the adulteress; for Pier della Vigna, the suicide; for Ciacco, the glutton. But when Dante—perhaps because of a vague feeling of imaginary complicity which is not surprising in one who delights in prophecy—begins to weep in the *bolgia* of the diviners and soothsayers, the gentle Virgil reproves him sharply; and Dante puts into Virgil's mouth the expression of this harsh judgement:

> . . . Ancor se' tu delli altri sciocchi?
> Qui vive la pietà quand'è ben morta:
> chi è più scellerato che colui
> che al giudicio divin passion comporta? [1]

> Are you still among the other fools? Here piety lives when pity is wholly dead. Who is more wicked than he who feels pity because of the punishment inflicted on sinners by the Divine Judgement?

We do not pause over the contradiction. Dante, who is sometimes moved to compassion by the punishment of the damned, would be (according to Virgil, which means according to Dante himself) a 'fool' and 'wicked.' What matters is the principle which is formulated here: the outspoken condemnation of pity. I do not know how far this condemnation is dogmatically justifiable, but coming from Dante it has an ill sound. Let us admit that the inmates of the Inferno are now unalterably and justly condemned, and that to excuse them or pity them would be an implicit censure of Divine Justice. But I think that a living man, who is likewise a Christian and a poet, passing through the region of the damned and thinking on his own sins which may one day imprison him also down there with those other

[1] *Inf.* XX, 27–30.

194

sinners, ought rather to weep, if only for himself, than delight in the torture of others and rejoice in its increase. Even if Filippo Argenti was in life a personal or political enemy of Alighieri, this attitude of cruelty after death toward one who is already suffering does no honour to the mind of the poet, and gravely compromises his title of true Christian. The Christian can and ought, at times, to inveigh against sinners, but it is unworthy of a follower of the Gospel to meditate vengeance against individuals even beyond the grave. Dante thinks of himself as invested with the dignity of a Christian poet who is destined for salvation; this is made clear by the poet himself at the beginning of his poem. Everyone remembers Virgil's account. Three ladies of Paradise are moved to pity for the poet lost in the forest, and they send Virgil to him to serve as guide. One of these ladies is no other than the Virgin; the third is Beatrice, the immortal Beloved; the second is Lucia, to whom Dante is 'faithful.' The poet describes Lucia in these few words—'enemy of every cruel person.'[1] She is identified by some as St Lucy, the Syracusan martyr; allegorically, she stands for illuminating Grace, or the like. But whatever she may be, she is foe to all cruelty. This is her special virtue. And Dante, her devotee, on that journey of purification, which he owes likewise to the intercession of Lucia, dubs 'fool' and 'wicked' him who feels pity; it is Lucia's *fedele* who, as he passes along, enjoys kicking the skulls and tearing the hair of the most desperately unhappy creatures—to the eyes and heart of a believer—that exist in the whole universe.

If we do not demand that the poet shall display pity

[1] *Inf.* II, 100.

195

at any cost, let us turn to the demands of justice, which the poet exalts and seeks. In the presence of the punishment of Francesca, Dante experiences something more than natural compassion—judging at least from the effects—for he straightway swoons. It is as much out of proportion to the cause as his ferocity against Bocca degli Abati. Is Dante perhaps indulgent toward the sins which he himself has committed or might commit? It would seem not. He has pity for Ciacco although he himself is no gorger of food; and he has no pity for Filippo Argenti who is as violent as he himself is. There is no just measure, therefore, in the mind of Dante; and to the suspicion of cruelty we must add the no less grave suspicion of a doubtful sense of justice.

29

DANTE AND CHILDREN

NOTHER proof that Dante does not always give perfect and active support to the teachings of Jesus is found in the opinion of children which he expresses in the *Convivio*. I do not think that anyone has noticed this contrast between Dante and the Gospels, and perhaps it was not apparent even to him. In any case, it is significant. 'Most men,' says Dante, 'live according to their senses and not according to reason, after the manner of children . . . so that . . . these men, who include, alas! almost everyone . . . are quickly desirous of something and quickly satisfied, are often joyous and often sad because of trivial delights and disappointments, are quickly friends and quickly enemies. They do everything in the manner of children, without the use of reason.'[1]

Here speaks the pure rationalist, the philosopher, and we may add, the illuminist: he who values above everything else the work of the intellect, and undervalues or ignores the freshness, the spontaneity, the richness of intuition. But Dante should have made reference, at least in passing and to justify himself, to the explicit testimony of Jesus on the spiritual worth of little children and of those who are childlike. The three synoptic gospels record the famous words: 'Suffer the little children to come unto me, and forbid them not, for of such is the kingdom of God. Verily, I say unto you, Whosoever shall not receive the

[1] *Conv.* I, iv, 3–5.

197

kingdom of God as a little child, he shall not enter therein.'[1]

These are the words of God Himself made man; no Christian can ignore them; even less can he contradict them. He can, however, recognize, as St Augustine did, the perversity of children, the heritage of the Fall; but in the text of the Gospels and in that of the *Convivio* they are not speaking of actual children, but of men who resemble children. According to Jesus, to resemble little children is an evidence of superiority in a man; according to Dante, it is an inferiority. Jesus says that only those who make themselves like little children are fit to enter the Kingdom of Heaven; that is, can reach the greatest perfection to which man can attain. Dante, on the contrary, speaks of the likeness with children as a detraction, an imperfection, a misfortune.

In this instance there speaks in Dante the man of earlier times who maintained that mature and clear intelligence was the highest faculty of man; and there speaks also, perhaps, the student of the rationalistic theology of Dante's own time. But a Christian to whom the Gospel is familiar is not permitted to ignore that there are faculties of the soul superior to reason—simplicity, meekness of spirit, unquestioning adoration, love. It is not said that with reason alone man shall reach beatitude or even the deepest truths. The Scribes and the Pharisees, in comparison with the unlettered disciples of Jesus, represented culture and intelligence; nevertheless Jesus condemned them, and Christianity won its victory through the instrumentality of ignorant fishermen in spite of the Doctors of the Law.

[1] Matthew xix, 13–15; Mark x, 13–16; Luke xviii, 15–17.

We may say that in the passage from the *Convivio* Dante was not thinking of the Kingdom of Heaven, that he had in mind lower and more human problems. But if we read attentively, we see that the implicit condemnation of men who resemble little children is a general condemnation, and has all the effect of a censure which admits no exceptions.

The question might be raised as to whether the psychology of the child sketched by Dante is entirely correct. It consists, according to him, in the brevity and inconstancy of the emotions: 'they are quickly desirous of something and quickly satisfied. . . .' But can we assert that reason itself escapes this changeableness? Is not the thinker besieged and dominated now by one argument, now by another? does he not waver often between assent and negation, between one thesis and its opposite? Is not the history of the human reason one of perpetual vacillations and obsessions? Granted that the rationalist remains longer in one mental position, is inconstancy to be measured by hours and not by years as well? In comparison with the eternal, that which changes in the course of a generation is as variable as that which changes in the course of a day.

But the fact remains, serious and significant, that Dante, speaking of the resemblance between grown men and little children, does not remember the impressive and well-known words of the Gospel. Even in the *Commedia*, the soul prone to deceive itself is compared, with an implication of inferiority, to an ignorant child who laughs and weeps without reason:

> . . . a guisa di fanciulla
> che piangendo e ridendo pargoleggia,

l'anima semplicetta che sa nulla

. . . .

Di picciol bene in pria sente sapore ;
quivi s'inganna. . .[1]

Like a little maid who, weeping and smiling, follows her childish
whims, the artless soul which knows nothing . . . at first tastes the
savour of some slight good ; by this it is deceived. . . .

Therefore, continues Dante, rulers and laws are
needed, the checks of reason.

Here also, Dante is too much concerned with the
human side, and does not think of the other and nobler
aspect of childish simplicity. This open contempt for
childhood, contrary to the spirit of Christianity, brings
him close to the arrogant pagan intellectualism. Once
more in Dante Aristotle over-rides the Gospel.

But fortunately not always. In the end, Beatrice
echoes the thought of Christ:

Fede ed innocenzia son reperte
solo ne' parvoletti. . . .[2]

Faith and innocence are found only in little children. . . .

It was time!

[1] *Purg.* XVI, 86–88; 91–92.
[2] *Par.* XXVII, 127–128.

30

THE VENDETTA

O N two occasions Dante refused to play the rôle of avenger. He did not avenge his father,[1] and he did not wish to avenge his father's cousin, Geri del Bello, who was killed, apparently, by one of the Sacchetti.[2]

Of the first case it may be said that there was no cause or reason for a true vendetta, and that everything is reduced to a malevolent insinuation of Forese Donati. In the other case, it is probable that the unhappy duty, according to the barbarous custom of the time, would not have fallen to Dante until after the nearest relatives had failed in their criminal obligation. However that may have been, Dante, as a Christian and moralist, knew that private vengeance was condemned by the law of the Gospel, and that the obligation of forgiveness was substituted for the old savagery of retaliation.

This much is true, at any rate, that Dante uses as an example of clemency the action of Pisistratus, who refused to take vengeance on his daughter's wooer.[3] The appetite for revenge is represented as one of the sins punished in Purgatory:

ed è chi per ingiuria par h'aonti
sì che si fa della vendetta ghiotto
e tal convien che il male altrui impronti.[4]

And there is he who seems so enraged because of some injury received

[1] The Tenzone, sonnet 6 (Rime, LXXVIII).
[2] Inf. XXIX, 22–36.
[3] Purg. XV, 97–105.
[4] Purg. XVII, 121–123.

that he becomes eager for revenge, and in such a state that he must
hasten harm for others.

Dante praises the fortitude of the 'good Marzucco'
who did not wish to revenge the death of his son.[1]

Notwithstanding these precepts and examples, we are
obliged to recognize in Alighieri a partiality for the
word *vendetta* and sometimes also for the feelings
associated with it.[2]

Dante ends one of his most famous canzoni, *Così nel
mio parlar voglio esser aspro*, with a line still more famous:

chè bell'onor si acquista in far vendetta.[3]
Because great honour is acquired in taking vengeance.

This poem, however, was written in a state of erotic
fury, and the verse quoted cannot be considered typical.
But we cannot offer this excuse for the passages in the
Commedia which refer to vengeance, and especially to
divine vengeance. The punishments which Dante records, whether terrestrial or infernal, are viewed almost
with satisfaction, and are called frequently and readily by
the word *vendetta*, which reveals thoughts of resentment and retaliation rather than of just punishment.
Elisha, who was 'avenged by the bears,'[4] and the arch-

---

[1] *Purg.* VI, 17–18.

[2] We must call attention, for the sake of fairness, to the fact that sometimes the word *vendetta* in Dante means 'punishment'; and punishment,
when it comes from God, is in its essence one of the forms of justice. We
should add that vengeance is demanded and exacted by the just men of the
Old Testament although even then it was clearly said that God reserved it
for Himself (Deut. xxxii, 35).

The word is found in the New Testament also in the sense of punishment.
For example, in the parable of the unjust judge, the widow says, 'Avenge me
of my adversary' (Luke xviii, 3). 'I tell you that he will avenge them
speedily' (Luke xviii, 8).

[3] *Rime*, CIII, 83.

[4] *Inf.* XXVI, 34.

angel Michael, who 'wrought vengeance for the proud violence,'[1] belonged to the scriptural tradition and are, at bottom, representatives of divine justice. But when the effect of this justice appears to the eyes of Dante in the *Inferno* not as grievous punishment but as actual vengeance, *vendetta*, the word sounds a little strange to modern ears. The *vendetta* presupposes and implies a wrathful mind, one which rejoices in harm to others; and such sentiments, appropriate to evil men, contradict all possible conceptions of the Christian God.[2] Dante, however, says of the damned that 'the divine vengeance hammers them,'[3] and that in another *bolgia* 'also for Medea is vengeance prepared.'[4] He sees the burning sand on which the blasphemers walk, and exclaims,

> O vendetta di Dio, quanto tu dei
> esser temuta. . . .[5]

> O vengeance of God, how much you should be feared!

Farther on, seeing the torture of the thieves, he cries,

> Oh potenza di Dio, quant'è severa
> che cotai colpi per vendetta croscia.[6]

> Oh power of God, how severe it is, that it rains down such blows for vengeance!

---

[1] *Inf.* VII, 11–12.

[2] That a clear distinction was made in the Trecento between *vendetta* (vengeance, revenge) and *punizione* (punishment), or *gastigamento* (chastisement), is proved by the following passage from Boccaccio: 'All that I do to you cannot properly be called vengeance (*vendetta*) but rather chastisement (*gastigamento*), inasmuch as vengeance (*vendetta*) should exceed the offence, and this will not equal it.'—*Decameron*, VIII, 7.

[3] *Inf.* XI, 90.

[4] *Inf.* XVIII, 96.

[5] *Inf.* XIV, 16–17.

[6] *Inf.* XXIV, 119–120.

Dante, at a certain point, was moved to pity by the punishments which he has seen:

E condollemi alla giusta vendetta.[1]

And I grieved at the just vengeance.

Although he represents himself as grieving at the vengeance, he makes those whom he recalls or meets demand vendetta. The widow does not ask Trajan for justice; she asks for vengeance:

. . . Segnor, fammi vendetta
di mio figliuol ch'è morto. . . .[2]

Lord, grant me vengeance for my son who is slain.

Hugh Capet twice asks God's vengeance on his successors, or rather makes direct appeal to the wrath (*ira*) of God:

Ma se Doagio, Lilla, Guanto e Bruggia
potesser, tosto ne saria vendetta
e io la cheggio a lui che tutto giuggia.

. . . .

O Segnor mio, quando sarò io lieto
a veder la vendetta che, nascosa
fa dolce l'ira tua nel tuo secreto?[3]

But if Douai, Lille, Ghent, and Bruges had power, there would quickly be vengeance, and I implore it from Him who judges all things. . . . When, O my Lord, shall I rejoice to see the vengeance which, hidden in Thy secret, makes sweet Thy wrath?

The same word is used by Cacciaguida when he prophesies the expulsion of the White Guelphs:

. . . ma la vendetta
fia testimonio al ver che la dispensa.[4]

But the vengeance will bring witness to the truth which administers it.

---

[1] *Purg.* XXI, 6. [2] *Purg.* X, 83–84.
[3] *Purg.* XX, 46–48; 94–96. [4] *Par.* XVII, 53–54.

Gentle Beatrice herself, in announcing the coming of the DXV, solemnly affirms 'that the vengeance of God fears not any sop.'[1] In allusion to the same judge and avenger, she says to Dante, who had been frightened by the cry of the Blessed, If you had understood the words of that cry

> già ti sarebbe nota la vendetta
> che tu vedrai innanzi che tu muoi;[2]

already would be known to you the vengeance which you shall see before you die.

Our surprise is even greater when that terrible word is used to mean the deed of the Crucifixion. Justinian recounts the history of the Eagle, of the Roman Empire, and having reached Tiberius, he says:

> . . . la viva giustizia che mi spira
> li concedette, in mano a quel ch'i dico,
> gloria di far vendetta alla sua ira.[3]

The Living Justice which inspires me granted [to the Eagle] in the hand of him of whom I speak, the glory of avenging God's wrath.

Afterwards Titus, by destroying Jerusalem,

> . . . a far vendetta corse
> della vendetta del peccato antico.[4]

. . . hastened to exact vengeance for the vendetta of the ancient sin.

Dante had already said the same thing in the *Purgatorio*:

> Nel tempo che 'l buon Tito, con l'aiuto
> del sommo rege, vendicò le fora
> ond'uscì 'l sangue per Giuda venduto.[5]

At the time when the good Titus, with the aid of the Most High King, avenged the gashes whence issued the blood sold by Judas.

---

[1] *Purg.* XXXIII, 36. The meaning of this famous *crux* appears to be that there are no limitations to obstruct the execution of divine vengeance.—Trans.
[2] *Par.* XXII, 14–15.
[3] *Par.* VI, 88–90.
[4] *Par.* VI, 92–93.
[5] *Purg.* XXI, 82–84.

Beatrice is aware of Dante's doubt and perplexity at the words of Justinian, and makes a long discourse on the mystery of the Atonement, using the same terms as the great Emperor:

> Secondo mio infallibile avviso,
> come giusta vendetta giustamente
> punita fosse, t'ha in pensier miso.[1]

> Through my unfailing insight, I know that the question, how a just vengeance could be justly avenged, has set you thinking.

Indeed, it needed explanation.

The theological doctrines of the Atonement numbered three: first, the Mystic (called also speculative and physical), derived especially from the Eastern theologies, according to which men were redeemed from sin by the fact of the Incarnation alone, that is, by the union of the divine and human nature which took place in Christ, and which elevated and purified our condition; second, that of the ransom from the Demon, which appears especially in St Augustine, according to which Satan, in consequence of Adam's sin, had become in a sense master of humanity, so that a great price had to be paid to free man from such servitude, and the price paid was the blood of Christ; and finally, the realistic theory, due mainly to St Anselm, according to which Christ has redeemed us by substitution, that is, by taking our place and, through His passion and death, offering to God that satisfaction which the human race owed to the Creator after the Fall but which we, being finite and sinful creatures, were incapable of offering.

Beatrice expounds this last theory, following the famous dialogue of St Anselm, *Cur Deus homo?* which is

[1] *Par.* VII, 19–21.

even to-day one of the classic treatises of the Catholic doctrine of salvation. St Anselm's teachings were accepted with some modifications and additions by St Thomas; both St Anselm and St Thomas always speak of 'satisfaction' (*satisfactio*) and never of vengeance.[1] The offering of the life of Christ is a 'gift' (*donum*) of the Redeemer, not a punishment inflicted by God. Dante's thought is, in general, the same as St Anselm's and St Thomas's: man has sinned deeply against God and God must obtain reparation; but man cannot by himself alone make infinite satisfaction for an infinite offence. It is necessary, therefore, that God should intervene in the person of Christ, who was man and God. The martyrdom of the Cross is a means of punishing human nature and by that expiation rendering it worthy of pardon. It is a voluntary act of love on the part of God: it is not and it could not be an act of vengeance, a vendetta.

In the words of Justinian, however, in the above-cited passages from the *Paradiso*, the theory of St Anselm becomes, at least in form, altered and distorted. God is angered, *irato*, against man, and it is honour, *gloria*, for Tiberius to serve as the instrument of God's vengeance, *vendetta*. God is angry and wishes revenge, and He avenges Himself against mankind by permitting men (Pilate, the vicar of Tiberius) to put to death His own Son. The fact that Titus justly takes vengeance for this vengeance, destroying Jerusalem and scattering the Jews, appears more natural—although first it is the glory of Tiberius to have permitted the vengeance and now the

[1] Dante, speaking on another occasion of the Atonement, says that Christ 'made satisfaction' (*sodisfece*); *Par.* XIII, 41.

vengeance for the vengeance (*la vendetta della vendetta*) falls upon the Jews and not upon the Empire. But that the Father should consider the crucifixion of His only begotten Son as vendetta, that is to say, as the outlet of His wrath against an Innocent Person who pays for the sins of mankind,—such a thought as this was never spoken by the Fathers or the Doctors of Christianity. Only Alighieri could have achieved the temerity of voicing it—that Alighieri who finds his inspiration more often in the harshness, the *terribilità*, of the Old Testament than in the gentleness of the New.

To the Christian understanding, the death of the Saviour is a spontaneous offering prompted by a divine and infinite love. Dante transforms it into a vendetta of God the Father. Even if we substitute the word punishment for vengeance, and argue that the poet wished to give more force to the idea and so used the tremendous, the too human *vendetta*, there remains in the mind of the Christian reader a vague confusion and the belief, natural under the circumstances, that Dante has expressed, with it may be an over-emphasis of form, the orthodox theory of the Atonement. And such distortion, even if unconscious, inclines us to think that the mind of Dante was too much disposed to see wrath in every judgement and vengeance in every punishment.

We must reach the seventeenth century, the century of the Jansenists, in order to find the word *vendetta* used in regard to the Atonement. 'En effet,' says Bossuet, 'il n'appartient qu'à Dieu de venger les injures. . . . Il fallait donc, mes Frères, qu'il vînt lui-même contre son Fils avec tous ses foudres; et puisqu'il avait mis en lui nos péchés, il y devait mettre aussi sa juste vengeance. Il l'a fait, Chrétiens; n'en doutons pas.'[1]

Bossuet, who is an orator, which means that he is an artist and poet, repeats the same word used by Dante; and Dante, led by his instinct for the effective and forceful word, gave to the theory of '*satisfactio*' the terrible aspect of *vendetta*.

Could we not sustain the argument that the *Commedia* itself is due in part to an idea of vengeance? Did Dante not use it in fact to avenge himself against those who were enemies of his person or his ideas?[2] Did he not conceive of the coming of the DXV, of the 'messenger of God,' as the coming of a terrible avenger? Dante, a Christian, too often forgot the divine injunction which Christ repeated so many times to men—Forgive your enemies.

[1] *Pour le Vendredi Saint* (26 mars 1660); Troisième point. *Œuvres Oratoires de Bossuet*; Edition critique de l'abbé J. Lebarq. Paris, Desclée de Brouwer, 1927, III, 385. The same ideas and expressions may be found in Massillon and Bourdaloue.

[2] Note how Dante speaks of Baldo d'Aguglione, author of the famous *reform* of 1311, which excluded the poet from among those recalled to Florence: *Purg.* XII, 105; *Par.* XVI, 56.

THE SHARP WIND OF POVERTY

ONE of the surest signs of the Christian is love of poverty or, at least, uncomplaining endurance in the midst of distress. A greater sign in the most perfect Christians is the voluntary search for poverty and, as a natural consequence, the decision to live on charity.

The two great religious orders, founded about half a century before Dante was born, held it an honour to be called Mendicants. Dante was well aware of this; in the *Paradiso* he speaks of 'the most dear lady' of St Francis, his spouse, the Lady Poverty;[1] and he called the Friars Minor the 'poor folk,' *gente poverella*.[2]

If an uncomplaining acceptance of poverty were the only virtue demanded of the Christian, Dante, with innumerable others, could hardly be considered a true follower of Christ. He recalls and praises the poverty of the Virgin Mary,[3] that of St Peter,[4] of Fabricius,[5] of Romeo da Villanova;[6] but when it comes to his own poverty, we do not find in his writings words of resignation or of rejoicing, but only complaints and murmurings. Dante approved of poverty—but only in others. His own lay heavy on his soul and humiliated him; and he did not scruple to remind others of his distress in tones of bitterness, in order that they might excuse him or sympathize with him or succour him.

[1] *Par.* XI, 112–114. [2] *Par.* XI, 94.
[3] *Purg.* XX, 22. [4] *Par.* XXIV, 109.
[5] *Purg.* XX, 26. [6] *Par.* VI, 139.

The earliest lament, probably, is that contained in the letter of condolence written to Oberto and Guido di Romena on the occasion of the death of their uncle, Count Alessandro, in 1304. 'As your servant therefore,' he says at the close of the letter, 'I excuse myself for not having taken part in the sad obsequies since neither negligence nor ingratitude kept me away but the unforeseen poverty which is the outcome of my exile. For poverty, like a pursuing wild beast, having despoiled me of weapons and horses, has driven me now into her den as into a prison; and although I exert every effort to escape, up to the present it is she who prevails and cruelly contrives to keep me always under her claws.'[1]

Some time afterward, possibly in 1306, in writing the first book of the *Convivio*, he expressed his complaint more openly. He says that he has journeyed through almost every part of Italy 'like a pilgrim, displaying against my will the wounds of fortune. . . . I am a ship without sail and without rudder, driven . . . by the sharp wind which blows from grievous poverty. . . .'[2]

Again, in the letter to Can Grande, which belongs to the last years, perhaps to 1318, Dante recalls his wretchedness: 'urget enim me rei familiaris angustia.'[3] And he adds quickly that from the generosity of the prince he hopes for aid to enable him to go on with his poem.

There is a veiled allusion here to hoped-for and perhaps asked-for contributions. The proud pilgrim may have been obliged more than once to make similar requests, in person and in a form more explicit. There was nothing so bitterly distasteful to Dante, nothing

[1] *Epist.* II, 7–8.   [2] *Conv.* I, iii, 4, 5.
[3] *Epist.* XIII, 88.

which inspired in him such commiseration, as mendicancy. Even in Canto XI of the *Paradiso*, in which he exalts St Francis, Dante is a lukewarm Franciscan, remote from the spirit and the rule of the Mendicants.

We have just seen in the *Convivio* how Dante considers it a supreme misfortune to go almost begging from town to town and from court to court; and all readers will remember the tone of desolation in the terzina of Cacciaguida's prophecy:

> Tu proverai sì come sa di sale
> lo pane altrui, e come è duro calle
> lo scendere e 'l salir per l'altrui scale.[1]

> You shall come to know how bitter is the taste of another's bread, and
> how hard a passage is the mounting and descending of another's stairs.

Bitter, therefore, that bread of charity which St Francis in joyfulness of spirit divided with his poor companion on the clean stone beside the cold fountain.[2] And 'hard' that mounting and descending of another's stairs, which for the *gente poverella* was, and is to-day, a duty and a joy.

We recall also with what grief and conscious sympathy Dante speaks of Romeo da Villanova who departed 'poor and old,' and how it seems to Dante a title to pity that Romeo should have gone 'begging his livelihood bit by bit.'[3] To have to ask for charity is such humiliation that, according to Dante, it has won salvation even for the proud Provenzan Salvani who, 'every shame laid aside,' stationed himself in the Campo of Siena to beg for money to liberate a friend, and with such sacrifice of

---

[1] *Par.* XVII, 58–60.
[2] v. *The Little Flowers of St Francis*, XIII.
[3] *Par.* VI, 139–142.

pride that 'he brought himself to tremble through every vein.'[1]

Humanly speaking, this fear of poverty on Dante's part and his bitterness and complainings are things that we understand and sympathize with. A man of noble family, heir to a patrimony small but sufficient to keep him from hunger and beggary and the servitude which they engender; unjustly deprived of his little property by pillage and exile; a man of learning and of great genius, forced to contract debts and to beg; in every moment of this life he must have felt embarrassment, scorn, grief, and shame at such necessity. But that which is understandable and pitiable in any man, in a man simply human and unthinking, or in a man of great but pagan mind, is understood ill and arouses little sympathy in the case of a Christian who sets up as his aim in his greatest work the recalling of mankind to Christianity, who often commends poverty in pagans and in Christians, praises the famous bridegroom of Poverty and those who followed him, and approves those who bring themselves to live by charity. If poverty is an evil, why praise it? If it is a good, why so many complaints about his own poverty? Why call it 'a pursuing wild beast,' 'cruel,' and 'grievous'?

[1] *Purg.* XI, 133–138.

SACRED AND PROFANE LOVE

HE Dante of the popular biography and the chromolithographic tradition is the man of one woman only, the servant of Beatrice, the ideal and monogamous lover, faithful to the one and only woman, to the Chosen One. But if we study Dante's life a little more closely and read his lyrical poems carefully, we shall ultimately perceive that more than three women had encompassed his heart.[1] His loves, whether Platonic or Ovidian, were several. Dante, like most men, was polygamous although he was married only once.

We are not saying—it would be an unwarrantable perversion of the truth—that we ought to see in Dante a forerunner of Don Juan Tenorio or of Casanova; but the fact is that on his own testimony or that of others there were, between named and unnamed, at least a dozen women in his life. And we may permit ourselves to think that there were a few more, since Dante would not have wished or have been able to refer in his poems to all his adventures.

The women named by him are seven in number: Beatrice, Violetta, Lisetta, Pietra, Gentucca, Fioretta, and Pargoletta. Then there are the three women to whom he refers in the *Vita Nuova* without giving their names: 'the gentle lady of very pleasing aspect' who was the first of his 'screens'; the other lady chosen by Love

---

[1] The reference is to the opening line of the canzone, *Tre donne intorno al cor mi son venute.*—Trans.

himself, who was his second screen; and finally, the 'piteous lady' who comforted him for the death of Beatrice. That makes ten. In addition, there is the beautiful girl of the Trentino, to whom, according to some, he dedicated the canzone, *Amor, da che convien pur ch'io mi doglia*. Last of all, there is poor Gemma Donati, his wife and the mother of his children. And that makes twelve.

It is possible, however, that the three unnamed women of the *Vita Nuova* may be identical with three named in the *Rime*. We observe that Lisetta is a temptress, not a woman beloved; that the adventure of the Trentino is a legend; and that Pargoletta is not necessarily a proper name since the word was commonly used to mean a young girl. Subtracting these, there remain always six. For an austere moralist, six are a few too many. I take no account of the exaggerated hypothesis of Imbriani that Dante had loved dishonestly his sister-in-law Pietra, the wife of his brother Francesco. But the recent discovery from a document in Lucca that Dante had a son Giovanni, has given rise to fresh doubts. Was Giovanni the son of Gemma or of some other woman? Whatever the truth of the matter, we hold the belief that there are still some unsolved mysteries in the life of Dante.

Some of these loves were probably mere literary longings, fictions or velleities, or stratagems for hiding actually existent love-affairs; about this we cannot be positive. But there is no doubt that Dante was a sensual man. If the cord with which he had once thought 'to take the leopard of the painted skin'[1] is the girdle of the Franciscan, and if the leopard symbolizes lust, as many

[1] *Inf.* XVI, 106 ff.

commentators think, then this passage is the confession of a guilty man. The testimony of Boccaccio, who must have known some contemporaries of the poet, could not be more explicit: 'Amid so much virtue and so much learning . . . sensuality found ample place, and not only in his younger years but even when he was mature. . . .'

The so-called *canzoni pietrose*, because of the sensual ardour which pervades them, could have been written only for a real woman of flesh and blood, and they are an indubitable proof of the truth of Boccaccio's assertion.

On the other hand, in Dante's major works the dominating figure is Beatrice, the woman made angel, who incites to virtue and whom Dante scarcely dares to look upon when, transfigured and exalted by death, she accompanies her 'faithful one'—unfaithful several times —to the heights of Paradise.

There is, therefore, no consistent parallel between Dante's life and his poetry. In his life Libido rules; in his poetry, Eros purified. Under such circumstances can we speak of duplicity? I think not. For Christians of the Middle Ages the carnal side of love, which they could not forgo, was considered something impure, shameful, not to be acknowledged; so much so, that they rarely sang of conjugal love, although it was sanctified by the sacrament of the Church, because implied in it was the union of the flesh as well as of the souls. The only love admissible, and expressible in written words, was spiritual love freed from carnal desires; a love that ennobled the soul that held it, and raised that soul to virtue and faith. Every poet of that time was perforce and without any hypocrisy a Janus: he did what he could not sing, and sang those sentiments or conceptions which were not opposed to the traditions of the 'faithful in love' or to the ascetic morality of Christianity.

One time only, in the poems for the girl of the Casentino, for the cruel Pietra, Dante found himself uniting life with art, the violence of passion with the forms of poetry. But when he wrote those canzoni, Dante was no longer young, and his unsatisfied desire made him forget the sacred rules of the poetry of love. And in this instance the singer of the angelic Beatrice appears as a frustrated faun who whines with unsatisfied desire in 'the hot ravine.'

THE DEIFICATION OF BEATRICE

*W*HETHER we like it or not, it is impossible to speak of Dante without facing the problem of Beatrice. It cannot be avoided. She is so omnipresent in his work, from the youthful little book of the *Vita Nuova* to the end of the third canticle of the *Commedia*, that if we wished to be silent on this point or to ignore it, it would be like arguing on the question of light without naming the sun.

There are hundreds of books about Beatrice, in large part useless or tedious, but all of them turn on these three problems: Was Dante's Beatrice a real woman of flesh and blood, or was she a pure creation of the poet's mind, a fantasy and symbol? If Beatrice was a real woman, was she the Beatrice who was the daughter of Folco Portinari and the wife of Simone dei Bardi, or some other woman unidentified? If she was a symbol only, or a real woman transformed into a symbol, what does she represent: Grace, the Holy Scriptures, Divine Wisdom, Revelation, Theology, or something else?

Of these three problems the second, we should say, has no importance beyond that of a curiosity more or less warranted. Whether Beatrice was of the Portinari family or another is of little aid in throwing light on the life of Dante or on the significance which that young girl had in his thoughts.

As to the first and third, we can say that there is virtual agreement among the most learned and trustworthy Dantologists: Beatrice, they say, was a real woman and only after her death became a symbol; and in the *Commedia* she is a symbol of the knowledge of divine things, or Theology. I, too, accept these reasonable conclusions, but I do not therefore consider that the discussion on Beatrice is closed or that there is nothing more to be investigated or questioned. There is a fourth problem, so it seems to me, which almost no one has stated. How and by what successive steps was Dante able to enlarge to more than human size the figure of a simple Florentine girl and wife until he came to regard her as higher than the angels and the blessed spirits, almost the equal of the Virgin, and a new mediator between humanity, personified in Dante, and the Almighty?

An elevation so out of the ordinary, an exaltation so unusual and incredible—and from the Catholic point of view quite inadmissible—has need, I think, of explanation. The point of departure is normal, but the point of arrival is so astounding as to create surprise that the problem of the transition from one to the other has not attracted more attention from the professional Dantists. The effect of habit, no doubt, which makes a thing seem natural and obvious when it is strange and even mysterious.

In the Provençal poets and in Guinizelli we find the first traces of the exaggerated idealization of the beloved. The woman is like an angel, and therefore worthy of Paradise; on the lover she has a wonderful effect, and that too in the moral sense. But Dante goes much further. His Beatrice, from the very first pages of the *Vita Nuova*, is a being apart, transcending humanity. The little maid, dressed in crimson, who appeared to Dante when she was but nine years old, is the 'youngest of the angels' of whom 'might be said those words of the poet Homer, She seemed to be the daughter not of a mortal, but of a god.'[1] She appears to him also as 'destroyer of all the vices and queen of all the virtues,'[2] and inspires in him such 'a fire of charity' that it makes him 'pardon whoever had injured [him].[3] She is so perfect that without her Paradise is imperfect:

> Lo cielo, che non have altro difetto
> che d'aver lei, al suo segnor la chiede,
> e ciascun santo ne grida merzede.[4]

Heaven, which has no other defect than lack of her, implores her of their Lord, and every saint asks the grace of her presence.

In the same canzone, the poet says that she is the 'hope of the blessed spirits,' so greatly 'desired in highest heaven' that Love himself asks:

> . . . Cosa mortale
> come esser pò sì adorna e sì pura?
> Poi la reguarda e fra sè stesso giura
> che Dio ne 'ntenda di far cosa nova.

How can mortal be so lovely and so pure? Then, gazing on her, he takes oath within himself that God meant to make a new creature.

'Cosa nova,' a new thing, something different from other mortals. 'Pride and wrath flee before her,'[5] and many who saw her pass said, 'This is no woman but one of the beautiful angels of heaven,'[6] and even greater things.

[1] *V.N.* II, 8. [2] *V.N.* X, 2.
[3] *V.N.* XI, 1. [4] *V.N.* XIX, 7.
[5] *V.N.* XXI, 2. [6] *V.N.* XXVI, 2.

Because, adds Dante,

> Vede perfettamente onne salute
> chi la mia donna tra le donne vede.[1]

Who sees my lady among other ladies sees every excellence in its perfection.

It is no wonder that when she died the whole city became a 'widow despoiled of every dignity,'[2] and that Dante wrote to the lords of the earth about the death of this superwoman. Even less should we wonder at Dante's intention, expressed at the close, 'to write of her that which has never before been written of any woman.'[3]

He kept his promise. All of the *Divina Commedia*, from the first to the last canto, is a monument to Beatrice, 'true praise of God.' It is she 'whose beauteous eye sees everything';[4] she who is 'the beloved of the first lover';[5] and even the wisest spirits in the heaven of the sun circle about her like a garland, gazing on her with delight.[6]

It must be said at once that this strange sublimation of Beatrice is, in a Christian writer, unexpected and disturbing. I should say, if the worshippers of Dante will permit, that it approaches sacrilege. Christianity recognizes in two beings only, but in ways substantially different, the ineffable union of the Divine with the human. In Christ who, although God, humbled Himself to assume the nature and form of man; and in Mary who, although an earthly being, was the Mother of Christ, of God, and almost shares in the homage due to

---

[1] *V.N.* XXVI, 10.   [2] *V.N.* XXX, 1.
[3] *V.N.* XLII, 2.   [4] *Inf.* X, 131.
[5] *Par.* IV, 118; cf. *Inf.* II, 76–78.
[6] *Par.* X, 92–93.

God through the fact that she, among all women, was chosen by the Holy Ghost as His spouse. To deify another terrestrial creature, as Dante does Beatrice, is an erotic and heretical extravagance. I say 'deify' not without reason, because, according to the poet, Beatrice is higher than the saints and angels, the source of every virtue, a being free from sin, almost a rival of the Virgin Mary, and through her power of saving Grace, like Christ Himself. We could almost say that Dante wished to make a Madonna just for himself, a private and personal Madonna, a mediator between himself and Mary, just as Mary is a mediator between mankind and Christ. Before Beatrice 'was a symbol,' writes Scherillo, 'she was a woman; and like the Virgin whom she so closely resembles, *tutta santa*, perfect and holy.'[1]

No other poet, either before or after Dante, has ever idealized a woman to this extent. It has occurred to no one else to transform a woman whom he loves into the specially chosen and preferred handiwork of God. Women almost deified appear often in the history of Christianity, but always associated with heresy. Simon Magus had with him the famous Helena of Tyre who personified, according to him, *Ennoia*, a direct emanation of God; and faith in Helena and in him was the prime condition of salvation. Montanus took with him the women-prophets Prisca and Maximilla, and they also were the mouthpieces of the Holy Spirit. The German heretic, Manasses, was accompanied by a woman who, according to his statement, was another Virgin Mary. In Dante's own time, the famous Wilhelmina, who died in 1282, was believed by certain fanatics to be the incar-

[1] Scherillo, *Dante*. Milan, Treves, 1921, p. 52.

nation of the Holy Spirit, and was succeeded by a certain
Maifreda as vicar. The Fra Dolcino[1] recorded by Dante
was united to a certain Margherita whom he called his
spiritual sister and whom he placed above all other
women.

Dante's case is different. He did not live with his all-
but-goddess, and only after her death did he dare to
make her a quasi-divinity, contemplated and honoured
under the veil of symbolism.

To find an instance similar to that of Beatrice we must
come to the nineteenth century, to Clotilde de Vaux, beloved by Auguste Comte. He too, after the death of the
woman, imagined that she had become, in some sort,
divine; and in the positivist cult which he founded, the
central figure was the lost Clotilde, transfigured into a
mystic symbol of regenerated humanity. But Comte had
abandoned Christianity and in the last years of his life
he was of unsound mind.

But Dante was a Christian and sane. And the deification of Beatrice, which we accept to-day without surprise because of long custom, remains one of the boldest
and strangest aspects of his great spirit.

To say that Beatrice is deified only in so far as she is a
symbol of Divine Wisdom is not sufficient explanation
for two reasons: first, because the poet attributes to her
supernatural and thaumaturgical qualities even in the
Vita Nuova, which is a story of love and not a theological
poem; second, because Beatrice in the *Commedia*, although
she may be a symbol, never really loses her concrete
human personality. She may be Theology or some other
symbol, but she is always, in her own remembrance and

[1] *Inf.* XXVIII, 55–60.

in that of the poet, the young Florentine woman who was loved on earth and who died.[1] The mystery remains; and there remains also our legitimate amazement before the quasi-divinity created by 'theologus Dantes.'

[1] See the allusion to her 'second age' and to her death. *Purg.* XXX, 124–125; Dante's 'ten years' thirst.' *Purg.* XXXII, 2; etc.

THE ODOUR OF SACRILEGE

ONE of Dante's most surprising customs—perhaps not yet noted—is that of applying to mortal creatures words from the Bible which refer, and ought to refer, only to Christ and the Virgin.

He adopts this singular practice, first of all, for his divinized Beatrice. When he writes in a sonnet which celebrates a vision of her in life,

e venne in terra per nostra salute,

she came to earth for our salvation,

he does no less than repeat an expression which in the apostolic symbol is used only for Christ.

The apparition of Beatrice in glory in the Earthly Paradise is accompanied by similar reminiscent phrases. When she is about to show herself, one of the four-and-twenty elders—he who represents the *Song of Songs*, or perhaps Solomon himself—cries three times, *Veni, sponsa, de Libano,*[1] 'Come with me from Lebanon, my spouse.' Words of the famous Song[2] which the Church adopts and repeats only for the Virgin Mary and for the Church itself. And almost at once all cry, *Benedictus qui venis,*[3] 'Blessed thou that comest'—the same words which the people of Jerusalem applied to Christ at His last entry into the fatal city.[4]

When Beatrice is about to pronounce the famous

---

[1] *Purg.* XXX, 11.   [2] Song of Solomon iv, 8.
[3] *Purg.* XXX, 19.   [4] Matthew xxi, 9.

prophecy of the DXV, she uses and applies to herself
the same words which Christ spoke of Himself at the
Last Supper: *Modicum, et iam non videbitis me; et iterum
modicum et videbitis me* . . .[1] 'A little while and ye shall
not see me; and again a little while and ye shall see me.'
Twice in succession, then, Beatrice—either as a woman
or as a symbol—is identified with Christ.

This heterodox honour is not reserved for Beatrice
alone. Dante likens to Jesus, and does it openly, the
man whom he has most hated on earth and the man
whom he has most loved—Boniface VIII and Henry VII.
Everyone remembers the famous lines, spoken by Hugh
Capet, on the assault at Anagni:

> veggio in Alagna intrar lo fiordaliso
> e nel vicario suo Cristo esser catto.[2]

I see the fleur-de-lis entering Alagna and Christ made captive in His
vicar.

Up to this point it is permissible, because Christ is
seized indeed, but in the person of His vicar, Boniface.
In the next terzina, however, Christ is substituted without reserve for the injured Pope, with a complete
repetition of the Passion which, in truth, did not occur
at Anagni.

> Veggiolo un'altra volta esser deriso;
> veggio rinnovellar l'aceto e 'l fele,
> e tra vivi ladroni esser anciso.[3]

I see Him mocked a second time; I see the vinegar and the gall
renewed, and Him put to death between living thieves.

At this point the Pope is no longer the vicar of Christ,
but Christ Himself who undergoes a second time His
sufferings and death.

[1] *Purg.* XXXIII, 10 ff. John xvi, 16.
[2] *Purg.* XX, 86–87.
[3] *Purg.* XX, 88–90.

The same thing is repeated in the case of Henry VII. So long as Dante calls him another Moses or a new David (*proles altera Isai*), there is no offence; they too were men. We can attribute the vigour of Dante's praise and prophecy to his being a partisan excited by the hopes of a speedy revenge, and go on. But the situation changes when he applies to Henry the prophecy of Isaiah which foretells the sufferings of the Redeemer,[1] and above all when he describes his visit of homage to the Emperor: 'Then my spirit rejoiced in thee while I said silently to myself, Behold the Lamb of God which taketh away the sins of the world.'[2] They are the same words which John the Baptist spoke when he saw Jesus coming toward him the first time.[3] And even if we can see in Dante another precursor, it is a little hazardous for a Christian to recognize another Christ in the Count of Luxembourg.

Henry, at least, was a Christian. But what shall we say when we see Dante declare that a worshipper of 'the false and lying gods' is the only one worthy to serve as a symbol of God? 'And what mortal man was more worthy than Cato to symbolize God? Certainly none.'[4]

But there is worse to come. Dante does not fear to liken himself to Christ and to appropriate to himself deeds which parallel those of Christ or words addressed to Christ. At the end of the first treatise of the *Convivio*,

---

[1] 'tanquam ad ipsum, post Christum, digitum prophetie propheta direxerit Isaias, cum, spiritu Dei revelante, predixit: Vere languores nostros ipse tulit et dolores nostros ipse portavit.' *Epist.* VI, 25.

[2] Tunc exultavit in te spiritus meus, cum tacitus dixi mecum: Ecce Agnus Dei, ecce qui tollit peccata mundi.' *Epist.* VII, 10.

[3] John i, 29.

[4] *Conv.* IV, xxviii, 15.

wishing to recommend to the reader the nutriment which
he offers, he exclaims: 'This shall be that barley bread
with which thousands will be fed, and full baskets of
the fragments will remain over for me.'[1]

It is possible to look upon this as a metaphor based on
the poet's recollection of the miracle of the loaves and
fishes; but we find a definite appropriation of a eulogy
spoken to Christ, in the famous line which Dante causes
to be addressed to himself by Virgil:

> Benedetta colei che in te s'incinse![2]
>
> Blessed is the womb that bare thee!

The plagiarism deliberately assigned to Virgil implies
two equalizations: Monna Bella (Dante's mother) is
another Mary; Dante, another Christ.

We need not dwell on these bold comparisons. In the
Middle Ages, which were nourished on Holy Writ,
biblical expressions applicable to contemporaries flowed
easily from the pen. But an expression which referred to
Christ could not be applied to any mortal without
evident sacrilege. Precisely in Dante's time the Church
had condemned the custom, which the Spiritual Franciscans and especially Pier Giovanni Olivi had, of finding a perfect parallel between the life of Christ and
the life of St Francis. And in that instance they were
speaking of a saint, and a great saint!

Probably Dante's intention was impeccable and he did
not think himself transgressing when he applied to a

---

[1] *Conv.* I, xiii, 12. Also the words which follow, on the light which shall
overcome darkness, repeat phrases of the New Testament which were used of
Jesus. Cf. I Peter ii, 9; and Paul, Eph. v, 8.

[2] *Inf.* VIII, 45. Cf. Luke xi, 27.

young Florentine wife, a sinful pope, a German emperor, and to himself, those words which in the revealed books refer to Christ and only to Christ. But an orthodox Christian, who sees in the Bible a work inspired directly by God, and maintains, therefore, that it should be used with infinite respect, cannot think that the passages having reference to the Eternal should be perversely misapplied to mortal and earthly creatures; and he cannot fail to perceive in those Dantesque assumptions of the divine in favour of the human, a certain unmistakable odour of sacrilege.

THE CHRISTIAN

*W*AS Dante a secret heretic or a perfectly
orthodox Christian? This is the problem
that most people propound when they speak
of Dante's religion. But there are, in addition, two
other problems, much more important and almost never
mentioned.

I will say at once in order to clear the field that I put
no faith in the intricate lucubrations of Gabriele
Rossetti[1] and his continuators and imitators. Dante was
not a member of any sect, and he did not belong to any
secret conventicle of heresiarchs. If we meet with ideas
and hopes in his works which do not seem wholly
orthodox to-day, it is not important. The Catholicism
of the fourteenth century is not that of the twentieth.
In Dante's bitterest invectives against the curia of Rome
and in his boldest prophecies—like that of the Eternal
Gospel—there appears to be nothing that could shut him
out from the community of the faithful. The more a
Christian loves the Church, the more he wishes to see it
purified and made worthy of reverence. To expect, as
Dante did, a renewal of the world through the coming of
the Holy Spirit, the Comforter promised by Christ in
the gospel of St John, is not in opposition to the
obedience which, until His advent, is due to the Church

[1] Not to be confused by English readers with his son, Dante Gabriel
Rossetti. Gabriele Rossetti, who came to England from Italy in 1824, was
later professor of Italian at King's College, London. He regarded Dante's
Commedia as a poem distinctly anti-Catholic, and gave it a fantastic interpretation.—Trans.

founded by the Second Person of the Trinity. St John the Baptist, who awaited and announced the coming of the Saviour, was not considered a heretic by the Hebrews; his death was due to the vengeance of the Tetrarch and his woman, not to the denunciation of the priests or to a sentence passed by the Sanhedrim.

Dante was a Christian and a Catholic both by birth and free will. He held in scorn the sowers of schism and every sort of heretic. But the other questions which we can and ought to raise about his religious attitude are these: Up to what point, in belief and in practice, was Dante a Christian? In what sense, taking into account the complexity of his mind, was he a Catholic?

We are in the habit of calling Dante the greatest Christian poet and of characterizing his greatest work as a poem essentially religious, whose purpose is to point out to wandering or feeble souls the way of salvation. These assertions are true, but they do not answer the two questions just now stated.

It is necessary to distinguish between the intellectual, doctrinal, and practical concurrence with Christianity and the complete Christian life. A man may be a Christian by faith, sincerely Christian, and fulfil all the devotions prescribed by the Church, and yet not be profoundly and completely Christian in the essential elements of the spirit and in his manner of thought and his conduct towards others. True Christianity is conformity to the life and teaching of Christ as found in the four gospels, and not merely acceptance of theological dogmas and of devotional practices. Very few, as we all know, succeed in achieving this conformity, and they are so few that the Church presents them for the veneration of the faithful under the name of saints. But the duty of being perfect even as God is perfect is a commandment laid upon all Christians without distinction. In this approximation to the evangelical type there are varying degrees.

There are Christians who, urged by the desire of aiding their brothers, summon men to the evangelical perfection while they themselves remain far from such perfection. Yet they cannot be accused of duplicity or of deliberate deceit. They are usually entirely sincere. They see the ideal and the necessity for adhering to it and reaching it, but they themselves lack the strength and the innate qualities which achieve the heights. They call all mankind to the summit while they themselves remain half-way up the slope, hindered by mists and by precipices. It is not that they lack the will to persevere to the top, but they exhaust all their ardour in appeals and entreaties. Others, sustained by a stronger flame of charity, unconsciously reach the clear light of the uplands, and from these heights they call to others, and aid more by example than by words.

Among those Christians who point the way to the summit which they have not yet reached, was Dante. And which of us could cast the first stone? How many of those who call and think themselves Christians, are certain of having advanced farther along the way than he? All are summoned to Christlike perfection, but in every century those who attain it are extremely few. Only the saints attain it, and even they not always in every phase of their life. Dante—let us say it with the frankness which it deserves—was not much of a saint. No one would think of blaming him for not having acquired holiness,—neither the saints who are full of loving pity for sinners, nor, even less, ourselves, cold and imperfect Christians that we are, far below Dante in other things besides genius.

But in approximating to the complete Christian life there are, we repeat, gradations; and after having examined some aspects of the soul and the life of Dante, we are forced to admit that he was further from the evangelical ideal than is generally believed—an ideal which, half a century before his birth, had had a wonderful renewal in St Francis and his followers. Dante did not have the essential virtues requisite for a true Christian, or else these virtues were opposed and weakened in him by passions which were in direct contrast.

The Gospel enjoins chastity, and Dante was given to love-affairs not altogether Platonic and poetic, and, according to his own son, to sensuality. The Gospel enjoins humility, and Dante was proud beyond measure, even to the point of praising himself in his works. The Gospel enjoins uncomplaining acceptance of poverty, and Dante bewailed the loss of his property and the scantiness of his resources. The Gospel enjoins forgiveness, and Dante yielded, at least in thought and in words, to feelings of revenge. The Gospel enjoins love for one's enemies, and Dante gave vent to his hatred for his adversaries in cruel words and atrocious imaginings. The Gospel enjoins kindness and gentleness, and Dante, at least in the scenes of the *Inferno*, showed himself unnecessarily cruel against some of those unfortunates who were already being severely punished by Divine Justice. The Gospel points to little children as an example to be followed, and Dante, from the heights of his rationalism, holds them in contempt.

This continual contrast between Christian perfection and the qualities which we find in the poet, gives us food for thought. No one thinks that Dante ought to have been a saint; but the divergence between what is demanded of the Christian and the attitude we find in Dante is greater than would be expected in the truly divine poet of the *Paradiso*. It is not enough to say that he was, as I believe him to have been, a faithful observant. He himself wrote in the *Convivio* that 'God did not wish us to be religious if not with the heart.'[1]

We must add to all this his custom, almost sacrilegious, of applying to human beings and even to himself expressions and words of praise, reserved in the Scriptures and in the liturgy solely for Christ or the Virgin. Furthermore, the deification of Beatrice, in whatever way the symbol may be interpreted, is always a puzzling and disturbing question.

This tendency toward deifying mortals belongs properly to paganism, and there are not lacking in Dante other signs of a mind which seems pagan by nature— such as his admiration, wholly of the ancient Roman stamp, for the *civitas* and the Empire; and his inclination to make pagans (often on slight foundations) participants in the Christian salvation—as Cato, Statius, Trajan, Rhipeus. There was in Dante not only the passion of the new humanist, but also the conviction perhaps that the just men who had lived in Paganism had been treated too severely by the Church; and he wished, so far as in him lay, to remedy it. And yet Virgil,

[1] *Conv.* IV, xxviii, 9.

the 'sweet father' who conducts him to Beatrice, is condemned to return to Limbo.

Dante's admiration for pagan poetry was unbounded and, in a Christian, exaggerated. Not only does he people the Inferno with mythological and poetic figures taken from the ancient poets—Cerberus, Minos, Phlegyas, Geryon, and so forth; but when he prays for aid in his undertaking, he addresses invocations to the Muses and Apollo[1] and not to that God who in the Gospel left to the world the loftiest examples of poetry. That the greatest Christian poet should constantly invoke Calliope, Urania, or even Euterpe[2] produces, to tell the truth, a rather curious effect. Dante believed himself to be descended from Roman stock, and it really seems at times that there lives again in him one of the pagan poets of the Augustan age.

There remains the other question—In what sense was Dante a Catholic? Dante professed Catholicism with sincerity, and followed by preference the theological teachings of Thomas Aquinas who is even to-day the pre-eminent master of Christian philosophy. But to understand the Catholicism of Dante it is necessary to examine not only that which to-day is recognized as Catholic by most people. Dante did not believe that all was well within the Church. He did not hold that all the priests and monks were saints. On the contrary, he went so far as to put popes and bishops into the Inferno. Nor was he of the opinion that Christianity consists solely of indulgences, of unconditional absolution, and

[1] Inf. II, 7; Purg. I, 7 ff.; Par. XVIII, 82 ff.; XXIII, 55 ff.
[2] The invocation to the 'virgins sacrosanct' and to Urania, Purg. XXIX, 37–42; to Calliope, Purg. I, 9. Some commentators believe that the 'diva Pegasea' of Par. XVIII, 82, is Euterpe.

of caressing pity. He had a horror of sin and frankly detested sinners. His Catholicism, in short, included a free criticism of the clergy and a spirit sharply aggressive. Dante, then, is the opposite of the modern pattern of the right-thinking Catholic.

We must keep in mind also that his boldly critical attitude towards pontiffs and prelates was not, even in his time, entirely original. Only after the Counter-Reformation, and especially after the Vatican Council of 1870, there arose in the Church a spirit of optimistic reverence, at least in the writings, toward the clergy and ecclesiastical authority even in matters which do not properly concern either the doctrine of the Church or the form of worship. Obedience in matters of dogma and discipline is right and necessary since it is implicit in the intrinsic nature of the Church; but perhaps the excessive timidity of the laity in all those questions which are outside the theology, the mysteries, and the liturgy, has not helped to hasten the necessary victory of Catholicism in the world. I fear that this lack of internal criticism is due not so much to an increase of reverence as to a cooling off of the spirit. It has facilitated from outside the Church criticism by non-Catholics, and has given occasion for apostasy, abandonment, increasing indifference, detachment.

Wherever there is love, there is also a desire to make better, and consequently a zeal for accusations and contests.

Every living body is subject to corruption if there is no courageous physician who from time to time cauterizes without pity. The Church, founded by Christ and aided by the Holy Spirit, is immortal and incorruptible in its principle and in its essence; but it is formed by men who are weak and fallible creatures. The Church always received a rekindling of life from outside persecutions and even from heresies; but above all from those Christians, whether they were saints like Peter Damian or simple scholars like Gerson, who dared to put their finger on the sores of their time. One of the physicians, and perhaps the most pitiless and the most famous, was the poet Dante Alighieri.

BOOK FOUR
Work

THE TWO SUNS

HEN Cacciaguida, in the heaven of Mars, looks forward through time, and praises his descendant for having, in his exile, made of himself a party by himself, that is, for having turned his back on all factions, it is no mere play on words, no boast on the part of the poet.

Dante, like all great spirits, could not long ally himself with any faction. In truth, he was neither the 'fugitive Ghibelline' of Foscolo nor the 'White Guelph' of Isidoro Del Lungo. Both by family tradition and by love for his native place, he was a Guelph during the years of his life in Florence. During his exile, especially after the coming of Henry, he appeared by the necessity of events and of his banishment, a Ghibelline. In reality, as well as in the *De Monarchia*, he is beyond Guelphism and Ghibellinism. A lofty mind like his could not remain at ease in those prison-shades of partisan intrigue.

Absolute Guelphism, expressed in the book of Ægidius Romanus and in the Bull of Boniface, *Unam Sanctam*, demanded the complete subordination to the papacy of all monarchs, including the Emperor. Absolute Ghibellinism, on the contrary, demanded that the prelates should receive their authority from the Emperor rather than from Rome, and saw in the Pope little more than the Emperor's chaplain.

Dante goes beyond both theories, fixing his attention on the good of humanity which both Pope and Emperor ought, in the last analysis, to serve. He distinguishes the two chief ends of man—earthly happiness and heavenly beatitude; and as basis for this distinction he affirms the mutual independence of the two powers which ought to lead the way to those two fundamental beatitudes. There should be two universal rulers: one for all men as members of a mundane society; the other for all men as souls destined to make part of an ultramundane society. The Emperor does not derive his authority from the Pope, nor is the Pope in any way subject to the Emperor. The Pope owes counsel and aid to the Emperor in spiritual matters; the Emperor owes reverence to the Pope as a son to a father.

Dante, with his Latin and Tuscan liking for clear and distinct ideas, boldly separates the earth from the sky. He separates political life from religious life; the search for the peace necessary in human life from the search for the salvation which concerns the life after death; the realm of justice from the realm of charity; the journey of the living from the triumph of the immortals.

To the two aims, the two ways, the two ideals, correspond the two sovereigns: the Pope, at the head of his bishops, who bases his sacred authority on Revelation and Theology; the Emperor, with the kings subordinate to him, who bases his human authority on Tradition (the Roman Empire) and Philosophy (*philosophica documenta*).

A magnificent conception which was called and is still called Utopian, but which really corresponds to the needs and desires of mankind. These two universal authorities, both supreme, each autonomous but concordant in essentials, which promise to the human race peace on earth and salvation in heaven, the one by means of Reason and Justice, the other by the light of Mysticism and the fire of Charity, are both necessary to the man who thinks of something besides his stomach, his shop, and the interests of his city.

Dante disliked the political meddling and the avarice of the prelates and the popes, but at the same time he saw in Boniface, even in Boniface struck down by French insolence, another Jesus injured by a new Pilate and a new Caiaphas. The Pope ought not to interfere with the government of the people, but the Emperor and the kings ought not to entangle themselves in the government of souls. The Pope is intangible and cannot be deposed by the Emperor, just as the Emperor cannot be driven from his throne at the will of the Pope. Both Pope and Emperor should give an accounting only to God.

From the Catholic point of view Dante's theory seems, in some respects, disquieting and dangerous. Cardinal Del Poggetto had some reason after the poet's death for causing the three books of the *De Monarchia* to be burned; they are essentially a reply to the famous Bull of Pope Boniface and a concise condemnation of every sort of theocracy.

The complete separation of the political from the religious power, advocated by Dante, is the first principle in that theory of the autonomy of the State which in modern times has changed with the Reform and the anti-clericalism of the Emperor Joseph II into the intrusion of the State into the affairs of the Church. Later still, in the French Revolution and in the Russian Revolution, we see the attempt of the State to substitute itself for the Church and to deny it all right to existence. Dante's theory, then, was a first step in progressive anti-clericalism: the State ought to be independent of the Church; the State has a right to supervise and direct the Church; the State transfers to itself the greater part of the offices of the Church; the State ignores the Church; the State ought to suppress the Church.

We might answer Dante that in the concrete man it is not always possible to separate that which concerns his present terrestrial and civil life from that which concerns his future celestial life. Men must earn heaven while living on earth. The terrestrial life, for ascetics and devout Christians, is only a painful preparation in a lower world for the higher life of heaven. If this life is wretched, full of suffering and sacrifice, it matters little —or so much the better! The present life is short, it is nothing more than a hard examination to be passed. What counts is the other life, the life eternal. In order to merit eternal life, we may find ourselves in given moments unable to fulfil our duty as citizens and as subjects when it is opposed to the duties laid down by the Gospel. Indeed for mystics, the most certain way of ensuring future beatitude is to withdraw entirely from the world about them, from all its laws and obligations, to retreat to a solitude or shut themselves up in a cloister, and consecrate themselves wholly to contemplation.

But Dante, who is both pagan and Christian, does not lose sight of the obligations and the purposes of the practical and social life which cœnobites have been unable to abolish. In order to construct his book logically, he is forced to separate himself from two saints who were dear to him and who had often been his teachers, St Augustine and St Thomas. For St Thomas the earthly good of the individual and of society is secondary to the eternal good; and, therefore, the authority which conducts us to this good, the priesthood, is superior to all others. Dante, on the contrary, assigns an almost equal value to the two felicities, and consequently to the two monarchs. In order to demonstrate his thesis he has recourse to Averroïstic principles: that the human intellect, since it can know all things perceptible to the senses, *ought* to know them all; but as this is impossible for the individual, it results that humanity as a whole knows them. Therefore there is a social end independent of the individual. And the distinction between religious truth valid only in the supernatural sphere, and political truth valid in civil communities, presents a certain analogy with the Averroïstic doctrine of the two truths.

Dante, then, in order to write the second book of the *De Monarchia* and to make the legitimacy of the Roman Empire directly derivable from God, had virtually to contradict the famous indictment which St Augustine wrote in the *De Civitate Dei*. For Dante, the earthly city —and in this he is profoundly Roman, or pagan—is not the city of the devil but a city almost as sacred as the city of God, and it has its rational foundations and its special virtues.

As we follow the poet's argument, which is indicated in the *Convivio* and repeated in the *De Monarchia*, we become aware that the contrast between the two conceptions is less marked than it appeared at first. According to Dante—and here he returns to an idea cherished by Augustine—man has a right to happiness. But there are two kinds of happiness: happiness in this brief vigil which we call life, and happiness in the other life. To this last we are guided by the Old and New Testaments and by the Pope. But the Gospel is not so universally accepted and practised that we can dispense with a sure guide who will lead the way to earthly happiness. Man wishes to be happy here below, but too often within him dwells the accursed love of riches, of power, of honours, which sets man against man, town against town, nation against nation. In the midst of such confusion, discords, and wars, man cannot be happy, because the first condition for happiness is peace. There is need, therefore, of a supreme authority set above the cities, the peoples, and the princes, which, lighted by philosophy, inspired by justice, free from all covetousness, will hinder dissensions, rivalries, and wars. This authority is the Emperor. Possessing all, he desires no more; being above all princes in honour and legitimacy, he fears no one; invested by God Himself and crowned by the Pope, he has full authority over all men and is subject to none. He alone, therefore, can conduct the human race to perfect peace, to happiness.

In the mind of Dante, the Empire is not so much a glorious abstraction as a guarantee against war. Dante hates dissensions and conflicts. Dante is a pacifist, and desires the Emperor because the Empire means peace. Even Christ, according to Dante, would not descend to earth until the world, under the imperial rule of Augustus, found itself after so long a time enjoying perfect peace.[1] As the complete pacification of mankind, that is, the abolition of hate and the declaration of love,

---

[1] *Conv.* IV, v, 8. The idea of peace returns constantly to Dante's mind. Cf. *Conv.* IV, iv, 4; IV, vi, 17; *De Mon.* I, iv, 2 ff.; xi, 14, etc.

is one of the greatest aims of Christianity also, it is clear
that Dante's pacifist ideal, urged upon the imperial
authority, was easily reconcilable with the aspirations
of his Christian heart. In brief, the Emperor is necessary
because men are not yet true Christians. If the teaching
of Christ had uprooted from their souls 'the blind greed
which bewitches them,' there would be no strife and
carnage and, consequently, no need of laws and emperors.

Unfortunately, those very men who ought to set a
good example and guide mankind to evangelical perfection, which means before all else the renunciation of
riches, have betrayed the Gospel and sought to make
themselves rich and powerful. Both the Church and the
Empire have been guilty. Constantine, by ceding a part
of the Empire to the Pope, was the first author of the
evil; and if the popes had been true followers of Christ,
they would have refused that gift. Instead, they have
begged for more, and have sought to displace the
Emperor and substitute themselves as supreme authority
over the princes. This usurpation, added to a thirst for
riches, has brought about a decline in the pontificate,
and rendered less and less efficacious its apostolic work
of spiritual renewal. Therefore, the complete separation
of the two powers is necessary. He who carries the
crosier ought not to carry the sword. The 'confusion of
rules' is the ruin of humanity, because to the many
causes of war already existing one more is added, contrary to reason and the Gospel. Kings are needed to
curb men and to force them to observe the laws; the
Emperor is needed to curb the ambitions of the kings
and to uproot every desire for war.

When Cæsar and Peter are equally obeyed, but in

two spheres strictly delimited, the world will be at peace and mankind will be happy in this life and certain of happiness in the life to come. Neither Pope nor Emperor has the right to give commands except in so far as they contribute to the spiritual and temporal good of their subjects. They are legitimate masters only in so far as they are the first servants of the human race under the all-seeing eye of God. The one is no greater than the other. They are two suns destined to illumine the dark forest of the earth. If they do not shine in full concord, man suffers and comes to grief. Upon them lies the terrible responsibility of the good and evil in the world.

Dante, raised on high by the majesty of his genius, takes his place above the one and the other, and pronounces them both unfaithful to their divine offices—the Emperor because he is remiss or timid; the Pope because he usurps property and powers not his own. Dante teaches them what they ought to be and what they ought to do for the happiness of mankind.

Neither Guelph nor Ghibelline, Dante forms by himself alone the party of the disregarded prophets. But he is convinced that he speaks in the name of the greatest authorities that he knows: Reason, History, the Gospel. His conception went beyond political science; it was Utopia. But it was among those Utopias which the greatest minds will dream of till the end of Time and which suffice for the glory of one man and one age.

PROFESSOR DANTE

AY his august shade pardon me, but I cannot refrain from saying it: with less genius there would have been in Dante the makings of an intrepid professor. I do not say teacher—for he was and is still a very great teacher—but rather a professor, just that! His genius as a poet got the upper hand of his pedagogical talents, but not always. The professor remained in the shade, overpowered but not killed.

Some think that Dante taught publicly at Verona and Ravenna, but we have no proofs and the most wary Dantologists do not believe it. It is unimportant. Whoever is born to be a professor carries his *cathedra* with him, invisible and permanent; and the great hall of a palace, the tavern, or the street serves him in place of lecture-room and university. Then there are the books which he writes; these can take on the method and the appearance of formal lessons, as often happens in Dante's writings.

All books teach or try to teach, but there are many ways of doing it. Dante's way very often recalls the methods of the professor in his lecture-room. It may well be that this meticulous method, founded on definitions, distinctions, and formal disputations, was suggested to him by the scholastics. The scholastics really taught school, and many of their writings are their courses of study or summaries of lessons prepared for their students.

Dante, on the contrary, is the lonely artist who writes in the vernacular Italian for everyone, and who yet feels impelled to stop every moment to give a lesson. The *Convivio* is in large part a series of brief lessons on morals, rhetoric, philosophy, and the history of philosophy, with an occasional interlude on politics or religion. The *De Vulgari Eloquentia* is an actual course of lessons, left incomplete, on linguistics and metrics, not without instruction also in theology and philosophy. The *De Monarchia* is a treatise on political science. The *Epistle* to Can Grande is an excellent lecture on the underlying meanings of literature. The *Quæstio de Aqua et Terra* is a public dissertation, serious and ample in treatment, on natural philosophy and physics.

In the *Commedia*, too, the professor appears at every turn, especially in the *Purgatorio* and the *Paradiso*. He uses every pretext to insert in the religious epopee of salvation a little lesson on ancient or modern history, on æsthetics, moral practice, astronomy, or the tenets of the Church. Yielding still further to this invincible passion for teaching, our poet pretends that he himself is a pupil and listens to the learned lectures which he himself puts into the mouth of Virgil, Beatrice, Father Adam, and others. He often uses figures of speech which recall the schools, like the famous one of the 'bachelor who arms himself but does not speak' (*Par.* XXIV, 46). Toward the end of the *Paradiso* (XXIV–XXVI), the starry heaven is transformed into an examinations-hall where Dante is methodically questioned before being admitted to the supreme visions. St Peter, St James, and St John examine the poet who answers, of course, astonishingly well. Only then Beatrice opens to him the entire vista in order to qualify him to contemplate the angelic choirs and the mysteries of the Trinity.

This pedagogical mania of Alighieri's corresponds, in essentials, to his apostolic design of enlightening his contemporaries and posterity with the truths in which he believed; but in part, especially in his prose writings which are more definitely doctrinal, it was the natural outpouring of one who has discovered new lands and rejoices to make them known to others.

Almost up to Dante's time, learning was a monopoly of the clergy and was almost always transmitted in Latin. Dante is one of the first laymen who mastered theological, philosophical, and classical culture, and who felt himself compelled to share these shining riches with his brothers in that vulgar tongue which was the only language understood by everyone. In an age of universal culture he could have spared himself the copiousness and the insistence of his lessons. In the midst of a people who were still almost ignorant, since the highest learning was the property of the men of the Church and was shut away from others by the barrier of Latin, Alighieri perceived the duty of making himself not only a prophet and master of life, but also a professor. He knew himself to be a poet and a great poet, but he wished to be also *Præceptor Italiæ*, schoolmaster to all Italy. What seems at times the pedantic prolixity of a parvenu of learning, happy to display his newly acquired treasures, is in Dante the fulfilment of a duty and, at the same time, a necessity in order that he may be the better understood by those unlettered laymen to whom he addressed himself. And the coruscating prophet—perhaps with more complacency than could have been expected from him—frequently brought himself to don, in prose and verse, the professorial gown.

DANTE, THE SORCERER

ON 1319, Matteo and Galeazzo Visconti, lords of Milan, wished to bring about the death of Pope John XXII by means of sorcery. They summoned a priest, Bartolommeo Canolati, reputed a sorcerer. He refused, however, to lend himself to this undertaking, and refused a second time, a year later, when he was called by the Visconti to Piacenza. Then Galeazzo, perhaps to excite the professional jealousy of the 'sorcerer'-priest, told him that they had sent for Master Alighieri of Florence to do the business —*magistrum Dante Aleguiro de Florencia pro isto eodem negocio pro quo rogo te.*

Probably there was no truth in the statement that Alighieri had been summoned. Nevertheless, it is clear from a notarial document that in 1320 Dante was thought, or possibly was thought, an expert in the black arts.

He was not the first learned man who had such a reputation. Virgil was so reputed; and so was Pope Sylvester II, and Roger Bacon, the famous Franciscan, who was contemporary with Alighieri. In those days it was sufficient for a man to have a reputation for extraordinary learning and to appear constantly absorbed in solitary investigations and meditations in order for the common people, and not only the common people, to give him the name of sorcerer. In the case of the Visconti it was something more. Dante had boasted, in certain verses written in the vulgar tongue, of having descended into hell. It was known also that he did not love Pope John XXII, against whom he had vented his wrath (or was about to do so) in Canto XVIII of the *Paradiso*.

We may recall, however, that Dante had already placed in the Inferno diviners and sorcerers, and that, therefore, he did not intend to have anything in common with them. On the other hand, this statement is valid only up to a certain point. Dante, as a Christian and a moralist, put into the Inferno every sort of sinner; but as a man—and the *Commedia* furnishes evidence of this—he himself was not guiltless of some of those sins. For example, among the lustful and the proud, to mention only these, he must have felt himself a fellow-sinner rather than a judge. In the *bolgia* where 'magic frauds' are punished, when our poet sees the sorcerers with their faces turned to the back so that their tears run down over their buttocks, he is moved more than usual and begins to weep. And it is just at this point that Virgil pronounces the pitiless condemnation of every pity. Those tears of Dante's, shall we say? were the natural compassion of a kindly soul. Or were they the tears of remorse? In short, was Dante entirely innocent among those ravishers of the future?

To me it seems that he was not. We can and we ought to distinguish between the common and vulgar fortune-teller, like Asdente, and the noble prophet like Joachim of Flora, enskied by Alighieri. But in each of them the primary wish is identical—the desire to announce, or the pretence of foretelling, things which have not yet happened. In the fortune-teller there is greed of gain, a foolish itch for notoriety, the aims of the charlatan.

254

In the prophet there is inspiration (sometimes supernatural), purity of purpose, and no self-interest. But
there is always a certain fellowship between the two as
there is between the sleep-walker of the market-place
and the witches in *Macbeth*, or between the bastard and
the legitimate son. Dante was a prophet and so proclaimed himself. His *Inferno* begins with the prophecy
of the Veltro. The *Purgatorio* ends with the prophecy of
the DXV. In the *Paradiso* his prophecies are confirmed
by Beatrice and St Peter.

We can go beyond this. Equally with workers in the
occult, Dante believed in astrology. He definitely admits
a direct influence of the stars on human affairs. 'And
since the composition of the seed,' he writes in the
Convivio, 'can be better or worse . . . and the disposition of the Heavens toward this effect can be good,
better, and excellent (varying according to the constella-
tions which are continually shifting), it results that
from the human seed and from these influences a soul
perfect or less perfect is produced. . . .'[1]

Even the birth of Christ was due, according to our
astrologer, to the favourable disposition of the stars:
'since the heavens began to turn, they were never in
better disposition than when He who made them and
rules them descended thence to earth; as by virtue of
their arts the astrologers can still calculate.'[2] And it is
the stars which announce and approve the early advent of
the One sent by God. Beatrice affirms it in the famous
passage:

[1] *Conv.* IV, xxi, 7. On the influence of the stars, see *Purg.* XVI, 73 ff.:
'The heavens initiate your movements.'
[2] *Conv.* IV, v, 7.

ch'io veggio certamente, e però il narro,
a darne tempo già stelle propinque,
secure d'ogn'intoppo e d'ogni sbarro,
    nel quale un cinquecento diece e cinque,
    messo di Dio, anciderà la fuia
    con quel gigante che con lei delinque.[1]

I see with certainty, and therefore I announce it, stars even now
moving near, secure from every opposition and hindrance, to appoint us
a time at which a Five hundred, Ten, and Five, a DXV, sent by God,
shall slay the infamous woman and that giant who sins with her.

This means, so the commentators explain, that stars
are about to rise which, free from every opposing and
unpropitious circumstance, will by their influence
render the time of their ascendancy favourable and
opportune for the coming of the messenger of God.[2]
Dante believed that he himself had been born under a
favourable conjunction of stars. Brunetto Latini is made
to say:

. . . . . . Se tu segui tua stella
non puoi fallire a glorïoso porto.[3]

If you follow your star, you cannot fail to reach the glorious port.

When Dante has mounted to the Eighth Heaven and
discovers the constellation of the Twins, beneath which
he was born, he breaks forth into a hymn of astrological
gratitude:

O glorïose stelle, o lume pregno
di gran virtù, dal quale io riconosco
tutto, qual che si sia, il mio ingegno,
    con voi nasceva e s'ascondeva vosco
    quelli ch'è padre d'ogni mortal vita,
    quand'io senti' di prima l'aere tosco;
    e poi, quando mi fu grazia largita
    d'entrar nell'alta rota che vi gira,
    la vostra regïon mi fu sortita.

---

[1] *Purg.* XXXIII, 40–45. [2] Vandelli's paraphrase.
[3] *Inf.* XV, 55–56.

A voi divotamente ora sospira
l'anima mia, per acquistar virtute
al passo forte che a sè la tira.[1]

O glorious stars, O light imbued with great virtue, from whose
influence I acknowledge that I have received all my genius, whatever it
may be; with you was rising and setting he who is father of all mortal
life, when first I breathed the Tuscan air; and then, when grace was
granted me to enter within the lofty wheel which turns you, your region
was assigned to me. To you my soul devoutly breathes the hope that she
may acquire virtue for the difficult task which draws her to itself.

Dante, it is clear, thought that he had been born under
a favourable constellation, and to it he addresses prayers
that he may receive new power.

We cannot, therefore, think Galeazzo Visconti entirely
wrong if in the mysterious explorer of the Hereafter, the
prophet and astrologer, he saw a supposed worker of
evil spells.

But Dante has an art no less wonderful and even more
powerful than that of the sorcerers. His magic art,
which is one with his poetic art, is necromancy.
Alighieri is the greatest necromancer in all literature.
All the characters in the *Divina Commedia*, except the
living and breathing visitor to the Other World, are
spectres of the dead, evoked with such effectiveness
through the powerful magic of Dante's art that even
to-day they appear alive to our eyes. Ulysses had to
pour blood at the entrance to Hades in order to give
some moments of life to those who had passed into the
realm of the dead. For Dante the power of his imagination sufficed to reanimate those dead bodies and to make
them speak in such a way that they seem more alive than
the living. In his own way Dante triumphs over death.

[1] *Par.* XXII, 112–123.

From the three kingdoms of the shades he has drawn forth those whom he wished. Supreme sorcerer, by the enchantment of his verse, he has brought them back among us on the earth; and here they will remain, phantoms alive and speaking, as long as there is a man able to understand his poem.

THE DEAD RESTORED TO LIFE

ANTE is the greatest poet of the dead. But on careful examination, we see that in his poem there is no such thing as death.

I mean, first of all, physical death; the fearful dissolution of the flesh, the decay of the body. That terrifying vision of the final destruction which appears so repellent and violent in the prose of Innocent III, in the poetry of Jacopone da Todi, in the frescoes of the Camposanto at Pisa; a vision which continues until the seventeenth century in the realistic and terrifying pages of John Donne, of Father Segneri, and of Daniel Bartoli—this is an aspect of death never found in the *Commedia*. In Dante, we are in the realm of the dead, but there is no charnel-house, no ossuary, no vermiculous destruction of the body, no uncovering of tombs. We are among the dead, but there is no stench of dead bodies, no whiteness of skeletons. All of Dante's dead have a body either tortured or shining, but in appearance whole, although not solid. Some of the dead are changed into branches, others into serpents, others into light and flame. But nowhere is there the evil smell of the cemetery or of the corpse in decay.

The dead of Dante resemble the living in almost every way. They speak, they remember, they lament, they prophesy, they teach. The earth and the life of earth are present to them even in the heights of the *Paradiso*. They are souls who suffer, hope, rejoice. They are not the dead who cause shuddering and fear. Only Buonconte gives a thought to his body dragged along by the waters, and Manfred to his corpse buried beneath the cairn. But all appear as if death had been only a very brief pause in life, like a simple moving from a temporary dwelling to a permanent one.

Dante, differing from the ascetics and the moralists before and after him, does not wish to teach the true life of the soul through the pitiable spectacle of the body. He does not wish to rouse terror, or rather he wishes to rouse it, but without the display of the charnel-house, representing for his purpose the torments of the souls in the new world which they inhabit. Not the earth, but the tombs are forgotten. Even from the burning sepulchres of the heresiarchs, the damned souls lift themselves to speak, upright and whole.

Why has Dante made no use of the fearful theme so dear to the ascetics of every age? Because the decay of the body, the vile and perishable sheath of the soul, has little importance for one who believes in a double survival.

Dante, as a Christian, believed in the everlasting life of the soul in Heaven. As a poet he believed in life perpetuated on earth by glory. The ancients coveted this last above all things. Ascetics desired only the first. Dante had a lively faith in both. Man, as he believed, does not die. He continues to live here below in his own works and in the memories of men. He continues to live hereafter either in torture or in beatitude. The death of the body is for him only an unimportant episode, the passing from one to another form of life.

Dante was too spiritual to give great importance to the abhorrent destiny of our mortal body. When the soul has departed, the body remains an insensible sheath which will be devoured by worms. But the soul knows nothing of that horrible dissolution, and does not suffer. To exhibit to the living the open tombs with their carrion excarnated and deliquescent might be a preacher's expedient to inspire humility or thoughts of the transitoriness of earthly things; but it was not worthy of a philosopher. Dante supplants these visions of the tomb by introducing us among dead who seem alive, among dead who have still the appearance and feelings of the living.

He was led all the more toward this because at the period when he began to write the *Commedia*, the beings most loved by him were already in the kingdom of the dead. His mother was dead, his father was dead; Beatrice was dead, the woman of his first love; dead his first and best-loved master, Brunetto; dead the first of his friends, Guido. All the life of his affections had been transferred to the other world. Those who had loved him and whom he had loved were now among the dead. In expectation of seeing them again, he wished to resuscitate them in fancy, to treat them as living, to move toward them in anticipation.

In this desire is to be found, I think, one of the initial motives influencing Dante's choice of theme—the journey in the realms of death; a theme common in literature from the time of the *Odyssey*. In order to call mankind to the true salvation, he could have written, as so many others did, a treatise on morals, a history of the world, a guide to mysticism. But these would have been abstract works and of little efficacy. As artist and as poet, he chose the world of the dead because it would permit him to give manifest life and potent words to the shades called forth in the poem. It is for this reason that in Dante the dead are alive, and are indeed the only living, freed as they now are for ever from the ephemeral prison-house of flesh and bone.

Nietzsche, who passes for a profound thinker, has defined Dante, in the *Twilight of the Idols*, as 'the hyena who composes poetry among the tombs.' The definition may seem a happy one or, at least, to have a semblance of truth; but it proves that Nietzsche did not read the *Divina Commedia*, or that he read it carelessly and hastily. The hyena feeds on dead bodies, and Dante is the opposite of a necrophagist. He does not give sepulture within himself to the dead, but he gives new life to those no longer living. He restores the dead to life, it may be for only a moment and with only a word, in that world so terribly alive, the world of the imagination, the world of eternal resurrection. To the disembodied shades he restores a body; to those mute through long silence he gives a voice. And he makes use of those dead to whom he has given an aspect of life, to teach the way of a nobler life to those still living. Dante, in short, not only writes poetry in the purely literary sense, he creates.

Reflecting on Nietzsche's known jealousy, I have found the key to his contemptuous judgement of Dante, given in these words from *Ecce Homo*: 'Dante compared to Zarathustra is only a believer and not a man who first creates the truth, a spirit which dominates the world, a fatality.'

Let us examine each word. 'Compared to Zarathustra': the clamorous prophet, born of Nietzsche's nostalgia, does not fear comparison with the Florentine and Catholic prophet.

He 'is only a believer,' that is, a *minus habens*, an unfortunate, a primitive. Nietzsche also is a 'believer,' but he does not lower himself, as Dante did, to believe in Christ. He believes in himself, he believes in Dionysius, he believes in the coming of the Superman.

'Not a man who first creates the truth.' Truth is not something to be sought for; it is not something which stands of itself, eternal, outside and above man. But man himself, a super-Protagoras, must create it in his own fashion, make it to his own measure, in order that it may serve to satisfy both his boasting and his extravagant speculations.

'Not a spirit which dominates the world.' An answer to this insolent and fallacious declaration has been made by a fellow-countryman of Nietzsche, Friedrich Gundolf, the greatest German critic of our time. In the introduction to his book on Goethe, he recognizes two great types of creators—the introverted and the expansive. The poet who, according to Gundolf, best corresponds to the first type is Dante. He continues, 'The introverted creator tends to transform the whole world into his own Ego, to remake it according to his own inmost image. He feels his Ego as the centre and symbol of the world, as happened in the case of Dante.'

Was Nietzsche, who was secretly jealous of Jesus in the field of religion, of Socrates in the field of philosophy, of Wagner in the field of art, jealous also of Dante, at least momentarily, in the field of poetry?[1]

---

[1] 'Nietzsche a été jaloux du Christ, jaloux jusqu'à la folie.' A. Gide, *Dostoievski*. Paris, Plon, 1923, p. 116. On the secret affinity of Nietzsche with those whom he opposed most violently, see E. Bertram, *Nietzsche. Versuch einer Mythologie*. Berlin, 1919.

40

THE *COMMEDIA* AS REVENGE

E could give, and others have given, a number of definitions of the *Divina Commedia*. Each of them, if not altogether senseless and foolish, is probably true in what it affirms, if not always true in what it tends to exclude. In a youthful essay, I myself ventured to define the poem in a phrase which seemed to me fresh and comprehensive. I called it 'a Last Judgement anticipated.'[1] I do not wish to-day to forswear or refute that ambitious definition. It may stand beside the others because it serves to recall one of the aspects under which we may study the *opus maius* of Dante.

But a poem like that, constructed by the patient and impassioned work of years, by a mind greater than the greatest in so many qualities, cannot be reduced to a single phrase. The aims which the poet set for himself were undoubtedly many, and there are likewise many aspects and characteristics which we can discover in the poem according to the emphasis we place upon one or the other of its elements.

One of the most original definitions of the poem, in my opinion, is that offered by Piero Misciattelli. The *Divina Commedia*, he says, 'is nothing other than a miracle performed by the Blessed Virgin to save the soul of Dante; a miracle glorified in verse by the sinner devoted to Mary. . . . Who first was moved to pity

[1] In *Dante vicario d'Iddio*, published in 1907; now reprinted in *Ritratti Italiani*. Florence, Vallecchi, 1932, pp. 7–17.

264

by Dante's lot? Who averted the danger of the "harsh judgement" hanging over him? The gentle Lady of Heaven, Mary. The *Divina Commedia* may be called a miracle of the love of Mary.'[1]

Such a conception is far from being arbitrary. It has the merit besides of putting into relief one of the starting-points of Dante's inspiration. Nevertheless, it is not possible to consider the *Commedia* solely as an *ex voto* to the Madonna. It is that certainly, but not only that. The sacred poem is a forest, and in the forest is a great abundance of plants and animals. It is a populous city, and a city cannot be reduced to a church-tower. It is the superposition of three realms, of three worlds; and no formula, however ingenious, clever, and illuminating, can include them all. But this does not mean that we should give up trying to find it. The whole truth, as complex as the work, will result from the sum of the multiple points of view, in so far as they do not contradict or nullify one another.

We might, for example, suggest a definition of the *Divina Commedia* which would emphasize especially the original subjective impulse which led Dante to write it. Every work of art is, in addition to many other things, an imaginary compensation which the artist offers to his unsatisfied soul. He who cannot fight writes a bellicose book. A man unloved consoles himself with poems or romances of love. One who cannot dominate the nations by force, tries to seduce and conquer them with his music.

[1] *Miracoli della gloriosa Vergine Maria*, edited with an introduction by P. Misciattelli. Milan, Treves, 1929, pp. xxxviii–xlii. On Dante's worship of the Madonna, see P. Domenico Bassi, *Maria nel poema di Dante.* Florence, Lib. Ed. Fior., 1931.

Applying this principle, we may define the *Divina
Commedia* as a retaliation and a revenge. Dante's temporal state did not measure up to his pride. Born of an
ancient family, he was poor and forced to take second
place. Desirous of excelling in the front rank, and of
commanding others, he had to content himself with
the duties of a subordinate and appear almost as a
beggar. He wished for the moral reform of the Church,
and became the victim of Boniface VIII. He hoped to
re-enter his native country, and his own city obstin-
ately repulsed him. He believed for a moment that
Henry VII might be the awaited deliverer, and then
saw the Emperor's undertaking come to a wretched
end.

Then was born in his mind the overpowering need of
a victorious recovery, of a revenge which should com-
pensate him for his humiliations and delusions. The
poor wandering pilgrim, compelled to accept the hospitality of the great, will judge from on high the kings
and emperors. The exile, victorious through the splendour of his poetry, will be recalled to Florence to receive the crown. The victim of Pope Boniface will
cause the covetous and simoniacal popes to be condemned by the voices of the saints. The humble
courtier of princes will make himself the announcer
and prophet of an approaching restoration of the world.
Inconspicuous, neglected, sacrificed in the temporal
order of the world, Dante will declare his unmeasured
greatness in the spiritual order. The *Divina Commedia*
is the proof of his claims; it is his refuge, his sublime
revenge. He is poor, but he offers as a gift that which
is worth more than gold. He is obscure, and one word

of his confers immortality. He was defeated in life, and reconquers a thousandfold in poetry.

Meanwhile he revenges himself for all his humiliations and all his injuries. He rends Florence which had banished him. He casts dishonour on Boniface who had caused his condemnation and exile. He distributes through the blackest circles of Hell his own enemies, the enemies of truth, and the enemies of the Empire. The power of his art is such that his vengeance goes on without end. The world which saw the birth of the poet is now dust and a few names. Dante alone is alive, proud, victorious.

41

HEAVEN AND EARTH

ANTE had the instinct and habit of greatness; not only of moral and intellectual greatness, but of that sort which seems to be bound up with the idea of quantity: a love of the immense and the immeasurable. It derived first of all from the very nature of his constructive and soaring genius—the spirit of an eagle which had at its service an architect of the universal and the sublime. It came to him also from the very air and attitude of mind of the period. The thirteenth century in which he was born, and which deserves much more than the fifteenth to be called the Renaissance, had seen the rise of the vast doctrinal system of Dante's master, St Thomas, and of those equally vast if less important of Roger Bacon, Vincent of Beauvais, and Brunetto Latini. The learned men of that time did not content themselves with essays, with contributions, and approaches. They were titanic, encyclopædic. They did not hesitate to undertake labours destined 'to describe the foundation of the whole Universe.'[1]

But perhaps no one undertook to weave and colour so immense a web as Alighieri did. Even more than most great men, he had the disposition to see and to think greatly. His impassioned imagination was scarcely content with the whole. If art, as someone has said, is an exaggeration, then no one was a greater artist than Dante. In his mind, a young girl becomes a divinity;

[1] *Inf.* XXXII, 8.

the little city of merchants, a terrestrial hell; a second-rate emperor becomes a new Moses, a new David, a Jove, a Titan, a second Christ. The Inferno is a gigantic crater which opens down to the centre of the earth. Purgatory is an immense mountain which rises from the unbroken expanse of ocean until, with the leafy boughs of the Earthly Paradise, it almost touches the first heaven.

Giants have a special attraction for Alighieri, whether they are imaginary and symbolic like the Old Man of Crete, monstrous like Geryon, arrogant and fulminating like Capaneus, terrible and rising tall as towers around the lowest pit of the Inferno like Nimrod, Ephialtes, Briareus, and Antæus. They make Dante shake with fear, but his imagination cannot picture them as less terrible. It almost seems as if he were attracted by that corporeal magnitude which suggests, even in these accursed giants, a confused idea of super-human majesty.

But the greatness most typical of Dante is not to be sought for so much in outward aspects and in imaginary creatures as in the conception of the poem as a whole. It is the only work among the great creations of human genius which really embraces in its plan and in the working out of that plan, the entire universe. That totality of subject-matter which appeared to be reserved for the vast compendiums of history, philosophy, and theology was transported successfully into poetry, for the first and last time, by Dante. There are poems and dramas which mingle together heaven and earth. In the *Iliad* we are present at assemblies of the gods on Olympus; in the *Odyssey* and in the *Æneid* we descend into Hades; in *Jerusalem Delivered* and in *Paradise Lost* we see intervention by celestial and infernal powers; in *Faust* there is a prologue in Heaven and an attempt to reach the mysterious realm of the Mothers. But these supernatural episodes remain fragments, incidental events, simple interludes: the poems and the characters who appear in them are almost always terrestrial. In the *Commedia*, on the contrary, there is all this present world but, even more, all the other world: the cavity of the earth, the other face of the earth, the nine heavens which revolve around it, and, finally, the supreme heaven, unimaginable and ineffable, where, radiant in its mystery, abides the triune Divinity.

As these three worlds are peopled by creatures who lived on earth and who remember the earth, and suffer or rejoice for what they did there, the poem reflects, almost as in a great mirror, all our life in all its manifestations, its activities, its sufferings, and its achievements. But in addition there is the life which is no longer life but death, which, in turn, has its own life, full of torture or of bliss; and there are all those worlds which are hidden from the eyes of the living—the world of the indifferent, the world of the blameless unredeemed, the world of the eternally damned, the world of those to whom liberation has been promised, the world of the blessed and the saints, the world of the angelic hierarchies and of the Virgin, the world and the super-world of the Love which moves every world. All the universe visible and invisible, physical and metaphysical, human and divine, subterranean and astral, is contained in the *Commedia*. All is there—from the lizard which runs across the road, to Eve, the ancient mother of the living; from the lark which sings as it rises from the furrow, to the Thrones and Dominations; from the little child who seeks its mother, to the Virgin Mother, daughter of her Son; from the 'evil worm' with the three crushing mouths, to the intolerable vision of the Trinity.

The history of the world from the fall of Adam to the latest misdeed in Romagna; biblical, classical, and contemporary history—all is contained, in allusions and flashes, in the three canticles of the *Commedia*. In addition, these contain, in fragments, a *summa theologica*, a treatise on cosmography, a *speculum* of Nature in all her aspects. Men of all races, of all times, of all religious faiths, people this epopee at once funereal and exultant; and all the beasts of the earth and birds of the air, real or symbolic, appear there.

Even to-day Dante's poem remains, in the universality of its subject-matter, the vastest of all those which the human mind has conceived and created. Works exist which try to represent, by means of legendary or realistic adventures, almost the whole life of man. But the *Orlando Furioso*, *Don Quixote*, the plays of Shakespeare, *Candide*, and the *Comédie Humaine*, all deal with terrestrial things, and they have as background and setting the countries and cities of the earth; and as characters, living human beings. In the *Commedia*, on the contrary, is presented all the known life of the earth and, in addition, all the other life of the world beyond. Men of every sort appear; but we see also the shades of the dead, the demons, the angels, the three Divine Persons. No other human book up to the present has surpassed the *Divina Commedia* in the vastness of its theme. Only the Old and New Testaments, which we owe to the inspiration of God, surpass it and overshadow it.

It is not surprising that Dante, toward the close of his superhuman labour, should call his work

> . . . 'l poema sacro
> al quale ha posto mano e cielo e terra.[1]
>
> The sacred poem to which both heaven and earth have set their hand.

Commentators explain 'heaven and earth' in two ways: Dante means either that the poem describes heavenly and earthly things, or that he was aided in composing it by heavenly knowledge (revelation and theology) and by earthly knowledge (science and philosophy).

It seems to me, however, that Dante may have meant something more, that he may have been transported by a thought so majestic in its implications that the commentators have not perceived it or have not dared to express it. The poet does not say that heaven and earth are the subject of his poem, but that heaven and earth have 'set their hand' to a poem which is not merely human but 'sacred.' Dante himself, toward the end of the *Paradiso*, must have been amazed by the grandeur, the power, and the profundity of the work which had 'made him lean.' Perhaps the thought flashed upon him that he was not the sole author of the great poem. Might he not have thought that he had at times been inspired directly by God, to whom he wished to lead back humanity corrupted and gone astray? Had Heaven, perhaps, to aid him in his sublime labour, set its own hand to the task—Heaven and He who in other times

[1] *Par.* XXV, 1–2.

inspired Moses and David, the Prophets and the Evange-
lists? Might not the *Commedia*, also, be a prophecy,
almost a continuation of the New Testament? Had
the words been given to him almost by supernatural
dictation? Had he an unseen collaborator whom he
called 'heaven,' that is, God? Is it not right, therefore,
that his poem should be called 'sacred,' just as the
Scriptures are called sacred because they were inspired
by God?

Perhaps he himself trembled and hesitated when such
proud thoughts as these rose in his mind. So he con-
tented himself with merely glancing at them quickly
and then veiling them. But the soul of Dante was indeed capable of such great pride and of such humility.
Of pride, because he thought, No human work is equal
to this of mine, worthy to be called sacred. Of humility,
because he would say to himself, Alone, without the
help of God, I could not have accomplished it.

He knew that true nobility of soul is a gift of Divine
Grace and that because of this some men are 'almost as
gods.'[1] Almost certainly Dante believed himself to be
one of these men 'most noble and divine,' that is,
almost God (*quasi Dio*). What wonder if he imagined
himself to be aided and inspired by Heaven?

[1] *Conv.* IV, xx, 3, 4.

42

THE DEMIURGIC POEM

*T*HE greatest wrong which we can do to Dante —one which many continually do him—is to classify his most important work as literature; although, of course, great poetry is literature. The *Divina Commedia* is a book like other books only in appearance, only in so far as it uses words as its vehicle for the transmission of ideas. In reality, at least in the intention of its creator, it is an act, a means of action, a work, an *opera* in the primary meaning of the word; that is, an attempt to change and transform material. In this case the material is man.

Dante has a love for perfect literary form, for 'bello stile' and 'dolce stile,' a passion for teaching, a longing for glory and for revenge. But his poem was not begotten solely from these motives. Dante did not wish to make a fine book which would amuse or instruct; and he would have been ashamed to be considered simply one of the main pillars in the temple of the Belles-Lettres.

Dante wished to act, to change the souls of men and the condition of the world. In his eyes, the *Commedia* is above all the instrument of this transforming operation, of this remaking of the human race. Only that it may attain this end, act more effectively on the spirits of men, it is powerful art and noble poetry.

Dante himself states clearly in his letter to Can Grande the purpose of the poem: ". . . finis totius et partis est removere viventes in hac vita de statu miseriae

et perducere ad statum felicitatis. Genus vero phylo-
sophiæ sub quo hic in toto et parte proceditur, est
morale negotium, sive ethica; quia non ad speculandum,
sed ad opus inventum est totum et pars.'[1]

Nothing could be more explicit than this. The *Commedia* is not to be a poem solely for æsthetic enjoyment
—art for art's sake—nor, as most people think, for
philosophical teaching, a book of instruction.[2] It is
to be a practical work, a work operative and formative,
a work which shall be not only poetically beautiful and
morally good, but which shall change the state of man,
and change it radically; which shall conduct man from
misery to happiness, from suffering to beatitude, from
present hell to future heaven.

It makes use of figurative language and metrical forms,
but it is not a literary work. It contains ideas and
theories, but it is not a speculative work. It reveals
itself in forms of beauty, but only in a subordinate
way is it a work of art.

The *Commedia* was to produce not merely admiration
and surprise; it was to produce a miracle—a fundamental change in the human race. Art in this instance
was not to illuminate; even less was it to amuse. It was
to metamorphose. Therefore the *Commedia* is outside
all the categories of human literature. It is useless to

[1] *Epist.* XIII, 39–40. The purpose of the whole and the part is to remove
those living in this life from their state of misery and to lead them to a state
of happiness. Now the kind of philosophy under which it advances in both
the whole and the part is a moral act, or ethics; since the whole as well as the
part was conceived not for speculation, but for a practical end.

[2] In the letter to Can Grande quoted above, Dante speaks of the *Commedia*
as *opera dottrinale*, because it contains certain theoretical teaching (*Epist.* XIII,
18). But this has to do with a means of subserving the chief end, which is
practical.

seek a definition of it, or a designation in the thickets of æsthetics. It is not a moral poem, nor an heroic fable, nor a mystic drama, nor even a simple Odyssey of the other world.

It is a writing, but only in so far as the written signs can serve as implements and tools of a transmutation not wholly intellectual. It is composed of words, but only in so far as the words can be translated into acts, and into acts such as to change the values of life and the face of the earth.

The *Commedia*, in short, is to be the book as instrument; as hammer, scourge, wings, remedy. The 'sacred' book which shall melt down and recast the hearts of men, and redeem those who are plunged in the 'black slime.' The book which is to mark a new epoch in the history of mankind, making happy the unhappy, and holy the sinful.

Dante is not only a writer, a philosopher, a moralist. He is a demiurge, a sort of rival of God. His purpose is to offer a supplement to the Bible, a sequel to the Apocalypse. He is a poet, but only in the primary and literal sense of the word as one who *makes*, who works —from ποιεῖν, to make, to produce. Although the author of the *De Vulgari Eloquentia* defines poetry as *fictio rethorica musicaque posita*,[1] the author of the *Commedia* returns intuitively and willingly to the most ancient conception which makes poetry synonymous with magic, something which possesses a miraculously transforming power. Dante is the new Orpheus. He

---

[1] *De V.E.* II, iv, 2. The meaning of this much-debated phrase seems to be —A product of the imagination of a rhetorical kind, composed in verse.— Trans.

wishes to tame wild beasts; or, rather, to make the evil good, the foolish wise, the mournful happy.

The fundamental problem for Dante, as for every truly great man, is this: Can the human soul be changed? and how?

And why change it? Because men suffer and make others suffer. Because the world is a place of vileness and of torture. Whoever loves men must perceive within himself, as an absolute duty, the need of working to make them less unhappy and the world less vile.

It is not enough to change the outward forms, the institutions, the teaching, the dominating castes. In order to obtain a true transformation, complete and enduring, it is necessary to change from the very bottom the character and the inherent powers of man, his feelings and his passions.

To wish to change the human soul means not only that we consider it base and weak, but that we possess a model to which we wish to conform it, in order that it may rise and free itself. For a Christian there is a model, perfect and divine, and its lines are drawn for ever in the Gospel.

But by what means can we bring about this funda-mental change, apparently impossible and yet necessary? Certainly not alone by moral teaching and preaching. It is not sufficient to say to men—Do this, and do not do that. It is not sufficient to praise innocence and love, and to rail against lust and idleness. Almost all men know approximately what is good and what is evil; but most of them are incapable of good and continue to wade in evil.

Dante understood perfectly this ineffectiveness of

pure theory. He was not content to repeat lessons already familiar to the mind.

The ordinary man, he thought, is by nature sensual. He is not moved by abstract ideas, by philosophical terms, by the syllogisms of ethics, by general sermons on the moral entity.[1] Man is bodily sense—above all, sight and hearing; and feeling—especially, fear and desire.

It is necessary to place before the eyes of men the ugliness of the present life, and to show in concrete forms, fearful and horrible forms, what the lot of sinners will be after death. It is useless to discourse in mystic phrases about the felicity of the blessed and the saints. It is necessary to make men see it, to make them hear, taste, and desire that bliss which will actually be found in the high heavens, in the light, the splendour, the flaming brightness, the harmony, the sweetness, the supreme ecstasy of the Empyrean.

In order that the *vision*, not merely the apprehension, of this triple life—the life of the damned, the hopeful, and the blest—may be reproduced for the living in a manner potent and irrefutable, carnal for the carnal, sensual for the sensual, the poet resorts to the power of poetry, to the enchantment of word-music, to the supreme miracles of art. In order to work upon men, he has need to terrify them and to charm them.

From this inspiration and this desire was born in the spirit of Dante the *Divina Commedia*, a book unique in

---

[1] Cacciaguida says to Dante: 'The mind of him who hears is not persuaded, nor does it feel confidence . . . in an argument which is not apparent' (*Par.* XVII, 139–142). That is, the mind is not moved 'by theoretical reasoning which is not clear, which is not rendered easily understandable and persuasive by clear examples.'—Vandelli.

the entire range of literature precisely because it is not only a book but something more than a book: one of the most heroic attempts that a man has ever made to reform and to save his unhappy brothers, to conduct the living, as the poet himself said, from a state of misery to a state of felicity.

The *Commedia* is a miracle of poetry which was meant to perform a striking spiritual miracle. Therefore it does not belong solely to the brief history of literature, but above all else to the strange and dolorous history of mankind.

43

THE VELTRO

No one who writes about Dante can refrain from pursuing the Veltro. He may shun the *piè fermo*, skip the *disdegno di Guido*, give over the *Pape Satan aleppe*, disregard Matilda and the *femmina balba*, avoid the Messenger from Heaven who opens the city of Dis with his rod. But he cannot ignore the Veltro (the Hound), and its twin-brother, the DXV, the Five-Hundred-Ten-and-Five.

The *Inferno* is not only a description of sufferings. For readers and commentators, it is an instrument of fresh tortures. Every Dantist is damned. He is condemned to everlasting research on the meaning of the Veltro. The problem is to strip from this famous hound the mask of the symbol, to discover his true name. No excuses may be made; there is no way of escape. A man must resign himself to the inevitable and say, as did the people of Dante's Florence, 'I submit!'

A harsh necessity for one who enjoys the full splendour of the poetry and the ascent to the heavens of its grandeur and its truth, to bring himself after such magnificence to the task of deciphering enigmas. He risks being mistaken for a trifler or a maniac, or for one of the devotees of learned pastimes and of esoteric toys. But that is of no moment. The messianic prophecies of the Veltro and the DXV are at the very centre of Dante's thought, and upon their interpretation depends in part the true meaning of the *Commedia*.

The undertaking may well seem hopeless. Hundreds of printed articles, long and short, deal with this famous mystery, but as yet there is no agreement. It is not possible to review in a few pages the history of the pursuit of that animal whose 'chief excellence . . . lies in his swift running';[1] and in any case that is not my present concern.

Whom does the Veltro symbolize? The candidates are not few: Henry VII, Duke Louis of Bavaria, the Khan of Tartary, Can Grande della Scala, Uguccione della Faggiola, Guido Bonacolsi of Mantua, the Emperor William of Germany, Cino da Pistoia, Castruccio Castracani, Pope Benedict XI, Garibaldi, Vittorio Emanuele II, an unidentified Ghibelline captain, an unidentified emperor, an angelic pope unidentified, Dante himself, or Christ returning. To-day most writers on the subject believe that it must refer to an emperor; few think that it means either a pontiff or the Redeemer.

Let me say at once that those who think that the Veltro means Christ seem to me nearest to the true interpretation. An attentive reading of the first canto of the *Inferno*, accompanied by some knowledge of the religious thought of Dante's period, quickly convinces one that no man, however powerful and perfect, can be concealed under the symbol of the Veltro. If, as almost everyone believes, the She-Wolf is Avarice, that is, covetousness in all its forms, and in the last analysis, the centre and essence of sin, it is not conceivable that Dante should expect from a mere man the miraculous and supernatural enterprise of driving it from the world and thrusting it back into the Inferno.

[1] *Conv.* I, xii, 8. Cf. *Inf.* XIII, 125–126.

Those who identify the Veltro as Henry VII, always cite those passages[1] where Dante speaks of the Emperor as superior to every desire because, since he possesses all, he can desire nothing. But they forget that the Emperor is the only one in this privileged position, that he alone is exempt from avarice. What of all other men? However submissive they may be to the will of a single ruler, they will always go on desiring the good things of earth, possessions. No emperor can stop his subjects from feeding on 'land and lucre.' The Wolf might be driven from the mind of the Emperor, but it would remain in every town; while the Veltro, as Dante says, must make it disappear from the face of the earth.

To expel completely from human life the chief cause of sin is not a task to be entrusted to a man, born in sin and from sin, even though he may be great and holy. The freeing of humanity from the Wolf, and from the Leopard and the Lion,[2] can be accomplished only through the act and favour of the Omnipotent, of God. But Christ, according to the Scriptures and the early Christian beliefs, will return upon the earth only at the end of time, for the Last Judgement, when the earthly history of the human race will be completed. Dante, however, definitely assumes that the Veltro will inaugurate a new epoch in the lives of men. If everything were ended for mankind, it would no longer be necessary to put the Wolf back into the Inferno, because the Wolf dwells within men; it is the avarice which consumes them, which is bound up with their existence.

---

[1] *De Mon.* I, xi, 13; XIII, 7. *Conv.* IV, iv, 4.

[2] Perhaps we should remind ourselves that the three beasts, which appear in *Inf.* I, are usually understood as representing Avarice, Lust, and Pride.— Trans.

When the last man is dead, avarice will automatically disappear.

If then we must think of the intervention of a Divine Person, but must exclude a return of Christ, we must necessarily turn to the Third Person, to the Holy Spirit. The first one to think of this interpretation, more than forty years ago, was a German, Paulus Cassel;[1] but he did not present arguments of a nature to be taken seriously. He based his reasoning mainly on etymological subtleties which caused him to identify the Veltro with words which signify *vento*, wind; so that the transition was easy from wind to breath and to spirit, and the Holy Spirit.[2]

An Italian, Filomusi Guelfi,[3] with greater insight and broader preparation, attempted to prove that the Veltro must be the Holy Spirit. Other arguments may be added, with advantage, to his discussion.

Let us return, meanwhile, to an examination of the perplexing lines.

Why should Dante have called the Holy Spirit a Veltro, a Greyhound? First of all, as others have already observed, because the use of the Wolf demanded the

[1] D. Paulus Cassel, *Il Veltro, der Retter und Dichter in Dantes Hölle*. Berlin and Guben, Sallischer Verlag, 1890; a pamphlet of 57 pages.

That Dante's Veltro might have reference to a religious reform of the world (and therefore to Joachimite Franciscanism) was the thought expressed by Rousselot (*Histoire de l'Evangile Eternel*. Paris, 1861); Kraus (*Dante. Sein Leben und seine Werke*. Berlin, Grote, 1897); J. C. Huck (*Ubertin von Casale und dessen Ideenkreis*. Freiburg i. B. Herder, 1903); P. A. Martini (*Dante Francescano*. Arezzo, 1921, pp. 17–18), and others.

[2] P. Cassel, pp. 25–26. The conclusion alone is important: 'Der Veltro ist für den Dichter das allegorische Bild des heiligen Geistes.'

[3] L. Filomusi Guelfi, *L'allegoria fondamentale del poema di Dante*. Florence, Olschki, 1910. Note especially pp. 24–32. I accept for the most part Guelfi's arguments, but in my discussion I proceed in another way, adding proofs which do not appear in his article.

use of one of its natural enemies—a hunting dog famous for its speed in running. We must not think it strange that Dante concealed under the name of an animal one of the Divine Persons. In Christian symbolism and in mediæval poetry, Jesus Himself appears as a fish, a lamb, a serpent, a lion, a dragon;[1] and Dante calls Him a pelican.[2] The Holy Spirit had already been represented as a dove, that is, under the symbol of an animal. It is possible that the selection of the Greyhound, the Veltro, as an enemy to the three beasts, had been suggested to Dante by the dream of Charlemagne in the *Chanson de Roland*:[3] Charlemagne is asleep and dreams of being attacked by a bear and a leopard, but 'd'enz de sale uns veltres avalat,' from within the hall a hound leaps down and bites the two beasts furiously.

Finally, the six letters in the word Veltro may conceal an allusion, not yet observed, to the doctrine of Joachim of Flora. We are aware that Joachim's prophecy of the coming kingdom of the Holy Spirit was known in Dante's time under the name of *Vangelo Eterno*, the Eternal Gospel.[4] In the words, *Vangelo Eterno* are concealed, in their proper order, the six letters which form the word Veltro:

VangEL eTeRnO.

[1] Cf. Remy de Gourmont, *Le Latin Mystique*. Paris, Crès, 1913 (2nd ed.), and other collections of mediæval poetry.
[2] *Par.* XXV, 113.
[3] LVII, 730. The first to make the comparison was E. Boehmer, *Il Veltro*. *Jahrbuch der deutschen Dante-Gesellschaft* : Vol. II. Leipsic, Brockhaus, 1869, pp. 363–366.
[4] The expression 'everlasting gospel' occurs in Revelation xiv, 6, and Joachim of Flora had used it. Gherardo da San Donnino established its use and made it popular with his *Introductorius in Evangelium Æternum* (1254), which was the collection of the'three works of Joachim with introduction and comments.

Let us say, however, that this is mere chance—
although nothing in the *Commedia* is left to chance—
and examine the information which Dante gives on the
liberator of humanity and the slayer of avarice.

The Veltro 'will not feed on land.' Who is it in the
Bible who is condemned to feed on land, earth, dust?
Tommaseo is the only one, so far as I know, who
remembered it in this connection. It is the serpent in
Eden; it is Satan: 'Dust shalt thou eat all the days of
thy life.'[1] The Veltro, then, is the opposite of Satan,
and this is another reason why we cannot identify the
Veltro with a man. The opposite of Satan could be
only the Divinity. The not feeding on earth signifies
also, refusing every temporal power. Therefore the
Veltro cannot refer to a prince: the Emperor possessed
a part of the earth.

Nor will the Veltro feed on *peltro* (literally, pewter);
that is, metals in general and, as the commentators
explain it, money. Therefore he will be the enemy of
wealth, the restorer of evangelical poverty.

For Joachim of Flora, and especially for his Franciscan
followers, poverty was one of the signs of the new era
of the Holy Spirit; an era which would be that of the
hermits, of those who renounce everything, and therefore, as the Franciscans of Dante's time declared, of
the Friars Minor.[2]

[1] Gen. iii, 14. Cf. Isaiah lxv, 25.
[2] The phrase used by Joachim of Flora is famous: 'Qui vere monachus est
nihil reputat esse suum nisi citharam.' (The true monk thinks nothing his
own except his song, his psalmody, his prayers.) *Expositio super Apocalypsim*,
f. 183, b.
The phrase is, of course, another affirmation of the monk's poverty.
A brief discussion of this passage, giving another interpretation of *citharam*,
occurs in the article entitled *Joachim of Flora : A Critical Survey*, by George La

This explains why Dante says of the Veltro that his 'dominion shall be between feltro and feltro.' Although there has been much cudgelling of brains over the meaning of *feltro*, it seems to me impossible to overlook the early commentators who are unanimous in saying that it is the name of a poor kind of cloth.[1]

With this interpretation of *feltro*, the passage would mean that the Veltro will have his habitation among people dressed in poor cloth, perhaps among the mendicant friars, among those who represent for Joachim and his followers the beginning of the era of the Holy Spirit.[2]

We find conclusive, therefore, the line in which Dante announces that the Veltro will not eat dust or money (*non ciberà terra nè peltro*), but wisdom (*sapienza*), love (*amore*), and power (*virtute*). These are, as Dante well knew,[3] the special attributes of the Three Persons of the Trinity.

As Dante knew also that the Three Persons are one substance only,[4] he reasons that to each of them belong those attributes which our intelligence, unequal to the

---

Piana. *Speculum, A Journal of Mediæval Studies*; April 1932: Vol. VII, no 2: pp. 257–282.—Trans.

[1] Those in accord on this point are Ser Graziolo, Jacopo della Lana, the *Ottimo Commento*, and Boccaccio. 'No one,' adds Filomusi Guelfi, 'will care to deny the authority of the old interpreters where it concerns the meaning of a word' (p. 26).

[2] See P. A. Martini, *Dante Francescano*. It is clear that the third age, according to Joachim, was that of the monks, and many Franciscans believed that he had prophesied the coming of St Francis.

[3] 'la potenza somma del Padre . . . la somma sapienza del Figliuolo . . . la somma e ferventissima caritate dello Spirito Santo' (*Conv.* II, v, 8).

It is clear that potenza = virtute, and carità (caritate) = amore. Cf. 'fecemi la divina Potestate, la somma Sapienza e 'l primo Amore' (*Inf.* III, 5–6); the divine Power, the supreme Wisdom, and the primal Love made me.

[4] *Purg.* III, 34–36.

mystery, discerns and distinguishes; so that to the Holy Spirit belong also the power (*virtute, potenza*) of the Father and the wisdom (*sapienza*) of the Son. He who unites in himself, as the Veltro does, almost as his nutriment and essence, the three manifestations of the single divine substance can be no other than one Person of the Trinity.

We turn now from heaven to earth. How and where will the supernatural power of the Veltro act?

> Di quella umile Italia fia salute
> per cui morì la vergine Cammilla
> Eurialo e Turno e Niso di ferute.[1]

He shall be the salvation of low-lying Italy, for which the virgin Camilla and Euryalus and Turnus and Nisus died of their wounds.

It seems as if the horizon suddenly closes in. The Holy Spirit must transform the earth, must drive avarice out of the world; but here, instead of the world, a definite and, apparently, restricted place is named. 'Low-lying Italy' may mean the plains of Lazio (Latium), the district in which Rome is situated; but actually the poet wishes to indicate Rome without using the name. Rome, in Dante's time, meant the Church, and by a permissible extension, Christianity. The Veltro would not come to save that ancient Rome for which the virgin Camilla died: that Rome is ended and lives only in memories and in ruins. The Rome present to the mind of Dante could be only Christian Rome, the seat of the universal Church, the capital of Christendom. To say that the Veltro will be the salvation of low-lying Italy is equivalent to saying that he will be the salva-

[1] *Inf.* I, 106–108.

tion of the Christian peoples; and all the more so when we remember that, according to the theories of Joachim's followers, the coming of the Holy Spirit would be marked above all else by a profound change in the Church of Christ which has its centre at Rome. Those who have died for this Rome are not the heroes of the *Æneid* but rather, symbolized in those Virgilian figures, the many Christian martyrs who, to found a Christian Rome, died gloriously 'of their wounds.' It is this Rome, which is the Church or the great society of Christians, that the Veltro, when he comes, will save.

The divine character of the Veltro is strongly re-affirmed in the last terzina which refers to him.

> Questi la caccerà per ogni villa,
> fin che l'avrà rimessa nello 'nferno
> là onde invidia prima dipartilla.[1]

He shall hunt Avarice through every town until he has put her back in hell whence Envy sent her forth.

Here is represented, if I am not mistaken, a divine addition to the Redemption. Christ, making Himself man and taking upon Himself the sins of the world, had redeemed mankind from the fault of Adam and had made possible the reconciliation with the Father. After the sacrifice on Golgotha, the way of salvation was open to every man, the grievous heritage of the Fall was cancelled. But in spite of this, not all men gained salvation. The way had been opened to them since they had been freed from the bond of original sin by virtue of Christ's blood. But they must of their

[1] *Inf.* I, 109–111.

own free will co-operate with Christ for their salvation by avoiding new sins and conforming to the teaching of the Gospel.

But there were always grave obstacles. Satan had not disappeared from the world. He continued to tempt mortals, especially by means of that avarice which, 'through envy,' he had unchained upon the earth. For this also, thinks Dante, divine compassion, which has no limits, will find a remedy. A Veltro will come, an anti-Satan, whose work will be the opposite of Satan's. Satan had sent out the Wolf from hell; the Veltro will put it back in hell. The Veltro will be another Saviour, a second Liberator, a continuator of Christ. He is, indeed, the Holy Spirit, proceeding from the Father and the Son.

Men, freed from the gadfly of avarice and from its devilish goadings, will be able the more easily to reach eternal salvation, and will not be forced, like Dante, to 'follow another road.' Christ had opened the road of salvation to all; the Veltro, the Holy Spirit, will remove the greatest hindrance which impedes most of those upon that road—the love of riches, of pleasure, of power. A marvel like this, the uprooting of every evil desire from the lives and hearts of men, could be accomplished only by a Divine Person, by the Paraclete whom many contemporaries of Dante were still expecting.

With this we complete our examination of the lines which Dante devoted to the Veltro; but the proof that the Veltro is identical with the Holy Spirit is not yet finished. There are abundant proofs.

First of all, let us consider the selection of the one who announces the coming of the Veltro. Virgil, as the Middle Ages and as Dante himself believed,[1] had prophesied, in the Fourth Eclogue, the incarnation of Christ, the Second Person of the Trinity. It was not without design that the poet entrusted to Virgil the duty of announcing another descent from Heaven, a second palingenesis of humanity.

It is said that Dante was the devotee of Saint Lucy who in the *Commedia* is Lucia, the messenger of the Virgin and of Beatrice; and it is thought that Dante considered her his patroness. But Lucia is not only the saint invoked by those who suffer from weakness or disease of the eyes. She is also the martyr who, more than others, makes repeated appeals for the protection of the Holy Spirit.[2] In the presence of the prefect Paschasius, the virgin of Syracuse solemnly recalls the words of Christ that the Holy Spirit will speak through the lips of those who are persecuted, and says that she is the temple of the Holy Spirit. She appears in this instance to be associated in a special way with faith in the Third Person. Of this her 'faithful one' could not have been ignorant.

If he 'who made the great refusal' is, as most believe, Celestine V, it is easy to understand Dante's severity (*Inf.* III, 58–66). The election of Pietro Morrone to the pontificate had been received with great rejoicing by

---

[1] *Purg.* XXII, 64–73.

[2] 'Said Paschasius: Then the Holy Spirit lives in thee? Lucia answered: Those who live chastely are the temple of the Holy Spirit. And Paschasius said: I will cause thee to be taken to a place of shame so that when thou art dishonoured, the Holy Spirit may then depart from thee. . . . And when they desired to drag her to the place of shame, the Holy Spirit stayed her going with so great a weight that they were not able to move her from the spot.'—Jacobus de Voragine, *Legenda Aurea*, ed. Levasti. Florence, Lib. Ed. Fior., 1924, I, 65–66.

the Spiritual Franciscans and by the Joachimists. His renunciation of the tiara was considered almost a betrayal, and certainly a calamity for the Church, since his successor was Boniface VIII, enemy of all those who awaited the triumph of the Eternal Gospel. Dante echoes this painful disillusionment and has given proof of sharing, even after many years, the ever-active sentiments of the expectant Spirituals.

It should be added that Dante hurled himself not only against Boniface who despised the Spirituals, but also against the other popes who opposed the Spiritual movement: Nicholas III,[1] Clement V,[2] and John XXII,[3] who was the most hostile of all.

The enemies of the Spirituals and of the Little Brothers of St Francis, that is, of those who were especially filled with the hopes derived from the teaching of Joachim, were looked upon as enemies by Alighieri also. The confession of his intimate thoughts could not be more explicit.

That Dante admired Joachim of Flora, the great prophet of the Holy Spirit, needs no pointing out. To have placed him in Paradise despite the condemnation which struck some of his doctrines in 1215 and 1255—leaving untouched, however, the orthodoxy of the founder of the flourishing order—is a proof of the sympathy which the poet had for him as a man and as a prophet.

We have already seen, in an earlier chapter, that Dante as a young man knew and almost certainly frequented the lectures of the famous Franciscans, Pier Giovanni

---

[1] *Inf.* XIX, 31–120.   [2] *Inf.* XIX, 82–87.
[3] *Par.* XVIII, 130 ff.; XXVII, 58.

Olivi and Ubertino da Casale. These two were among the most ardent and outspoken upholders of the theories of Joachim, adapted as those theories were to the times and to the ideals of the Minorites. In the *Commedia* there are traces of their writings, especially of the *Arbor Vitæ crucifixæ*,[1] which is now considered one of the sources of the poem.

We should not argue that because Dante censured Ubertino da Casale he did not admire him. The famous passage in the *Paradiso* (XII, 124–126) which contains the censure delivered by the same Bonaventure who points to the shining light of Joachim, links the names of Casale and the Cardinal of Acquasparta:

> ma non fia da Casal nè d'Acquasparta,
> là onde vegnon tali alla scrittura,
> ch'uno la fugge, e l'altro la coarta.

But [the good friar] will not come from Casale nor from Acquasparta, whence come those who so interpret the writing that one relaxes it, and the other makes it more stringent.

---

[1] For the resemblance between Olivi and Dante, see U. Cosmo, *Pier Giovanni Olivi e Dante* (*Giornale Dantesco*, VI, 1898, pp. 112 ff.); P. F. Sarri, *P. di G. O. e Ubertino da Casale* (*Studi Francescani*, Jan.–Mar. 1925); F. Tocco, *Il canto XXXII del Purgatorio*. Florence, Sansoni, 1902. (The appendix contains a part of Olivi's unpublished commentary on the Apocalypse.)

There is an abundant literature on Ubertino. For the comparisons with Dante, see the studies of Huck and of Sarri; U. Cosmo, *Le mistiche nozze di Frate Francesco con Madonna Povertà* (*Giorn. Dantesco*, 1898, pp. 61 ff.); also his *Noterelle Francescane* (*Giorn. Dantesco*, 1899, pp. 69–70); Kraus on Dante (pp. 738 ff.); E. G. Gardner, *Dante and the Mystics*. London, Dent, 1913 (especially pp. 343–348). Of special importance are P. A. Martini, *Ubertino da Casale alla Verna* (in *La Verna*, Arezzo, 1913, pp. 193 ff.); A. Donini, *Appunti per una storia del pensiero di Dante in rapporto al movimento gioachimita* (in *Annual Reports of the Dante Society*, 1930. Cambridge, U.S.A., Harvard University Press, 1930, pp. 49–69); F. Casolini, *Ubertino da Casale e Dante* (in *Annuario del R. Istituto Tecnico C. Cattaneo in Milano*, 1928–1929. Milan, 1930).

The 'writing' (*la scrittura*) is the rule of the Order of St Francis, and it has been believed until the present that Dante was accusing Acquasparta of relaxing this rule (*la fugge*) because it seemed to him to be too strict, and that he was accusing Ubertino da Casale of restraining or contracting it (*la coarta*), that is, of wishing to make it even more stringent and severe. But another interpretation has now been given to these lines.[1] 'Either we are greatly mistaken,' writes Donini, 'or the one who restrains it, makes it more strict (*coarta*), is Acquasparta, who by introducing laxity into the order constrains or forces (*sforza*) the spirit of the rule; and he who "relaxes" it (*la fugge*) is Ubertino da Casale. When John XXII was elected pope . . . Ubertino found himself in an impossible situation and was persuaded to desert the Franciscan order and to enter the Benedictine. In 1317, therefore, he had timidly "fled from" the "rule" of the Franciscans and could no longer say with the true Friar Minor,

> I'mi son quel ch' i' soglio.
>
> I am what I was wont to be.

'Not a few of Dante's contemporaries shared this severe estimate, perfectly justified by the conduct of Ubertino; and this helps to make clear once more to which side Dante's sympathies inclined in the contest between the authority of the Curia and the later followers of Joachim.'

In other words, Dante blames Ubertino not because he is one of the Joachimite Spirituals, but because he

[1] A. Donini, *Appunti per una storia del pensiero di Dante in rapporto al movimento gioachimita*, pp. 59–60.

had abandoned his post of battle in the Franciscan Order.

To make clearer the influence of the Joachimite Franciscans on the conception of the Veltro, we should remember that the first cantos of the *Inferno* were written, as some Dantists think, before the exile, that is, at a time when Dante's mind held in fresh and vivid remembrance the teachings and the conferences at Santa Croce. Even the form of the first canto, less perfect than the rest of the poem, confirms this hypothesis: Dante was younger then and less a master of his art. According to the opinion expressed by Barbi, which seems to me most reasonable and which was accepted by Parodi, the actual composition of the *Inferno* was begun about 1307; but it is not improbable that Dante had already conceived the general plan of the poem a few years after the death of Beatrice, that is, before 1300.

The death of Henry VII (1313) and other experiences, and long contemplation, must have weakened Dante's hope in the descent of the Veltro, understood as a spiritual revolution brought about by the Holy Spirit, and must have led him to the conclusion that there was needed first an effective human force, political and military, to put in order the practical affairs of the world and, in particular, those of Italy and Rome. If the corruption of the Curia and its complicity with the enemies of the Empire were the main obstacles to the reform of humanity, then it was necessary to restrict the papacy to its proper and just authority, to punish and reform it. There was need, therefore, of a powerful temporal prince, an emperor more able and more fortunate than Henry; there must be a leader, a *Dux*, who would be not a direct manifestation of God, like the Veltro, but 'a Messenger of God.'

The Five-Hundred-Ten-and-Five, the DXV, mysteriously announced by Beatrice,[1] is therefore not one and the same with the Veltro. It is rather his instrument, his harbinger, his forerunner.[2]

Towards 1300 Dante was still under the influence of the Joachimists, and with them awaited the Third Kingdom. In 1313 or 1314 he realized that this new kingdom could not come to pass unless they should first slay the 'fuia,' the corrupt Roman Curia, guilty of simony and usurpation. Whoever the person was whom Dante had in mind—and perhaps we shall never know with certainty—there is no doubt whatever that he was thinking of a prince 'sent by God,' who would put all things in order and prepare a new era of peace like that which obtained under the Emperor Augustus, an era which had been chosen for the incarnation of the Second Person of the Trinity.

The so-called prophecies of the *Commedia*, therefore, are two in number: one at the beginning of the *Inferno*, which refers to a direct intervention of God for the suppression of avarice and of sin in general; the other at the end of the *Purgatorio*, which announces the early coming of a strong and upright prince, perhaps an emperor, sent by God to purify the Church and to give peace to all men. The Veltro is a divine being and the moment of his coming is not known; the DXV is a

---

[1] *Purg.* XXXIII, 37–54.
[2] That the DXV is distinct from the Veltro is the view held also by Filomusi Guelfi, *L'allegoria fondamentale*, etc., p. 29.

human being, sent by heaven, and his coming is imminent.

In any case, Dante hoped until the very end for a change in the history of the world, and perhaps in his mind now one, now the other hope, dominated by turns. The period was 'the last age of the century,'[1] and a decisive happening could not long delay.

Let us understand, however, that Dante could not be called a true and complete Joachimist. To have shared, at least during a period of his life, in the supreme hope which Joachim held does not necessarily mean that Dante accepted Joachim's allegorical and numerical fantasies. Dante was too much a rationalist to lose his way completely in the daring exegesis of the visionary of San Giovanni in Fiore. Usually his thought moves more clearly in the ordinary enclosures of Scholasticism, and he could not accept completely a doctrine which in its essential character disregarded culture and reason. Dante draws inspiration from the *Apocalypse*, but without ever forgetting the *Summa* of 'good Brother Thomas.' When he has need in the *Paradiso* of a mystic guide, he chooses St Bernard, who was, it is true, a mystic, but at the same time a man of wisdom.

In Dante, however, side by side with the realist, is the Utopian who, in his hatred for the present. trusts eagerly in the future. This second self of his must have loved Joachim in spite of everything. We can understand, therefore, how he could accept and make his own certain ideas and prophecies of Olivi and of Ubertino. Dante shared with the Joachimists their passion for prophecy and their hatred for the reigning

---

[1] *Conv.* II, xiv, 13.

popes. In the Veltro he symbolized their common hopes—a reform of the Church *ab imis*, the defeat of the Wolf, the triumph of Poverty. All this was to result from the advent of the Third Person.

Later he placed his hopes in the *Dux*, as he had earlier in the Vangelo Eterno; but there remained in his heart an undying admiration for the abbot 'endowed with the spirit of prophecy.' This does not mean, however, that he herded with the Joachimite agitators. An admirer of Joachim always; but a sectarian never.

THE ALLEGED OBSCURITY

IT is commonly said that Dante—and by Dante is meant the *Commedia*—is very obscure. I do not share this opinion. The poem is not always easy reading, but difficult reading is not the same thing as obscurity. Every book is difficult which demands of the reader a serious preparation, but it is difficult only for him who is not prepared. By preparation difficulties are conquered and obscurities disappear. In a certain sense every great work is obscure for anyone who attempts it without the viaticum of knowledge necessary for understanding and appreciating it. This is equally true of those works which seem more readily comprehensible than the *Commedia*. To understand the Homeric poems we must know the Greek dialects, have something more than a superficial notion of archæology and mythology, acquire an idea of the Mycenæan civilization, of Greek and Phœnician history and of the common traditions. And Shakespeare, although he is more modern than Homer and Dante, is not understood and cannot be fully enjoyed unless we have a little acquaintance with Elizabethan English, with ancient and English history, both the authentic and the legendary, and at least an approximate knowledge of the thought of the Renaissance.

The alleged obscurity of the *Commedia* derives, mainly, from the ignorance of the readers. If a reader does not know a little Latin, if he has not studied in the texts and in dictionaries the word-forms peculiar to the

Florentine vernacular of the Trecento, if he is not familiar with the history of Florence, of Tuscany, of Italy, and of Europe in that period, if he has only a vague and inaccurate notion of the classical myths, of the Bible, and more especially of mediæval mysticism, scholasticism, and apocalypticism, he need not be surprised if he finds difficulties and obscurities in every canto. And the notes of the commentators do not always help to untangle the difficulty because the reader is often lacking in the knowledge necessary for understanding the annotations.

This brings us to the second point in the charge of obscurity in Dante. In addition to whatever is contributed to this legend by the ignorance of readers, there is also the too great erudition and vanity of those who wish to interpret the *Commedia* when no interpretation is needed. A large number of those who devote themselves to the study of Dante—many of them amateurs and therefore the more annoying—have a mania for solving riddles, for unveiling secrets, for interpreting the mysteries which are, or seem to be, in the 'sacred poem.' Many times they busy themselves with expressions which have almost no importance for the right understanding of the *Commedia* from the point of view either of æsthetics or philosophy. A well-known example is the 'sì che 'l piè fermo sempre era 'l più basso' (*Inf.* I, 30). Other times they discuss mysteries which Dante himself noted as inexplicable; for example, the words of Nimrod:

Raphel may amech zabì almì,[1]

---

[1] *Inf.* XXXI, 67.

of which Virgil expressly says:

> chè così è a lui ciascun linguaggio
> come 'l suo ad altrui, ch'a nullo è noto.[1]
>
> Since every language is to him as his is to others, which is understood
> by no one.

Now and again they tire themselves over problems (the 'disdain' of Guido, the three beasts of Canto I, Matilda) which have a certain importance for the understanding of the poem, but upon which all authorities are in approximate agreement, sufficient for a general understanding of Dante's thought. The three beasts, for example, are certainly three sins, grievous sins, which hinder a man from following the true road. But to be obliged to decide if the leopard is really luxury (or lust, to use the more modern word), as most think, or vainglory, or envy, is not a thing which matters very much for understanding the general lines of Dante's thought and enjoying the beauty of the poem. But the mystery-makers are moved less by the desire to shed more light on the *Commedia* than by their eagerness to furnish an outlet for their acuteness, their fantastic imagination, and erudition, and by their vanity in wishing to appear more expert and successful than those who preceded them; and occasionally they are urged on by some nice point of honour or by a spirit of contradiction.

Only one of these enigmas deserves to be taken seriously and probed to the very bottom. It is the crux of the Veltro and the DXV, because this constitutes the centre of the great prophecy which we name the *Commedia*. The others are easily solved, or else they are not

---

[1] *Inf.* XXXI, 80–81.

worth the fatigue of contriving solutions still more ingenious and sophistical.

Only in the instance of the Five-Hundred-Ten-and-Five, the DXV, the poet observes and admits in his own words that it is an enigma, and he makes Beatrice say so:

> E forse che la mia narrazion buia,
> qual Temi o Sfinge, men ti persuade
> perch'a lor modo lo 'ntelletto attuia;
>   ma tosto fien li fatti le Naiade
> che solveranno questo enigma forte.[1]

> And perhaps my utterance, obscure like that of Themis and the Sphinx, persuades you the less because in their manner it dims the understanding. But soon events will be the interpreters who shall solve this difficult enigma.

The prophecy of the DXV in relation to that of the Veltro is in truth the single obscurity which is intentional and complete. The other warnings given by Dante, cited by the specialists in enigmas as justification for their pretentious labours, are not, if carefully read, admissions of deliberate obscurity. When, for example, after the apparition of the head of Medusa, Dante says:

> O voi ch'avete l'intelletti sani
> mirate la dottrina che s'asconde
> sotto 'l velame de li versi strani; [2]

> O you who have sound understandings, consider the teaching that is hidden under the veil of the strange verses;

he does not mean that such knowledge is inscrutable or unattainable. It is enough to have a sound understanding, well-balanced and unimpaired, and the veil of the strange verses, unusual and allegorical, will be lifted without effort. If Dante had wished to hide that know-

[1] *Purg.* XXXIII, 46–50.　　[2] *Inf.* IX, 61–63.

301

ledge, he would not have roused the attention of the reader by saying, 'Mirate,' which means 'Behold,' 'Consider,' 'Admire.'

Even less likely material for the mystery-makers is the other terzina which urges the reader to greater attention:

> Aguzza qui, lettor, ben li occhi al vero,
> chè il velo è ora ben tanto sottile,
> certo che 'l trapassar dentro è leggero.[1]

> Here, reader, sharpen your eyes well to the truth, because the veil is now so very thin that to pass within is certainly easy.

Dante rouses the attention of the reader not because the meaning is difficult. On the contrary, it is true that to pass within is easy. But he 'sharpens our eyes' because we might pass on without stopping to consider the allegory of the two angels in green raiment, with green wings and truncated swords, who descend to drive away the serpents.

Dante, then, is not obscure except to the ignorant or the fanatic. One time only he is deliberately and inherently obscure—and with reason. He had to hide the exact meaning of a prophecy that would have seemed suspect to some over-zealous inquisitor. At that time hostilities against the Joachimite Spirituals were still going on; and although Alighieri may have been profoundly convinced that there was nothing heterodox in his expectation of the Veltro, he preferred to be understood by only a few. At this time he had rather too many enemies, and to draw other enemies upon him would have hindered or diminished the spread of his poem; and this would have reduced the good which he planned to accomplish by means of the *Commedia*.

[1] *Purg.* VIII, 19–21.

POET BEYOND EVERYTHING

D ANTE employed his life in many ways—in the exercise of arms, in public business, in councils and embassies. He wished to teach philosophy, to conduct mankind toward a moral revival, to announce a spiritual regeneration. But his deep and abiding vocation was poetry. God meant him to be, above all else, an artist. And with the colour, the light, the fire of art, he was able to accomplish the highest of his missions.

His youthful work, the *Vita Nuova*, was written to give unity and background to his first verses. The *Convivio* came into being as a commentary for other verses. The *De Vulgari Eloquentia* is an introduction to the art of poetry. When Dante wrote in prose, he was, unconsciously, a poet. Here is a line which bears the true Dantesque stamp:

> con certo giro vallava li abissi.[1]

It might be a verse from the *Commedia*, but it is part of a sentence from the *Convivio*.[2] Here are others taken from the same prose writing:

> e poi, continuando la sua luce
> caggiono, quasi come nebulette
> matutine a la faccia del[lo] sole.[3]

. . . .

---

[1] To translate this and the following examples would be to destroy the metrical quality which is the point under illustration.—Trans.
[2] *Conv.* III, xv, 16.   [3] *Ibid.* II, xv, 5.

303

ahi mirabile riso della . . . donna. . . .
che mai non si sentìa se non de l'occhio! [1]

. . . .
recan sete di casso febricante [2]

. . . .
sì come valli volte ad aquilone
. . . dove luce del sol mai non discende. [3]

Other lines like these could be found, equally vigorous and effective. If any change is needed in the prose
to render the line metrical, it is sufficient to add or
take away a word, or a syllable only, and we have
hendecasyllables which would not disfigure even the
'sacred poem.'

But it is not enough to say and to repeat that Dante
is a poet beyond everything, a very great poet, noble,
sublime. It remains to be seen through what qualities
of language and style, peculiar to himself, he is so far
above other poets, and so different. On this point very
little has been written, although the literature about
Dante is endless. The best known critics—omitting for
the moment those who have devoted themselves solely
to the historical, ethical, philosophical, and mystical
content of the poem—have concentrated their attention
on the principal figures of the *Commedia*, and have
written analyses, enthusiastic and more or less successful, of the most famous episodes and of the most
popular cantos. We do not wish to condemn entirely
these attempts at thorough understanding and interpretation of Dante's poetry in its most creatively successful
moments, because the poet shows himself especially a
creator when he endows those dead, whom he most
loves or admires, with a posthumous life which seems

[1] *Conv.* III, viii, 12.   [2] *Ibid.* IV, xii, 5.
[3] *Ibid.* IV, xx, 8.

304

to us to be real. In these analyses we can find skilful suggestions which help us the better to enjoy the beauty of certain conceptions or expressions. In the more notable instances they are collaborative interpretations of the poetry, the prose of art added to Dante's art in verse.

Less frequently we find studies on what we may call the plastic and musical qualities of Dante's verse, on the tone and colour of his language, on its resonance, on the wholly original character of his expressions. Dante is regarded as a sculptor, as an architect. He is not sufficiently studied as an artificer, an artisan, a musician. Keen observations are found here and there in the commentaries, which point out Dante's extraordinary success in the selection and disposition of words, but these observations are not co-ordinated under general principles so as to constitute an introduction to Dante's technique.[1]

Studies like the famous ones of Parodi, for example, on rhyme in the *Commedia*,[2] are valuable in so far as they contradict the foolish opinion that the poet alters the form of a word or invents new ones because of the exigencies of the rhyme. But these are not enough.

Poetry is admittedly inspiration and reflection. When it flows into verse it is also art; that is, it is material manipulated and moulded in definite and determined ways. It is also, to speak plainly, a craft; nor is it thereby degraded. By the very manner in which the artist uses his craft to reveal his visions, he discloses

[1] See, however, the recent article by G. Bertoni, *La lingua di Dante. Nuova Antologia,* 16 Feb. 1933.
[2] *Rima nella Divina Commedia. Bull. della Soc. Dantesca.* N.S. III, pp. 81–156.

not only his experience and his skill but the character of his genius and the physiognomy of his soul. The poet does not select words and images haphazard. Whoever has a limited mind and an unresponsive heart may make use of the most impressive and glowing words which sleep in the dictionary, but his prose will be a dead mosaic and his poetry will be as empty and dull as his mind. If the soul is lifeless, what it produces will be lifeless.

As far as this relates to Dante—a fertile and living mind and a master-craftsman—the fact that the work of criticism has been directed more to the figures and episodes of the poem than to the distinctive and permanent characteristics of the poetic diction, has given rise to an error not yet entirely corrected. It is the belief that the artistic value of the *Commedia* diminishes from one canticle to the next. In the *Inferno*, where the figures in the scene are more numerous and more strikingly presented, and most akin to us through common sins, Dante's æsthetic vigour is thought to be at its maximum. In the *Purgatorio*, although there are still some episodes warmly human in their appeal, we are farther from the earth, and too many theoretical disquisitions begin to cloud the clear sky of art. In the *Paradiso*, except for certain imagery and some famous invectives, theology too often takes the place of poetry, the abstract of the concrete, contemplative moralizing of pure inspiration.

This notion of a descending scale in the *Commedia*, which many still accept either openly or tacitly, is one of the worst stupidities in the ordinary criticism of Dante. The truth is exactly the opposite. Dante is a

great poet *always*, and in *all three* canticles. But if his
art has attained in any one place to the most sublime
and overpowering perfection, it is precisely in the
Paradiso. Moving ever nearer to God, the poet approaches more closely to the highest heaven of
poetry.

Two things have contributed to this absurd belief in
the falling off of the *Commedia*: first, the positivistic
atmosphere of half a century ago, which led to an over-
valuation of actuality and realism, and therefore to the
ascribing of major importance to the violent figures of
the *Inferno*; and, secondly, the fashion of to-day which,
believing Catholicism to be dead and a thing of the
past, assumes the privilege of ignoring it, and therefore
renders readers incapable of appreciating the lyric sweep
and the significant beauty of the last canticle, which,
more than the other two, and not alone for its subject-
matter, deserves to be called sublime.

As people read the *Paradiso* and do not understand it
or understand it imperfectly—being almost entirely
ignorant of the theology and Christian mysticism—
they suppose arbitrarily that the fault is in Dante
instead of in themselves, and think, foolishly, that
theology diminished and congealed the inspiration of
the poet. Even if out of curiosity or shame of their
ignorance they take the trouble to learn something about
Catholic thought, it is insufficient to help them to an
immediate comprehension of the profound poem. There
is always lacking the greatest and the best—a tested and
living faith in those truths which the poet believes, sees,
and represents. And further, that which flames brightly
in his verse seems dull, that which is a miraculous effort

to speak the unutterable becomes wearisome didacticism, and all the splendour of the *Paradiso* gives them the impression of a ruined church under a wintry sky, where the only gleams of light among the rubbish come from the gilding of the altars and the jewels of the votive offerings and the images. For this reason I said at the beginning that it is a great aid to the understanding of Dante and his art to be a Christian, and a Christian not merely by birth or in name.

We can admire the *Iliad* without believing in the Hellenic mythology because Homer is not a theologian, and is not concerned about the salvation of souls and the moral restoration of the world. He pretends rather to be an historian and to provide examples of heroic life for the lords who listen to him.

The case of the *Divina Commedia* is different. We are confronted with a work which is meant to be, in a certain sense, a supplement to the Bible, a universal sermon, a pointing out of the way to God, the veiled announcement of a new era of history. The journey through three worlds is only the pretext for an undertaking which surpasses every preceding vision. One of the fundamental personages of the *Commedia* is Beatrice, who typifies the knowledge of divine things; and the initial prophecy foreshadows the advent of the Third Person.

The *Commedia*, then, is a poem religious and moral in its essence, and he who does not believe passionately in that moral and in that religion will have difficulty at every turn in understanding the inner and compelling beauty which in every canto inspires and permeates the words, the rhythm and the rhyme, but which is still more luminous in the last cantos. For here the poet is about to reach his goal, to mount to the vision of that triform Light where every individual human will, sublimated and perfected, loses itself in the Divine Will.

HERE is no secret in Dante's art. His is a soul that strives and struggles in the words, and gives to the poetry his own clear imprint, the tone and flavour which are Dante's and only his.

For poetry, in so far as it is a means of transmitting the fire of one spirit to another, is made of words and of nothing but words. Every poet, however, has his own vocabulary and his own verbal and musical atmosphere, so that a group of words used by him, even though they may be words which are on everybody's lips and in everybody's books, take on another aspect, give out another sound, arouse other images; seem, in short, the discovery and the property of the one poet.

Such are Dante's words. The words which we find in the work of most writers seem employed at second hand; they are dingy from over-use, without significance of form or sound. Those of Dante seem to have been engraved and coined expressly for that moment's use, to be fresh from the mould, untouched coin, still bright and shining. It seems as if Dante were the first to draw them forth from the dark forge of the common language and to give them a living aspect, an unexpected emphasis, a vital significance. While most writers turn all that they touch into glass, mud, or dust, in Dante's poetry the most lowly words become bronze, iron, silver, or gold.

More than any other writer Dante restores the youth-

MASK OF DANTE, FRONT AND PROFILE

The so-called Death Mask, formerly belonging to Baron Kirkup. [*Photo: Alinari.*]

ful vigour of words. Although he employs the Florentine idiom of his day and, when this is inadequate, has recourse to Latin, and where Latin fails, turns to the Italian dialects or to gallicisms, and helps himself, in short, to linguistic material already existing, he gives the effect, this Dante of ours, of creating by himself, in his own manner and for his own use, a new language entirely for himself. He creates some new words, but to all the others he gives a new aspect with the light of his inspiration. His are potent words, almost incantations or *mantram*. Not only are they words which depict, but words which command, destroy, renew.

This fertility in words is not, in Dante's case, the laboured outcome of deliberate and calculated selection. It comes naturally from the emotions which animate and move his soul. According to the passion which at the moment tortures or exalts him those words flow from his pen which best correspond to that passion and are best adapted to express it. There is a transfusion of the spiritual force to the syllables, the vowels and consonants of the chosen words. The sound of the words comes forth from the very tone of the soul. The poet's anger blazes in the syntax of the verse, in the position of the words, in the prevalence or repetition of a certain letter. His contemplative rapture is reflected, as a torch in a mirror, by a sudden mellowness of cadence and of rhythm which steeps all the words in a strange and unexpected sweetness. Dante's passionate glow is revealed not only in thoughts, in sentences, but in every verse, in every expression, in the threadbare material of verbal usage which his amazing genius masters and elevates. His anger wrenches the syntax, his contempt is revealed

in the choice of syllables, his adoration gives spacious-
ness and soaring flight to a terzina. Here a verb is filled
with repressed fury, there an adjective hides secret pity,
in that clear imagery which is as delicate as the fall of
petals in the sunshine there is a suggestion of love, a
shy outpouring of tenderness.

Rules of rhetoric do not help us to understand this
art. We need the intuitions of a psychology which
probes beneath the surface.

> L'oltracotata schiatta che s'indraca
> dietro a chi fugge. . . .[1]

In the sound of that verse, in the angry rush of
syllables, in the threatening r's and t's and contemptuous c's, do we not hear the outburst of scorn and
hatred which Dante felt at the thought of 'the insolent
race who were fierce as dragons behind the fugitive,' the
Adimari family who had always been his enemies?

He contemplates the starry and moonlit sky. Clear
and shining, it exalts his thoughts to holy sorrow and
heavenly joy; and behold! the liquid verse pours forth
triumphant and serene in the lightness of its l's and n's,
and carries us drifting along on the moving air of the
infinite:

> Quale ne' plenilunii sereni.[2]

These two examples show the opposite extremes of
Dante's feeling and expression. Always great in the concrete formulation of a dogma, he is still greater in the
expression of harsh, and almost coarse, violence, or of
delicate and almost angelic sweetness. There is in his
nature at times a force almost peasant-like and rough-

---

[1] *Par.* XVI, 115–116.   [2] *Par.* XXIII, 25.

hewn, familiar and even vulgar, which reveals itself in the 'harsh, hoarse rhymes'; and in contrast, there is such a refinement of verbal and musical harmonies as to make us think of a saint who, awaking in the morning after dreams of paradise, stands at the threshold of his cavern and speaks his gratitude to the rising sun, to the world which shakes off slumber, surprised in the fresh mantle of its touching beauty. And in those moments, as we read the terzinas, we do not know what to say or to do. We wish to cry aloud in amazement or to weep in admiration, to embrace and to kiss him, our Dante, if only he were present here, if he could be brought to life again for at least a moment by our jealous affection.

> Quale allodetta che 'n aere si spazia
> prima cantando, e poi tace contenta
> dell'ultima dolcezza che la sazia.[1]

> Like a lark which flies through the air singing at first, and then is silent, content with the last sweetness which satisfies her.

Such is he, the poet so often divine; such are we insignificant men, when in the depths of our hearts we feel his song as it flies on inspired wings, the song that delights and satisfies.

If in equal measure we set over against the harsh and threatening verses those of a melting tenderness, we shall not be able to decide which is more admirable in Dante, the bolts of lightning let loose from the thunderous clouds, or the delicate light which, like a silent nun, is perceived as whiteness against whiteness, 'a pearl on a white forehead.'

Another element in Dante's mastery of words lies in

[1] *Par.* XX, 73–75.

his natural aversion for all that is abstract and trite. He speaks almost always in figurative language, as do all demiurgic poets; but at times in Dante the figure is reduced to a word. That word, however, is never trite or ordinary; it is taken from the rich earth, from the daily life, and carries with it the unmistakable stamp of a colourful and terse concreteness. Even when he has to explain philosophical or theological ideas or to name divine persons, Dante makes no concession to the pallid, sacrosanct vocabulary. A saint is *drudo della fede*, a paramour of the faith; spiritual rewards are *buone merce*, good wares; the intellect is *fiera in lustra*, a wild beast in its lair; Paradise is *un albero*, a tree; the grace of God is *l'eterna ploia*, eternal rain; the Church is *orto di Cristo*, Christ's garden; God is *l'ortolano eterno*, the eternal gardener, who, like the Virgin, *pregna*, conceives, and *partorisce*, gives birth to ideas.

Does Dante, for example, wish to refer to original sin? He uses no name and no common and prescribed image:

> . . . nel petto onde la costa
> si trasse per formar la bella guancia
> il cui palato a tutto 'l mondo costa.[1]

. . . in the breast whence the rib was taken to make the fair cheek of her whose palate all the world pays for.

There are two persons, Adam and Eve; and two facts, the sin and the fall. Dante substitutes four parts of the human body: breast, rib, cheek, palate. The thought remains the same, but it is all renewed by the imagery of the body Instead of repetition in abstract terms, we have here a concrete and plastic evocation due to the

[1] *Par.* XIII, 37–39.

naming of those bodily members which each of us possesses and knows.

Could any two things be more unlike than religious faith and money? Yet Dante, in a bold metaphor, succeeds not only in representing faith as money, but he makes it almost visible and tangible.

> . . . Assai bene è trascorsa
> d'esta moneta già la lega e 'l peso;
> ma dimmi se tu l'hai nella tua borsa.
> Ond'io: 'Sì, ho, sì lucida e sì tonda,
> che nel suo conio nulla mi s'inforsa.[1]

'Very well have the alloy and the weight of this coin been estimated; but tell me if you have it in your purse.' Whereupon I answered: 'Yes, I have, and so shining and round that I have no doubts of its stamp.'

In another it might seem irreverent, but in Dante's poem even St Peter speaks in the money-changer's language of the great treasure of the Christian, and the talk seems natural and the effect more striking.

When we think of charity in the religious sense of love, and wish to express the idea in figurative language, into the mind of each one of us come such words as fire, flame, spark, and the like; words that have now lost their force in this connection although they still serve for ordinary use. But Dante uses another figure. Wishing St John to ask him how much he loves God, he makes him speak in this bold metaphor:

> Ma di' ancor se tu senti altre corde
> tirarti verso lui, sì che tu suone
> con quanti denti questo amor ti morde.[2]

But say further if you feel other cords drawing you towards Him, so that you may make known with how many teeth this love bites you.

Love of the creature for his Creator is not, it seems, the gentle aspiration compounded of sighs and languors

---

[1] *Par.* XXIV, 83–87.   [2] *Par.* XXVI, 49–51.

as in so many Christians of the modern sort. It is nothing less than a wild beast, a beast with teeth, with teeth that bite. A little later Dante calls the impulses toward such charity 'bitings' (*morsi*)—almost like remorse and mental torment.

Some readers have been shocked by such brutal expressions. They wish perhaps that Dante had said, just as any one would say: 'Tell me what motives induced you to love God and what is the measure of your love.' Dante's expression has a vigour and power worthy of a prophet of the Old Testament. The other expression would go very well in the homily of a chaplain.

Dante sees everything, even the most lofty conceptions, in a plastic and living form. Like the ancient Greeks, he has an instinct for using visible detail instead of pallid generalities. His poetry is very rich in tactile values and colourings, stamped with all the aspects of being, and especially with the aspects of nature. The *Commedia* is a theological poem, but it is translated into the language of the stars and of rude country life, into a celestial idiom and an idiom tart and juicy, smacking of the warm earth. From this comes the undying enchantment of his language, harsh and heavenly by turns.

Dante's force of character, the vehemence of his loves and hates, appears in every verse and gives to his expressions, polished and rough alike, a weight, an emphasis, an emotional power, which no one has been able to imitate or equal. He thinks in a way peculiar to himself, *Dantescamente*; he writes in his own language, *Dantesco*. Where he has directed his eye and hand, he has made everything his own, and there is no imagery or word which will not carry to eternity the imprint of his seal. Even those things which he borrows from others he takes possession of and marks with his own personality. He becomes their lawful owner by right of imperial conquest.

It would be possible to reprint the *Commedia,* setting opposite in a parallel column all the passages from the Bible, the Latin poets, and the mediæval writers of which there are deliberate or unconscious reminiscence in Dante's poem. There are cantos where we find a parallel passage for almost every terzina. And yet no one would derive the idea that the *Commedia* is a patchwork of well-joined selections, for the reason that the stylistic transformation which they have undergone is so great and of such a nature that the passages take on another tone, another value, a wholly different colouring and harmony. The greater part of the material which forms the substance of the poem is derived from Dante's own thoughts, from his experience of life, from his contemplation of the world. The rest comes from his reading; but even this portion is so thoroughly disintegrated and recomposed by his genius that his versions or citations take on in that magic atmosphere features and intonations purely Dantesque.

A solitary and meditative pilgrim through the mountains and the plains of Italy, he has discovered for himself, with his own eyes and quick perceptions, the aspects of nature and the creatures of the earth. All reappear amid the furrows or on the heights of his poem with the bright freshness of primordial beings. If the prologue of the poem is a dark forest inhabited by terrifying beasts, the remainder, and especially the *Purgatorio* and the *Paradiso*, is a great country tranquil and sunny, mountainous and wooded, but with flowery uplands and leafy hedges; and all of it resounds with the call of flocks, the song of birds, the rush of torrents and of flooding streams.

When in the tenth heaven the poet declares himself conquered by his arduous theme, and yet wishes to give at least some shadowy suggestion of what he sees, he touches one of his greatest heights, creating a river where lights, metals, precious stones, perfumes, flowers, and flames are mingled in the supreme incandescence of an art which wishes to utter the unutterable.

> E vidi lume in forma di rivera
> fulvido di fulgore, intra due rive
> dipinte di mirabil primavera.
>   Di tal fiumana uscìan faville vive,
> e d'ogni parte si mettean ne' fiori,
> quasi rubin che oro circunscrive.
> Poi, come inebriate dalli odori,
> riprofondavan sè nel miro gurge.[1]

And I saw light flowing like a river, gleaming with brightness between two banks painted with the wonders of spring-time. From this stream rose living sparks, and on either side they were settling into the flowers, like rubies which gold encircles. Then, as if drunk with the odours, they plunged again into the marvellous swirling flood.

When a poet with his meagre human words represents so divinely the divine tumult of the blessed spirits, and with so few lines, which seem woven of pure light, not of heavy syllables, succeeds in expressing that which the fancy can scarcely imagine, he may justly feel content with his victory. But Dante is not satisfied. In the last cantos of the *Paradiso*, just where he manifests his power at its utmost, he feels and confesses his incapacity, the inadequacy of words, the failure of his genius.[2] He no

[1] *Par.* XXX, 61–68.
[2] *Par.* XXIV, 23–27; XXX, 99; XXXI, 137 ff.; XXXIII, 67 ff.; 121 ff.

longer prays to the pagan muses but to God, for help and inspiration:

> O somma luce che tanto ti levi
> da' concetti mortali, alla mia mente
> ripresta un poco di quel che parevi,
>   e fa la lingua mia tanto possente,
> ch'una favilla sol della tua gloria
> possa lasciare alla futura gente.[1]

O supreme Light, that dost uplift thyself so high above mortal conceptions, give back to my memory a little of that which Thou didst appear, and make my tongue so powerful that it may be able to leave but one spark of Thy glorious light for the race yet to come.

But the ineffable wonders press him even further, and the poet declares himself vanquished:

> Oh quanto è corto il dire e come fioco
> al mio concetto! e questo, a quel ch'i'vidi
> è tanto, che non basta a dicer 'poco.'[2]

Oh, how deficient is my speech and how feeble to accomplish my conception! and this in comparison with what I saw is so slight that to call it 'little' is inadequate.

Finally, before the shining mystery of the Trinity, Dante abandons every hope of success and admits his failure:

> All'alta fantasia qui mancò possa.[3]

Here power failed the lofty fantasy.

He has struggled through canto after canto to express the inexpressible, to describe the indescribable, to translate into human words the music of the divine light. Now all his power is broken. In the face of the

---

[1] *Par.* XXXIII, 67–72.   [2] *Par.* XXXIII, 121–123.
[3] *Par.* XXXIII, 142.

ineffable final glory, nothing avails save the renunciation of the artist and the dignity of silence.

The masterpiece of one of the greatest poets that ever lived closes with the confession that his poetry has failed.

BOOK FIVE

Destiny

UNFRIENDS AND ENEMIES

*W*E are accustomed to a reverential attitude, sometimes excessive, in the presence of Dante. There are those who speak of him as if he were a being of another race more estimable than ours. In contrast to this, we find that, even in his own lifetime, the divine Dante was ridiculed or censured by a number of people—treated, in short, like any other man, or rather, we should say, like one who did not deserve great respect from anyone.

It began with the outburst of Dante da Maiano. To the first sonnet written by the eighteen-year-old Alighieri (*A ciascun' alma presa e gentil core*)[1] da Maiano replied with one of unseemly advice, and in addition called the young poet delirious.[2]

Then came his first friend, Guido Cavalcanti, who addressed to him, doubtless with good intentions, words which are anything but respectful:

> I' vegno il giorno a te infinite volte
> e trovote pensar troppo vilmente ; . . .
> or non ardisco, per la vil tua vita
> far mostramento che tuo dir mi piaccia.[3]

I come to you many times a day and find too much baseness in your

---

[1] The first sonnet in the *Vita Nuova*. English readers unfamiliar with the original are referred to D. G. Rossetti's translation.—Trans.

[2] Dante da Maiano's sonnet may be found translated in Rossetti's *Dante and his Circle*, which is easily accessible. The sonnet begins, 'Of that wherein thou art a questioner.'—Trans.

[3] For the entire sonnet, see Rossetti (*Dante and his Circle*): 'I come to thee by daytime constantly.'—Trans.

thoughts. . . . Now, on account of your unseemly life, I do not dare to show that your rhymes please me.

Dante receives even worse treatment from Forese Donati in the famous *Tenzone*.[1] It may be said in explanation that in those days Dante was still young and not yet famous. But he was already known, I think, when Cecco Angiolieri, the mad but talented Sienese poet, launched against him the famous sonnet of retort which is, we must admit, one of the most successful among all those evolved by that cracked brain. What an assured onslaught in the closing terzina!

> E se di questo voi dicere piue,
> Dante Alighier, i' t'avarò a stancare,
> ch'eo so' lo pungiglione e tu se' 'l bue.[2]

And if you wish more of this, Dante Alighieri, I have enough of it to wear you out, for I am the goad and you are the ox.

He did not escape attacks, sometimes ironical, sometimes openly hostile, from Cecco D'Ascoli.[3] If we may believe the tradition, he was made the butt of jokes at the court of Can Grande della Scala in Verona by Gonnella or some other buffoon. According to the chronicler Foglietta, he was thrashed at Genoa by clients of Branca d'Oria in revenge for his pungent criticism of their patron: 'Brancae clientes, tantam verborum

---

[1] The *Tenzone* was discussed in Ch. 14 of this volume. Four of the sonnets of the *Tenzone* are translated in *Dante and his Circle*, Appendix to Part One.—Trans.

[2] For the entire sonnet see *Dante and his Circle*: 'Dante Alighieri, if I jest and lie.'

Cecco Angiolieri, the 'scamp of the Danteans,' appears in the *Decameron*, IX, 4.—Trans.

[3] *L'Acerba*, the best-known poem of Cecco D'Ascoli, contains a number of contemptuous references to the *Commedia*.—Trans.

324

petulantiam re tandem coercendam censentes, hominem in publico deprehensum male mulctarunt.'[1]

Certain prophetic words of Cacciaguida seem to refer to an attempt, or at least to an intention, on the part of Dante's fellow-exiles, to assassinate him in revenge for his desertion of them.

> E quel che più ti graverà le spalle
> sarà la compagnia malvagia e scempia . . .
>   che tutta ingrata, tutta matta ed empia
>   si farà contra te; ma, poco appresso,
>   ella, non tu, n'avrà rossa la tempia.[2]

And that which will weigh most heavily on your shoulders will be the company of evil and worthless men . . . who, all ungrateful, mad, and malevolent, will turn against you; but soon after, their foreheads, not yours, will be red for it.

Already Brunetto Latini, in Canto XV of the *Inferno*, had alluded to the hatred of the Guelph factions for Dante, and had said to him:

> La tua fortuna tanto onor ti serba,
> che l'una parte e l'altra avranno fame
> di te; ma lungi fia dal becco l'erba.[3]

Your fortune has such honour in store for you that the one party and the other shall have hunger for you; but the grass shall be far from the goat.

Fame, not hunger in the sense of desire to have him back again in this or that party; but hunger in the sense of wishing to devour like a lion, to tear to pieces, to kill.

---

[1] U. Foglietta, *Clarorum Ligurum elogia*. Romae, apud heredes Antonii Bladii, 1573, p. 254.
Branca's clients agreeing finally that such insolent language should be checked by energetic measures, caught the man in public and thrashed him soundly.—Trans.

[2] *Par.* XVII, 61–62; 64–66.

[3] *Inf.* XV, 70–72.

For Dante, then, there was no lack of injurious treatment contrived by human hatred. The divine poet, whom all the world now honours, was from his eighteenth year until his death subjected at one time or another to scorn, bitter reproaches, vilification, injurious attacks, and bodily assault; he was even threatened with violent death.

When you see many people enraged against a single man, draw near. Sometimes it is a disgraced man without protection. More often it is proud pre-eminence abjectly feared. Dante, because of his consecration to a lofty ideal, could not escape the detestable experience of persecution from the mediocre and the base.

FAILURES

RIVETED in the heads of average folk is the idea that a great man must be great always and everywhere; perpetually victorious; in whatever he does, at the head of the class and first in the race. The full and exact biographies which reveal the, inevitable shortcomings, do not succeed in changing this half-Plutarchian, half-romantic notion.

The truth is entirely different. Every man pays for his greatness with many littlenesses, for his victory with many defeats, for his richness of genius with many failings. Every great genius is, on one side at least, a failure, a *raté*. And if he appears never to be a *raté*, it is difficult to believe him a genius. Even Goethe, who seems in his genius to be good fortune personified, is a *raté* as a writer of romance (except in *Werther*) and as a physicist in his theory of colours.

Dante could not escape this law. In at least two things he was a failure.

He was a failure, first of all, as a man engaged in public affairs. Although he was ambitious and conscious of his ability, he did not hold either before or after his exile, within his *patria* or without, any but small and unimportant offices. His embassy to Boniface VIII was a failure. His attempt to unite the exiles in order to bring about their return to Florence was another failure. A third failure, and greater than the rest, was the finish of his hopes for the Empire with the ill luck and death of Henry VII.

He can be called a failure also as a religious man. He intended with his poem to instil wisdom into mankind and to point out to them the road which ascends to God. But the *Commedia* was admired above all as poetry or as a document of history, and neither then nor afterwards did it have any appreciable influence on the habits of his contemporaries and posterity. He thought that he would be the herald and, like another St John the Baptist, the forerunner of the new King of the World who was to come, swift as the Veltro, to reform sinful humanity. And now after six centuries we are still expecting, and expecting in vain, the real-. ization of that sublime hope. Dante, however, thought that at least the coming of the leader was near at hand, the *Dux* who would have prepared the way for the Veltro.

And, finally, the greatest success for a Christian is to come near to holiness and to acquire it. But Dante, although he was a Catholic in good faith, remained until the last embroiled in earthly passions, ruled by his strong desire for earthly glory, shaken by his inveterate hatreds. He never, even remotely, attained the complete purification of the saint.

We may say then that he failed as a statesman, as a White Guelph and as a Ghibelline, as a moral reformer and as a Christian. In recompense, he was successful as a poet. But he owes this eminence, at least in part, to the last and the gravest of his failures. A saint who is in earnest would not deign, even if he were able, to write poems, however certain he might be that his work would be greater and more beautiful than the *Divina Commedia*. The saint who has his mind fixed on the absolute has something better to do than to put together canto after canto of rhymed verses.

DANTE'S SOLITUDE

$\mathcal{I}$T is certainly not my intention to recreate in the old romantic manner a Dante always grieving, groaning, and weeping over real and imagined evils; his face distorted by unending anguish, his eyes red and wet with tears—the wandering victim of a continuous and merciless persecution.

On the other hand, we cannot think of him as a man without our hearts being moved to compassion at the thought of what formed so great a part of his life. Dante was great not only through his genius but through his sorrow. And his genius was, I do not say generated, but purified by his sorrow.

We know entirely too little about the outward events of his life to be able to enumerate all the causes of that deep melancholy which was his companion through long years and which sometimes broke forth in bitterness and desperation. Without resorting to invention, contenting ourselves solely with established facts which have been sifted out of the biographies and the poet's own writings, we can guess with sufficient certainty what he must have suffered from the time of his adolescence until his death.

In the first place, Dante was always terribly alone. His mother died when he was still an infant. Of his father we know little except that he was an ordinary man in every sense of the word, and incapable, even if he had lived longer, of understanding his son. For the woman who inspired in Dante the loftiest and the purest of all his loves, the young poet was able to show only a distant courtesy; she was the wife of another, and died when Dante was scarcely twenty-five years old. With the first of his friends, Guido Cavalcanti, he was not in complete harmony for, if the tradition is true, Guido was a sceptic and an epicurean, and he looked disdainfully upon the divine Beatrice. In any event, he died 'in the midst of the journey of our life' when Dante was thirty-five years old.

Dante's other Florentine friends, a certain Lapo Gianni for example, lacked the mental and moral stature which would have enabled them to be the poet's companions in those lofty places which he sought. Dante could talk with them of *ballate* and of young maidens, he could divert himself in their company, but no more than that.

The aged master, Brunetto, who taught him 'how a man makes himself eternal,' vanished from the earth when Dante was not yet thirty years old; and, in any case, Brunetto's mind was not so profound nor his life so pure that he could give to his disciple more than the desire for glory.

We have record of a brother, Francesco, who often comforted and aided him; but what kind of man he was and in what relations of affection he stood with Dante we have no means of knowing.

We know even less of Dante's wife, poor Gemma Donati. No one can say if Boccaccio's gossip about Gemma has any foundation in truth. The very words of the biographer seem to exclude the idea. But it is probable that Dante passed many years, perhaps the whole period of his exile, at a distance from his wife.

For a time he was separated from his sons as well. Was it the discreet Gemma who for reasons good or bad was unwilling to depart from Florence? Or was it the poet himself who wished to spare her the privations and miseries of his wandering life and so did not wish her with him? But if she was in truth near him during any part of his exile, was she able to understand his greatness and adequately comfort his spiritual solitude? And why is she never recalled, even indirectly, by her husband or her sons?

We need, in short, some trustworthy information before we can picture the joys and sorrows of Dante's life as a husband and a father. There remain a few things written by his sons, Pietro and Jacopo, but we must admit that they contain no trace of the paternal genius, and no trace of his wisdom and vigorous character. It seems certain that the sons lived some time with their father, probably in the last years of his exile. We can therefore easily suppose that Dante was not spared the unhappiness of realizing their intellectual mediocrity. They did not understand him or they half understood him, or perhaps even less: so that even with his sons the great solitary remained spiritually alone.

We may say too that he was solitary when with his party-associates, in Florence in the period of his office-holding, and in the first years of his exile. Those Florentine Guelphs thought mainly of saving money, of heaping up florins, of using public office for the advantage of their family, or at most of the faction to which they belonged. No one looked more than a year ahead or farther than the walls of the city. They were astute and profiteering politicians, intensely proud and quarrelsome. Their souls were barren of higher light. They nourished no vision of a civil and religious ideal which should transcend their little daily needs.

Dante seemed a partisan like so many others. He loved Florence more than every other city, more even than Rome. Rome was a sacred symbol, the seat of the Empire and the Church. Dante venerated her with sincerity and ardour, but his veneration lacked that almost sensual love which he had for his native place.

Dante, however, felt himself to be not only Florentine and Guelph, but Roman, Italian, Christian. He contemplated political problems from a more lofty point of view. He could not find himself in accord, even in his early maturity, with the corrupt and short-sighted dabblers in politics whom he found in his party. Led by his burning desire to recover his native city, he united for a time with the exiles who were in arms; but he learned very quickly how 'malevolent and foolish' was their companionship, and so once more he remained alone.

He was alone among the clergy who did not understand the imperial dream and who could not, most of them, approve his prediction of the Third Kingdom.

He was alone among the rhymers and grammarians of his time who thought of art only as a courtly ornament or a conventional tribute of love or an outlet for pedantic display.

He remained alone always. In the wanderings of his exile he seems never to have met with other spirits capable of consoling his scornful and overwhelming solitude. He was received kindly by noblemen and princes; he enjoyed the intimate friendship of soldiers and writers; he held discussions with notaries and monks, and contests with bullies and buffoons. In the last years he had friendly protectors, learned admirers even, and perhaps a few disciples. But no one of all these many persons who knew him could understand him fully, even less could they love him as he needed to be loved. Henry VII, who, for a moment, was his hero, must on closer acquaintance have been a disappointment to him; and the hesitations of the Emperor and his premature death must have grieved profoundly the Florentine prophet.

Only Giotto, as an artist, can be considered his equal. The painter could have been a not unworthy friend to Dante; but we know too little about the relations existing between these two great men, and not enough about the mind of Giotto outside of his painting, to feel certain that a true and inspiring friendship developed between them.

From another point of view we cannot blame Dante's contemporaries for the painful solitude in which he lived. Of men like him there is perhaps only one to a century; and even so, not every century; and only death unites those solitaries who were made to live together.

But there have been great spirits who, lacking equals, have found at least warmth of affection and unswerving loyalty. They have had friends, brothers, disciples, compounded all of reverence and love. There can be in simple souls, in default of intellectual power, a depth of sympathy which is worth the other and which can comfort it. But around Dante we see no one. All are mediocre: mediocre patrons, mediocre adversaries (excepting Boniface), mediocre friends, mediocre sons.

In the centuries after his death, about his name will cluster mediocre disciples, mediocre imitators, mediocre commentators, mediocre statue-makers. The only one worthy of him was Michelangelo, who wished to carve with his own hands a fitting tomb for Dante, and was not permitted.

WHERE IS DANTE NOW?

ℱEW, I believe, have thought or think about Dante's present fate, beyond this world.

That handful of white dust which is the last remaining trace of what was once his body, is enclosed in a commonplace little temple in Ravenna —but his soul, where is it now?

He who before his death, by right of his genius and his faith, passed through the three realms of the dead like a dreaming pilgrim, in which realm to-day does he, in fact, abide?

For those who are not Catholics this question has no meaning. It may even seem futile or ridiculous. But for a Catholic this problem, even if it is necessarily insoluble, has its meaning and its reason.

I, for one, addressing myself to him in verse on the occasion of the sixth centenary of his death, said that he had been welcomed in Paradise:

> Ora se tu dalla stanza serena
> dove fiammeggi insieme a Beatrice,
> degno conviva dell'eterna cena
> rivolgi il viso. . . .[1]

If from the heavenly abode where you gleam like a flame beside Beatrice and take your place, a worthy guest, at the eternal feast, you turn your face. . . .

But can we be quite sure that Dante now enjoys that beatific vision which he celebrated in his third canticle

---

[1] Prayer to Dante on the Sixth Centenary of His Death (1921), in *Poesia in versi*. Florence, Vallecchi, 1932, p. 201.

with such marvellous semblance of actuality? He was not a saint. According to the absolute standard of the Gospel, he was not even a perfect Christian. In most respects he was, like all of us, a sinner. We know this from his life and from what can be discovered from his works. He had, and perhaps still has, to expiate his sins.[1]

So far as a mortal is permitted to scrutinize the inscrutable ways of Divine Justice, we reject the idea that Dante is among the damned in hell. His sins, though heavy, were not such as to merit, so it seems to me, eternal punishment. But it is entirely probable that he had to spend some time in Purgatory. Is he still there at this moment, or has the infinite mercy of God, whom he loved and praised in verse, already drawn him up to form a drop in that stream 'gleaming with brightness'? Will six centuries of purgation have sufficed to make him a 'citizen' of that celestial Rome where Christ is Roman? Ought we still to pray for him and offer sacrifices for his liberation, or may we be permitted to hope that he now has no more need of our loving prayers? Does he suffer still, or is he at last filled with the eternal rejoicing which he pictured in the glories of the blest?

In either case, what does he think now of his greatest work? What emotions did he experience, whether of

[1] Dante knew that he must spend a time in Purgatory (*Purg.* XIII, 133–138), but was certain of ultimately mounting to Paradise, as we know from what Beatrice is made to say: 'before you sup at this wedding feast' (*Par.* XXX, 135). Antonio Pucci (a writer of the fourteenth century), in his *Centiloquio*, supposed, on the contrary, that Dante was still in Purgatory: 'If Dante's soul is spending in Purgatory its wintry time of expiation, I pray Christ, whence comes every grace, that of His mercy He will draw it thence and lead it to the bliss of eternal life.' (Solerti, *Vite*, etc., p. 7.)

amazement or of shame, when for the first time he was able to compare the vision of his imagination with the absolute reality which was before him?

In what circle of Purgatory, probably different from that Purgatory which he had imagined, did he pass the long years, or centuries, of expiation? Did he indeed meet there some of those souls whom he placed in Purgatory through his just discretion as a poet? What discourse did he have with his companions, with those whom he had already known on earth, and with those who came a long time after he came?

One thing above all I should like to know. Now that he is freed from passions and ambitions of every sort, what judgement does he pass on his poem? Does he smile at his pride as an artist, at his fierceness as a partisan? Does he still keep in his soul, freed now from the prison-house of the flesh, a certain affection for that great work which through so many years 'made him lean'? Or, following too late the example of the saints, does he judge it unequal to its argument, unjust and deserving of censure, nothing more than a heap of empty rhymes, a blind outlet for his pride, a weak attempt and a miserable failure to lead mankind to the light and to enclose in words too human for their purpose some spark of divine truth?

Does the *Divina Commedia*, in short, still seem to him a title to spiritual merit, or is it a cause of remorse and humiliation? Does he look upon it from on high with the nostalgia of a poet not as yet completely purified, or does it seem to him in the unspeakable brightness of the Empyrean a wretched note-book filled with meaningless and fast-fading scrawls?

338

But in whatever way the great Shade judges his own work, we know, we who are still dragged along by that life 'which is a running unto death,' what it has been for thousands of souls and is still for us—one of the boldest and most successful attempts to recreate the vision of Jacob. The *Commedia*, although it is a human work, is a ladder rising from the hunting-grounds of wild beasts to the garden with flowers of flame. Therefore we Christians, we poets, cannot think of Dante without our souls being flooded with love and gratitude. We forget his sins, we pardon his mistakes. We remember only the misfortunes and the greatness. We are moved always more and more by the profound tragedy of his stormy and storm-driven genius, by the ever-increasing miracle of his rugged and metaphysical poetry.

In whatever region of the empire of the dead our Dante suffers or rejoices, we feel an impulse to pray. To pray for him, if it is not yet granted him to contemplate the triune light which he has already seen in his vision. To pray to him, as to a gracious intercessor among the saints, on behalf of poets, if the Virgin Mother whom he so greatly loved has helped him to mount to the eternal city of her Son.

And suddenly at the end of this my pleasant labour, I feel compelled to address a prayer to him. I ask him to pardon me if I have been it may be over-bold in weighing and measuring his soul; to pardon me above all if I, of so little worth, did not know how to speak worthily of the noble greatness of his genius.

AUTHOR'S NOTE

CITATIONS from Dante's works are based on the critical edition of the Società Dantesca Italiana (Florence, Bemporad, 1921).

For the *Vita Nuova*, the critical edition of Michele Barbi has been used (Florence, Bemporad, 1932). This forms Volume I of the *Edizione Nazionale delle Opere di Dante*.

For lack of space no attempt has been made to list the works consulted. Readers are referred to the bibliography compiled by M. Barbi, in *Dante. Vita, opere e fortuna* (Florence, Sansoni, 1933), pp. 130–142.

Acknowledgments should be made for aid derived from the valuable *Studi Danteschi* (Florence, Sansoni, 1920 *et seq.*), directed by M. Barbi, of which sixteen volumes have been issued.

A few notes especially for the general reader have been added by the translators.